Anatomy of a Liberal Victory

Anatomy of a Liberal Victory: Making Sense of the Vote in the 2000 Canadian Election

André Blais
Elisabeth Gidengil
Richard Nadeau
Neil Nevitte

broadview press

National Library of Canada Cataloguing in Publication Data

Main entry under title:

Anatomy of a Liberal victory : making sense of the vote in the 2000 Canadian election / André Blais ... [et al.].

Includes bibliographical references.
ISBN 1-55111-483-6

1. Canada. Parliament—Elections, 2000. I. Blais, André

JL193.A58 2002   324.971'0648   C2002-901697-5

Broadview Press Ltd. is an independent, international publishing house, incorporated in 1985

North America
Post Office Box 1243, Peterborough, Ontario, Canada K9J 7H5
3576 California Road, Orchard Park, NY 14127
Tel: (705) 743-8990; Fax: (705) 743-8353;
e-mail: customerservice@broadviewpress.com

United Kingdom and Europe
Plymbridge North (Thomas Lyster Ltd.)
Units 3 & 4a, Ormskirk Industrial Park, Burscough Rd, Ormskirk,
Lancashire L39 2YW Tel: (1695) 575112; Fax: (1695) 570120;
E-Mail: books@tlyster.co.uk

Australia
St. Clair Press, P.O. Box 287, Rozelle, NSW 2039
Tel: (02) 818-1942; Fax: (02) 418-1923

www.broadviewpress.com

Broadview Press gratefully acknowledges the financial support of the Book Publishing Industry Development Program, Ministry of Canadian Heritage, Government of Canada.

Typesetting and assembly: True to Type Inc., Mississauga, Canada.
PRINTED IN CANADA

Contents

Acknowledgements

The Canadian Election Study is a huge endeavour and we have incurred many debts throughout the project, from its inception to this very day. Research of this scale requires substantial financial support. We were fortunate to obtain funding from the Social Sciences and Humanities Research Council of Canada (SSHRCC) and we gratefully acknowledge this support. We would also like to thank two partners, Elections Canada and the Institute for Research on Public Policy (IRPP), for their enthusiastic interest in the study and for their financial support. We are heartened by their commitment to supporting rigorous research on the working of electoral democracy in Canada.

The 2000 Canadian election came much earlier than we (and most analysts) had anticipated. Following our advice, the Institute for Social Research (ISR) at York University, which was in charge of the huge fieldwork, had planned for a 2001 election. They learned that political scientists are as good at predicting the date of an election as economists are at forecasting GDP growth. David Northrup, the ISR's director, did everything that could be done to accommodate us at very short notice, including agreeing, at the very last minute, to work with Jolicoeur & Associés, who did the fieldwork in Quebec. We deeply appreciate ISR's commitment to the Canadian Election Study.

Our respective universities—the Université de Montréal, McGill University, and the University of Toronto—are crucial supporters of the project. They contribute to the funding of the study. Most importantly, they agreed to provide some time release so that we could complete this book and many other publications in a timely fashion.

The Canadian Election Study benefits from the wisdom and advice of an experienced and talented group of researchers who compose our advisory board. We wish to express our gratitude to Herman Bakvis, Lynda Erickson, John Fox, John Helliwell, Jon Krosnick, Pippa Norris, Vincent Price, David Sanders, and Jeffrey Simpson. Our only regret is that the early election call prevented us from benefiting from their advice in the initial stages of the project. A very special thanks to Patrick Fournier who, in the fall of 2000, spent countless hours helping us prepare drafts of the survey questionnaires.

Finally, we express our gratitude to the students and research assistants who worked with us on the collection and analysis of huge data sets. We thank Agnieszka Dobrzynska, Frédérick Bastien, Charles Lor, Mathieu Turgeon, Éric Bélanger, Catherine Côté, Thierry Giasson, Cameron Anderson, Christopher B. Cochrane, Delton Daigle, Elizabeth Goodyear-Grant, and Antoine Bilodeau for their enthusiastic commitment to the study. A very special thanks to Agnieszka and Frédérick, who were involved in all stages of the study and whose contribution was outstanding. It is deeply rewarding to have students who share our passion for social science research.

Lastly, we have greatly appreciated the strong commitment of Michael Harrison and Barbara Conolly to the project, and the expert editorial skills of Laurna Tallman.

Introduction

On November 27, 2000, Jean Chrétien became the first Prime Minister since Sir Wilfrid Laurier to win a majority of seats in three successive federal elections. It is tempting to dismiss the Liberal achievement in the 2000 election as a victory by default. After all, the right had clearly failed to unite and the opposition remained fragmented. Worse, the new Alliance leader, Stockwell Day, had failed to live up to expectations and had run, by most accounts, a lacklustre campaign. This particular reading of the 2000 election implies that, once the "fight for the right" is resolved and the party system returns to a "steady state" (Nevitte et al., 2000), Liberal dominance will come to an end. But what this winning-by-default interpretation overlooks is an important thread that weaves through Canadian electoral history over the last half century: Liberal dominance *is* the steady state of the Canadian party system. Since 1945, the Liberals have won a plurality of the vote in 14 out of 18 federal elections.

This book aims to explain why the outcome of the 2000 election produced another Liberal victory and does this by developing a systematic account of why Canadians voted as they did in November 2000. The goal is not only to provide insight into the roots of Liberal dominance, but also to re-examine some of the conventional wisdom about voting behaviour in Canada. One prominent interpretation of vote choice in Canada emphasizes the weakness of social cleavages and the flexibility of partisan ties (Clarke, Jenson, LeDuc, and Pammett, 1979; 1984; 1991; 1996). That approach focuses consequently, on such short-term factors that influence voters' choice of party as leaders, the state of the economy, and the issues of the day. Certainly, no account of Canadian voting behaviour can afford to ignore the potential for considerable volatility (LeDuc, 1984). The impressive string of Liberal successes over the last 50 years, however, suggests that there are significant elements of continuity and stability in Canadian voting behaviour. The lesson we draw from this longer record is that it is also important to consider what possible role such longer-term influences as fundamental values and ideological beliefs might have on the vote.

At one level, providing an account of an election seems simple enough. Each voter indicates on a ballot which party's candidate he or she prefers, the candidate with the most votes in each constituency is elected, and the party with the greatest number of elected candidates forms the government. But at another level, elections are remarkably complicated events to explain. Voters have to sort through a myriad of considerations in order to decide how to mark their ballots. The decision-making process is further complicated by the fact that citizens are bombarded constantly with partisan appeals. Political parties do not confine themselves just to presenting their own positions on the issues or to extolling the virtues of their leader. Mixed in with these messages are warnings about the shortcomings of their competitors, the wrong-headedness of their positions on issues, the questionable values that they represent, and the dire consequences for the country and for individual citizens should one of these parties somehow gain office. Some voters pay attention to these messages, other do not. Some voters are well-informed about election issues, others are not. Some voters are misinformed. Consequently, no single factor can provide an explanation for why voters voted as they did, or why some parties did better than others.

To make the complicated task of deciphering the meaning of the election more manageable, we have developed a multi-stage analytical framework, which is elaborated in Chapter 5. The approach identifies a wide variety factors, or considerations, that may have induced voters to vote a particular way in the 2000 election. We do not assume that each of these considerations was important for individual vote choice, still less for the outcome of the 2000 election. Indeed, one of our tasks is to show that some of them had relatively little impact.

The question of why some *parties* were more successful than others is different from the question of why *individual voters* voted as they did. The distinction between these two questions is not merely a fine intellectual nuance; it has very practical ramifications for how we go about the business of interpreting the election. Obviously, if any specific factor has no impact whatsoever on individual vote choice then it cannot affect the outcome of the election. But the important point is that factors that affect individual vote choice are not necessarily the same as those that influence the final outcome. It is quite possible for a factor to have a significant effect on how people vote and yet have no net impact on the outcome of the election. To illustrate the point, consider the Alliance party's position on tax cuts. To assess whether the issue helped (or hurt) the Alliance what first needs to be established is whether opinions on taxes had any independent effect on vote choice. If the Alliance stance repelled as many voters as it attracted to the party, then it is entirely possible that such an issue position could have a significant impact on individual vote choice and yet have no net overall effect on the Alliance vote share. What is required is a simple methodology that allows us to ascertain the net overall effect on the parties, as well as the gross individual effect on voters. Both perspectives are needed to make sense of the election. Adopting this approach allows us to determine, for instance, how much of the Liberal victory can be attributed to, say, partisanship in constrast to, for example, perceptions of the economy.

It is not possible, or even useful, to try to provide an exhaustive account of all the factors that may have had some effect on the vote for all voters. A more useful strategy, in our view, is to try to make sense of the election by focusing on those factors that seem to have had the greatest impact on the greatest number of voters. The framework we use not only allows us to address the important questions that have been raised about the 2000 election but also enables us to draw from it a number of important implications for theories of voting.

To understand what made Canadians decide to support one party rather than another, or even to vote at all, we rely heavily on empirical survey research evidence from the 2000 Canadian Election Study (CES). The study consists of a three-wave survey conducted by the Institute for Social Research at York University and Jolicoeur & Associés. It includes a rolling cross-section survey with 3,651 interviews, a post-election survey with 2,862 of the campaign survey respondents, and a self-administered, mail-back questionnaire filled out by 1,535 of the post-election respondents.

These survey data are rich and useful for at least three reasons. First, the large sample size makes it possible not only to look at the whole electorate but also to examine specific subgroups. Because of the strong regionalization of the vote in Canada, it is important to recognize possible variations in the factors that affected vote choice in the different regions. The most crucial question in the election was whether the Alliance would succeed in making inroads in Ontario. For that reason, we pay particular attention to why Ontario voters were more reluctant than Westerners to vote Alliance.

Second, the CES interviewers spent a good deal of time talking to each of our respondents, about half an hour during the campaign interview and another half-hour in the post-election interview. In total, respondents were asked some 400 questions in these two interviews combined. This means that it is possible to explore the play of a myriad of considerations in vote choice.

Third, the campaign survey allows us to determine whether the campaign itself had an impact on vote choice, and, if so, how. About 110 respondents were interviewed each day of the campaign, so it is possible to see whether opinions about the issues, feelings about the leaders, and vote intentions moved during the campaign, and to determine which campaign events were responsible for these changes. The primary focus of this book is on the final vote decision, but an account of the election requires a consideration of how the campaign itself may have affected the outcome.

In addition to these survey interview data, we also develop and draw on two other complementary sources of systematic evidence that allow us to probe other vital facets of the election. Elections involve a dynamic interaction between parties and voters: voters can only react to what the parties offer them and so parties are in the business, during campaigns, of communicating to voters what they are offering. For that reason, the place to begin is with an examination of the parties' messages. To understand what messages the parties were conveying to the voters, we undertook a systematic content analysis of party platforms, press releases, websites, and televised ads, as well as the televised leaders' debates.

Similarly, it is impossible to make sense of the election without taking stock of the information that television news was providing during the course of the campaign. The main source of information about elections for most voters is television, and especially television news. To understand what kind of information was most readily available to voters, we performed a systematic content analysis of the nightly television news broadcasts: CBC's *The National*, CTV's *National Edition*, SRC's *Le Téléjournal*, and TVA's *Édition Réseau*.

Chapter 1 outlines the main arguments that each party used to curry public support. We set out the parties' positions on the major issues, and identify which issues each party stressed and which they avoided. Party messages, of course, are not confined to issues. We also ascertain how much emphasis each party gave to its leader. The final part of the analysis focuses on how parties interacted with each other. Campaigns are strategic battles between political parties competing to attract votes. Of particular interest here is which parties were attacking and which parties were attacked, and what form those attacks took.

Even with the advent of new communication technologies, such as the Internet, political parties are still heavily dependent on the media, and particularly television news, for getting their messages out to voters. Some parties will be more successful (or more fortunate) in this respect than others. Chapter 2 examines the messages that were presented to voters on the nightly television news broadcasts. We indicate which of the parties' messages were, and were not, transmitted to voters, and which issues and leaders received the greatest attention.

Then the focus shifts to the voters themselves. The first choice that a citizen has to confront is whether to vote or not. One truly striking, and troubling, feature of the 2000 election was that a very substantial number of Canadians decided to stay home on 27 November 2000. The average turnout in federal elections between 1945 and 1988 stands at around 74 per cent. Turnout dropped to 67 per cent in 1997 and dropped yet again to 61 per cent in 2000. This is clearly a very significant change. Chapter 3 looks at the reasons so many Canadians decided not to vote in this election. A key question here is whether the low turnout simply reflected the fact that it was a "boring" election or whether the low level of voter turnout was attributable to deeper, structural factors.

Attention then turns to those who did decide to vote and the question of what motivated them to vote for one party rather than another. Chapter 4 begins by placing the election in context. We show how the outcome of the election was both similar to and different from that of 1997. We also examine the evolution of vote intentions between 1997 and the beginning of the 2000 campaign. Then there is the matter of the campaign itself. We assess how much impact the campaign had on the overall evolution of vote intentions and identify which campaign events mattered, and which did not. Particular attention is paid to what happened to the Alliance Party, but we also ask whether—and how—the campaign saved the Conservatives.

The rest of the book focuses on the factors that affected vote choice. Chapter 5 proposes an analytical framework that builds on a causal sequence of eight factors, or considerations, that can contribute to vote choice. Each of the following chapters is devoted to one of these explanatory factors, beginning with the most long-term and moving progressively towards those that were specific to the 2000 election.

The first factor concerns voters' social background characteristics. Voters from different regions, religions, and ethnic backgrounds often vote rather differently. Knowing which groups are the most, and the least, supportive of the various parties is the logical first step in making sense of the vote. This is the subject of Chapter 6.

Chapter 7 deals with the question of whether the underlying values and beliefs lead voters to view some parties more positively (or less negatively) than others. We document which values and beliefs are the most electorally salient, and then determine to what extent these values and beliefs "explain" the social bases of party support. This is an important question. It is not enough to know that some groups are more likely than others to support a given party. What needs to be understood is why they do. Does the strong support for the Alliance in the West, for example, indicate that Westerners adhere to a different set of values?

Next, we consider the question of partisan loyalties. We all know people who think of themselves as supporters of a particular party and who tend to vote for that party in election after election. But we also know people who do not feel any attachment to any of the parties. Chapter 8 estimates the size of these two groups. A central question here is whether the Liberal Party has many more partisans than the other parties, and how much this contributed to the Liberal victory.

Chapter 9 turns to consider the short-term factors that were specific to the 2000 election. The first of these is the economy. The prevailing assumption is that the fate of the incumbent government hinges very much on the state of the economy. Chapter 9 tests the proposition that the main reason for the Liberal victory was that the Canadian economy was in good shape. We examine how Canadians felt about the economy and ascertain the effect of these economic evaluations on their choice of party.

Theoretically, an election presents voters with the opportunity to choose the party that best defends their positions on the major issues of the day. Chapter 10 examines the distribution of opinions on the major issues of the 2000 election. How much support was there for tax cuts or for increased spending on health and education? Did Canadians think we should be tougher with criminals? How did they feel about abortion? We then establish whether opinions on these issues had an impact on vote choice independent of prior predispositions such as party identification.

Instead of looking at the parties' positions and supporting the party that seems most likely to defend their views, voters can focus on what the incumbent party has, and has not, accomplished during its mandate and vote to re-elect it, or not, depending on whether its performance has been satisfactory or unsatisfactory. The fact that the Liberals were re-elected seems to suggest that Canadians were basically satisfied, but was that really the case? Chapter 11 presents the Liberal report card, and we determine whether perceptions about the government's performance over the previous three years really did contribute to the Liberal victory.

On election day, Canadians do not just decide which party will form the government, they also determine which person will become Prime Minister. Chapter 12 looks at the relative popularity of the various party leaders and assesses the specific impact of the leaders on the outcome of the election. We pay particular attention to the evolution of leader evaluations over the course of the campaign and to the personal qualities that Canadians liked or disliked in their leaders. The spotlight is on voters' reactions to Jean Chrétien and especially to Stockwell Day. *Was* Stockwell Day particularly unpopular, and was this why his party failed to break through in Ontario? And, above all, what role did his personal religious convictions play?

Finally, in Chapter 13, we estimate how many voters voted for a party other than the one they really preferred. In a "first past the post" system like Canada's it is tempting for voters to vote strategically. If their first-choice party/candidate has no chance of winning in their constituency, then citizens may decide to vote for their second preference in the hope of defeating a party/candidate that they particularly dislike. In the context of the 2000 election, we have to ask whether this hurt the two weaker parties, the Conservatives and the NDP. Did these two parties fail to do better because voters did not want to "waste" their vote on parties that had no chance of winning? Or, was the problem simply that these two parties were the first choice of relatively few voters?

Before addressing these questions, we need to understand what voters were reacting to when they were making up their minds how to vote. What were the parties telling voters about themselves and about their opponents? This is the subject of Chapter 1.

CHAPTER 1

The Parties and Their Messages

In an election campaign, politicians talk all the time. Party messages are the starting point of our inquiry. Our ultimate objective is to understand why Canadians voted the way they did, and the first logical step is to take stock of the options they could choose from. There were five major parties running in the election: the Liberals, the Alliance, the Conservatives, the New Democratic Party (NDP), and the Bloc Québécois, the latter confined to the province of Quebec. What were they telling voters?

That very general question can be formulated into four more specific ones. First, and most obviously: what were the parties' positions on the major issues of the day? An election is very much a debate about what should and should not be done about the various problems the country is faced with, and the parties are thus led to indicate what solutions they propose. The second question concerns the relative priority given to the various issues. The parties have to decide which issues they will emphasize and which ones they will say little about during the campaign. An election is also very much about the leaders and their personal qualities. So the logical third question is: How much emphasis did the parties put on the leaders in the campaign? Finally, the parties and their representatives have much to say about their adversaries. The question, therefore, is: Who attacked whom, on what issues?

We assume that the parties' messages stem from a combination of ideological preferences and pragmatic considerations. Pragmatic considerations are obvious. Parties want to get as many votes as possible. For that reason, they shun away from positions that are clearly unacceptable to the mass public. But politicians also have policy preferences. And they have to pay attention to party members, who often have strong ideological concerns. As a consequence, parties present policy packages that lean in a distinct ideological orientation while remaining as centrist as possible (Strom, 1990; Wittman, 1990; Blais et al., 1993). Ideological orientations should have greater weight on the construction of party programs. Concerns with votes should be paramount during the campaign. By that time, it may be too late to change the party's position on an issue, but it may be possible to tone it down or amend it slightly.

What can be done most easily during a campaign is to emphasize certain issues at the expense of others. The parties want to focus media and voters' attention on "winning" issues and they try hard to avoid "losing" issues. What are the "winning" and "losing" issues? A winning issue is an issue that the party feels it can benefit from, either because its position is particularly popular—or that of another party is particularly unpopular—or because it is an area where it has strong credibility—or another party has weak credentials (Budge and Farlie, 1983; Petrocik, 1996; Nadeau et al., 2000).

The strategic choices that the parties make during a campaign are not limited to the issues. They must also decide how much emphasis to put on their leaders and which parties to attack. We may assume that the parties will want to put their leader at the forefront, if they believe that this will give them more votes, that is, if the leader is particularly popular. The reverse holds if the leader is unpopular. Likewise, a party will target whichever adversary appears vulnerable, and that should be the party having supporters who seem most easily convertible.

We examine four *sources* of messages: programs, press releases, TV ads, and the televised leader debates. The party programs, which are elaborated before the campaign starts and which present party positions on the major issues of the day, can be construed as the parties' "ideal" agenda about what should be done to make Canada a better country. "Ideal" does not mean that programs are immune from pragmatic considerations about which ideas can and cannot be sold to the public; it rather means that the content of the programs is under the sole control of the parties and that they are not constrained by the vagaries of the campaign (Norris et al., 1999: 62). For their part, press releases, TV ads, and televised debates are produced during the campaign and reflect the parties' tactical choices.

The Parties' Programs

The programs were entitled *Opportunity for All: The Liberal Plan for the Future of Canada*, *A Time for Change: An Agenda of Respect for All Canadians* (Canadian Alliance), *Change You Can Trust: The Progressive Conservative Plan for Canada's Future*, *Think How Much Better Canada Could Be: The NDP's*

Commitments to Canadians, and *Plate-forme du Bloc Québécois: Un parti pris pour le monde*. Each paragraph of the party programs was coded, with the coders indicating which issue(s) the paragraph dealt with. If more than one issue was mentioned in a paragraph, each issue was registered. Figure 1.1 presents the relative importance of various issues in the party programs.[1] The percentages correspond to the percentage of total references to each issue. They do not add up to 100 per cent because many issues with very few mentions are omitted.

The programs provide a fairly accurate reflection of the Canadian political landscape. The differences between the priorities advanced by the different traditional federal parties (Liberals, Conservatives, NDP) reflect, above and beyond their similarities, their ideological positioning. The New Democrats focused on social programs and the environment, while the Conservatives paid more attention to crime. Further to the right, the Canadian Alliance gave top priority to public finances, and said very little about the environment. The Bloc's agenda reflects both its status as a sovereignist party and its label as a party of the centre-left. This supports the view that social issues belong to the left and the economy and security to the right.

An interesting exception to the above pattern is the issue of health care. This was the dominant concern of Canadians at the time of the election. As many as 84 per cent of the respondents to the Canadian Election Study indicated that improving health care was very important to them personally in this election. No other issue came close to being as important. The political parties were probably aware of these preoccupations at the time they prepared their programs, and all of them, including those on the right of the political spectrum (the Conservatives and the Alliance), felt obliged to show that they had similar concerns. As a consequence, the two right-wing parties devoted as much attention to health as did the NDP. The party that put health highest on its agenda was the Liberal Party. The outlier was clearly the Bloc, which systematically avoided an issue that it considers to be within provincial jurisdiction. Another intriguing exception is the importance given by the NDP to a traditional "right-wing" issue, public finances. Of course, the party gave it a different "leftist" spin, which is examined below.

The party programs testify to the dominance of a small number of issues at election time. The questions of health, public finances, the economy, social programs, crime, and the environment represent nearly two-thirds of the themes. It is interesting to note that crime

Figure 1.1   Issues in Party Programs

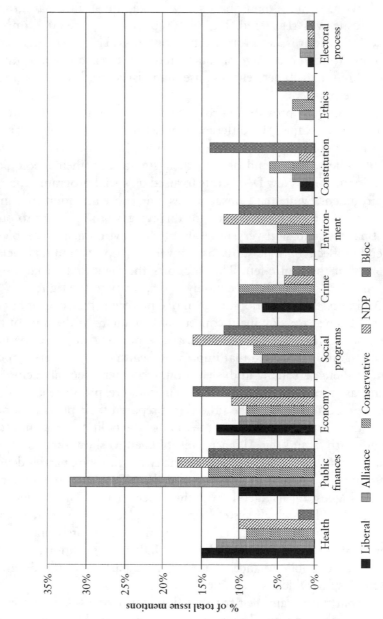

did not figure very prominently even within the Alliance and Conservative programs, despite the fact that the issue was very high on voters' agendas. Indeed, 72 per cent of our respondents said that fighting crime was a very important issue, only 12 percentage points less than for health, and more than for creating jobs (68 per cent) and for cutting taxes (54 per cent).

The near-invisibility of certain issues that would have some prominence during the campaign, such as abortion, the electoral process, ethics, and the constitution, is also striking. Finally, there was very little reference to policy domains, such as commerce, international relations, defense, Aboriginal affairs, immigration, transportation, and culture.

Figure 1.1 tells us which issues the parties were talking about. But *what* were they saying exactly?

Health Care

The Liberal Party claimed paternity over medicare in its platform, affirming that "medicare is a profound testament of Canadian values" (*Opportunity for All*, 15) and committing itself to preserving its integrity by opposing the use of public funds to finance private hospitals as well as the establishment of a two-tiered system. On health funding, the Liberals' position consisted of stressing the health care action plan adopted in September 2000 and which "commits all governments to respecting the fundamental principles of medicare and to working collaboratively to build a modern, sustainable health care system" (*Opportunity for All*, 15), a goal made possible by increased federal transfer payments. And it indicated that it would not allow any province to contravene the principles of medicare.

All these commitments were also made by the NDP, who made three additional commitments: immediately increasing federal cash transfers to 25 per cent of total public health spending, creating a national home-care plan, and creating a pharmacare plan. Clearly, the NDP was positioning itself as the party that was willing to do most for health.

What about the right end of the political spectrum? Interestingly, the Alliance Party first reiterated its support for the five principles of the Health Care Act. As for funding, it promised to "replace federal-provincial confrontations with a more co-operative approach" (*A Time for Change*, 15) and it called for five-year agreements with the provinces that would make it impossible for the federal government to unilaterally cut the transfers to the provinces. The party did not indicate, however, when and how much more money it was willing to give to the provinces. The Conservative Party's position was along the same lines: its platform specified that the party would add a sixth principle to the Health Care Act: stable funding.

In short, the Liberals were saying that they would fight to maintain the public health system, the NDP was promising to do more, and the Alliance and the Conservatives were declaring their support for the Health Care Act and their dedication to a more collaborative relationship with the provinces in this area.

Public Finances

The parties also differentiated themselves in a fairly clear manner on fiscal issues. The Canadian Alliance proposed the most significant tax cuts ($134 billion in five years) as well as substantial modifications to the tax regime (namely the adoption of a 17 per cent flat tax for taxpayers earning less than $100,000). The Liberal Party promised a $100-billion tax cut over the same period and targeted reductions in tax rates for those earning between $60,000 and $100,000. The Bloc Québécois set a more modest objective: a $73-billion tax cut, targeted at those earning less than $80,000. Even more modest was the cut promised by the Conservatives ($56 billion), who also indicated that they would eliminate the capital gains tax. This last proposition stands in contrast with the NDP's program, which argued against the exemption of capital gains and in favour of increasing the progressivity of the personal income tax by limiting tax cuts to taxpayers earning less than $60,000.

The parties also differed on the question of debt repayment. The positions of the Liberals, the Bloc Québécois, and the NDP were quite similar. The three parties said they would progressively reduce the debt-to-GDP ratio to 40 per cent (Liberals), 42 per cent (NDP), and 48 per cent (Bloc) by 2004-05. By contrast, the right-wing parties expressed a greater desire to reduce the debt. The Conservative Party advocated a law to eliminate the national debt within 25 years, while the Alliance committed itself to devoting 75 per cent of the budgetary surpluses to debt repayment.

Again, we observe a greater concern to reduce taxes and the debt on the right than on the left. But clearly the Liberals had decided to position themselves not too far from the right by announcing substantial tax cuts in the budget speech delivered by Finance Minister

Paul Martin a few weeks before the election was called. It is fair to assume that the Liberals wanted to neutralize an issue that usually advantages the right.

Economic Policy

The NDP and the Alliance held the most distinct positions on this issue. The NDP recommended changing the Bank of Canada Act to orient monetary policy towards job growth, extending the role of the Federal Business Development Bank to encourage community-based enterprises, and putting in place stricter price controls over monopolies such as Air Canada. At the other end of the ideological spectrum, the Alliance advocated the elimination of business subsidies, a sell-off of government shares in Petro Canada, the privatization of Via Rail, and an end to Air Canada's monopoly. The Liberal Party, for its part, stressed the importance of government initiatives to enhance research and stimulate regional development, while the Conservatives proposed the establishment of a "Canadian Institute for Learning and Technology" (*Change You Can Trust*, 14) Finally, the Bloc Québécois argued that the federal government should give Quebec its proportional share of federal expenditures slated for research and development.

Social Programs

The main party positions on social policy concerned increasing the number of public housing units (Liberals, Bloc, and NDP) and putting in place programs to encourage funding for education (establishing a registered apprenticeship system in the case of the Liberal Party, changes to the loans and bursaries system in the case of the Alliance and Conservatives, creating a "Canada Education Accessibility Fund" in the case of the NDP). Particularly noteworthy was the Bloc Québécois's insistence on reforming the employment insurance program.

Crime

The parties differed on two main issues: the balance between deterrence and rehabilitation, and gun control. On the latter, the Alliance position was clear, with Stockwell Day's party proposing to "repeal the Liberals' costly firearms law (C-68) that does nothing to enhance public safety" and to "replace it with a practical firearms control system that is cost effective and respects the right of Canadians to own and use firearms responsibly" (*A Time for Change*, 19). Adopting the opposing view, the Liberal Party, the NDP, and the Bloc Québécois expressed their intention to maintain the existing legislation, while the Conservative Party indicated it would make some adjustments.

Fighting crime constituted an important part of the Canadian Alliance platform, which proposed, among other things, the tightening of the parole system, the lifetime surveillance of sex offenders and repeat violent offenders, and the possibility of sending to adult court young offenders aged 16 (14 for more serious crimes). The Conservative Party came with similar positions, and attacked the Liberal government for cutting funding to the RCMP. Their stand was a strong contrast to the policies of the Bloc Québécois and the NDP, which stressed the rehabilitation of young offenders and insisted on intensifying the fight against organized crime and on helping victims of crimes, a position similar to that of the Liberal Party. A stark contrast between the two right-wing parties and the three others.

Environment

The environment was another visible theme in the party platforms. The NDP recommended many environmental-protection measures. It recommended initiatives to encourage the development of public transportation, reduce greenhouse gases, establish a water-purification fund, and make it mandatory to label genetically modified foods. The Liberal program emphasized the need to tighten standards regarding vehicle exhaust and to improve municipal infrastructures, whereas the parties more to the right were less explicit regarding their environmental policies. Clearly, the environment belongs to the left, in Canada as elsewhere.

Constitution

The constitution was virtually absent from the parties' platforms with the exception of the Bloc Québécois, which denounced the federal government's intrusion into provincial areas. The Conservatives and the Alliance committed themselves to a more collaborative approach with the provinces.

Ethics

There was also little discussion of ethical issues in the party platforms. The opposition parties did refer, however, to the widespread favouritism that, they alleged, plagued the subsidies offered by the Department of Human Resources.

Electoral Process

The Liberal and NDP platforms were silent on this issue. The Bloc Québécois proposed that the federal government adopt the kind of party financing legislation that is already in place in Quebec (only individuals are allowed to contribute). The parties on the right paid more attention to the issue. The Conservative Party, like the Canadian Alliance, said there should be more free votes in the House of Commons (the Alliance argued that all votes should be free, except for the budget and votes of non-confidence) and advocated the establishment of a Parliamentary ethics bureau. Lastly, the Canadian Alliance proposed the election of senators and asserted that citizens should have the right to force referendums "to put their priorities on the national agenda through a Canada-wide vote" (*A Time for Change*, 20).

Abortion

Only the Bloc Québécois and the NDP talked (briefly) about abortion.[2] The Bloc revealed its position by making direct reference to Stockwell Day: "the arrival of a party leader on the federal stage opposed to the free choice of women on the voluntary interruption of pregnancy leads us to specify that the Bloc Québécois is against the recriminalization of abortion and in favor of free access for women to abortion" (*Un parti pris pour le monde*, 80; original in French). The NDP advocated "a comprehensive reproductive health policy that recognizes women's right to control their own bodies and opposes recriminalization of abortion" (*Think How Much Better Canada Could Be*, 17). Interestingly, the Alliance was completely silent on this sensitive issue.

The Press Releases

Through their programs, the parties established their basic policy orientations. These orientations have to be fleshed out in the course of the campaign, and, most crucially, the parties must respond to the positions staked out by their adversaries as well as to unforeseen events. Throughout the campaign, they prepared press releases that reiterated or clarified their positions and/or underlined "flaws" in their adversaries' statements. Typically, each party issued one or two releases per day. The most "active" party was the Liberal Party, with 69 press releases, and the least active was the Conservative party, with 27. The Bloc Québécois had 64, the Alliance 56, and the NDP 32.[3]

These press releases were analyzed along the same coding scheme as the party programs. The press release constituted the unit of analysis. Figure 1.2 indicates the percentage of total references to each issue for each party. Again, the percentages do not add up to 100 per cent because many minor issues are omitted.

Perhaps the most striking finding in Figure 1.2 is the strong emphasis given to health care. Health emerged as the top issue in the press releases of the Liberals, the NDP, and the Conservatives. The parties seem to have realized that this was a dominant concern in the electorate and they decided to talk a lot about the issue. And, not surprisingly, the party that was most vocal was the NDP.

There were two exceptions. The Alliance and the Bloc Québécois did not say much. In the case of the Bloc, this was a conscious decision not to talk about an issue that the party thought was (and should be) a provincial responsibility. In the case of the Alliance, however, there is every reason to believe that the party would have liked the election to focus on almost anything else. They tried to say as little as possible, but of course their adversaries would not let them off the hook. Health is a "left" issue, and it was a tough issue for the party furthest to the right.

The Liberal Party's message became more defined during the campaign. The party continued to present itself as the defender of medicare and identified two threats to its integrity, privatization of hospitals and the emergence of a two-tiered system, but it personified these threats, associating them with Stockwell Day and the Alliance. The Alliance's response was to reassert its commitment to the public health system. The NDP was arguing, for its part, that the Liberals had already initiated a two-tiered system and that it was the only party fully committed to public health care.

The other dominant issue in the press releases was public finances. Every party talked a lot about fiscal issues, and the Alliance was the most talkative. Not surprisingly, since taxation is a right-wing issue.

Figure 1.2 Issues in Press Releases

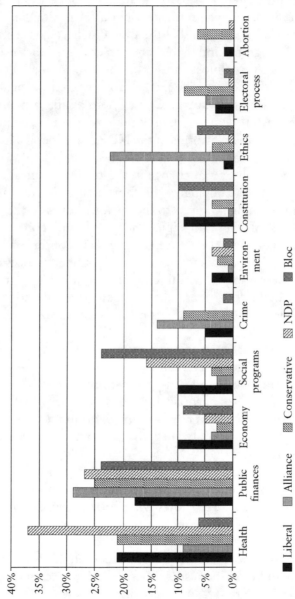

But, the Liberals and the NDP do not seem to have avoided the issue. We may surmise that the Liberals did not feel on the defensive, because they had just announced huge tax cuts. The case of the NDP is more intriguing. The party decided to make the question of tax equity a major campaign theme, right after health care.

Figure 1.2 also shows that the Bloc Québécois focused very much on social programs and the Alliance on ethics. In the case of the Bloc, the emphasis was almost entirely on the reform of employment insurance. The Alliance, for its part, clearly wanted to make ethics, and most especially the Auberge Grand-Mère affair,[4] a main issue in the campaign. And there was finally the environment, which had some importance in the platforms of the NDP and Liberals, but which was shelved off the agenda throughout the campaign.

Was there substantial change in the parties' tactical agendas over the course of the campaign? The short answer is "no." We compared the relative emphasis given to the various issues in the first and last two weeks of the campaign, and we found comparatively little change. There was one exception, which concerned the Alliance. While the Alliance talked mainly about public finances at the beginning of the campaign, it shifted course and came to focus more on crime and ethics. Perhaps Alliance strategists came to the conclusion that public finances was not as much a "winning" issue as they had hoped.

It is also interesting to see how many of the press releases were promotional—the party selling its own positions—and how much was in the attack mood—the party pointing out flaws in an adversary's position. Not surprisingly, the government party was the only one whose messages were mostly promotional (57 per cent); all the other parties were mainly "negative," about 60 per cent of their messages being attacks.

Who was attacking whom? The first point to note is that most of these attacks were personalized and that the target was usually a party leader. Table 1.1 shows what proportion of total attacks was directed towards each leader.[5]

The strategies of the parties were absolutely clear. In their attacks, the NDP, the Bloc, and the Alliance focused almost entirely on Jean Chrétien and the Liberals on Stockwell Day (except in Quebec). The Conservative Party was the only one to distribute its attacks almost equally between two targets, Chrétien and Day. Apparently Conservative strategists reasoned that they had to disqualify the two major party leaders in the voters' minds in order to get their support.

Table 1.1 Distribution of Attacks on Leaders in Party Press Releases

	Liberal	*Alliance*	*Conservative*	*NDP*	*Bloc*
Chrétien	0	94	48	77	97
Day	78	0	37	21	1
Clark	7	4	0	2	2
McDonough	1	0	7	0	1
Duceppe	14	2	7	0	0
Total attacks	76	139	71	149	154

Note: Cell entries are percentages. The table should be read in the following way. There were a total of 76 attacks on leaders in the press releases prepared by the Liberals. Among these 76 attacks, 78% were targetted at Stockwell Day.

The Liberal attacks on Stockwell Day were not particularly focused, though the favourite themes were health and public finances, the two top issues of the election (results not presented). The Liberals did also raise the issues of abortion and referendums, accusing the Alliance leader of having an hidden agenda.

The Alliance attacks on Jean Chrétien were concentrated on two issues, public finances and ethics. The latter issue came up because of new information that emerged about the Grand-Mère affair during the campaign. Clearly, the Alliance thought that this was a great opportunity to question the integrity and credibility of the Prime Minister.

The Conservatives attacked both Chrétien and Day. Attacks on Chrétien focused on fiscal matters and those against Day on abortion, referendums, the death penalty, and immigration. The party was trying to establish itself as the party of the "moderate" right and to depict the Alliance as "extremist."

As for the NDP, its main line of attack on the Prime Minister was, not surprisingly, health. The NDP accused Chrétien of having already introduced a sort of two-tiered health system. And the Bloc criticized the Liberal leader for its mismanagement of the government surplus and of the employment insurance program.

The examination of press releases confirms that the parties fought the electoral battle mainly on two issues: health and public finances. Health was the dominant issue for the Liberals, the NDP, and the Conservatives, while the Bloc and the Alliance tried to downplay it. This was a particularly tough question for the party on the right end of the political spectrum. Two other issues that had not figured much in the party platforms emerged: the question of ethics, with the new revelations about the Grand-Mère affair, and referendums and abortion, because of the suspected hidden agenda of the Alliance. One issue that was a top concern among voters, crime, got little attention. And one other issue disappeared almost entirely: the environment.

The press releases also indicate that the Liberals and the Alliance wanted the election to be fought between the two of them, which led them to largely ignore the other party leaders. The Bloc and the NDP focused their attacks on Jean Chrétien. The Conservatives for their part decided to attack both Day and Chrétien, an indication that they perceived themselves in between the Liberals and the Alliance and that there were possible gains to be made on both sides.

Televised Ads

The most direct way for the parties to communicate with the voters, and to tell them why they should vote for them, is the TV ad (West, 1997). We were able to obtain the ads put up by the parties during the campaign.[6] The Liberal Party was much more active than its adversaries on this front, perhaps because of greater financial resources. The party aired a total of 20 different ads, compared with 8 by the Alliance, 5 by the Bloc and the Conservatives, and 3 by the NDP. Because there were relatively few of them, we do not present a detailed quantitative analysis of the issues that were dealt with in these ads, especially as the patterns were similar to those that emerged in the press releases.

There were, however, some interesting differences. The Liberals put even more emphasis on health in their ads than in their press releases, and their line of attack was very much Stockwell Day and the two-tiered system. The Alliance ads were much less "negative" than its press releases. While the latter included many attacks against Jean Chrétien, the ads were "softer," stressing the merits of Stockwell Day and its party.

The Conservative strategy was exactly the opposite. It was all negative, and it entirely targeted Jean Chrétien. As for the NDP, the party did talk a little about the environment in its ads. And the Bloc focused, once again, on Chrétien and the employment insurance program.

In designing their ads, the parties were faced with another difficult strategic decision: how much visibility to confer on their leader? The parties came up with very different choices. At one end of the spectrum, we find the Conservatives. Joe Clark was completely absent from all the Conservative ads. Apparently, Conservative strategists believed that the best way to attract voters was not to show the Conservative leader but rather to convince them that both Jean Chrétien and Stockwell Day were unacceptable. At the other end, there was the Alliance. Stockwell Day appeared in each and every Alliance ad and he could be seen most of the time during these ads. This was part of the soft, personalized approach that characterized the Alliance ads. The party must have felt that Day's personal style carried well on television. In between these two extremes were Jean Chrétien and Gilles Duceppe, who were quite visible but not as omnipresent as Stockwell Day. Finally, Alexa McDonough, while not being as invisible as Joe Clark, did not feature prominently in the NDP ads, presumably because she was not perceived to be very charismatic.

This analysis of televised ads points to an additional message that the Alliance was attempting to convey; this message was that the party had a "good" new leader. For the Liberals, the ads offered another opportunity to hammer home the idea that health was the dominant issue and that Stockwell Day and the Alliance could not be trusted on this issue. The Conservatives went completely negative, relentlessly attacking the Prime Minister. For the NDP, the ads provided an occasion to talk a little about the environment.

The Leader Debates

The televised leader debates provided the parties with another golden opportunity to tell voters all the good reasons they should have to support them rather than their opponents. As is now the norm in Canada, there were two successive leader debates at mid-campaign, the first in French on November 8 and the second in English on November 9. These debates did not allow the leaders to impose their agenda, because they had to respond to the questions raised by the journalists. They had the possibility, however, to make some crucial points.

Our intention is not to review the two debates in any detail but only to identify additional dimensions of the ideological battle. Two aspects of the French debate were particularly noticeable. First, language barriers turned the French debate into a three-way fight among Jean Chrétien, Joe Clark, and Gilles Duceppe. The implicit message for the largely Quebec audience was perhaps that the NDP and the Alliance were not really "in the game" in Quebec. Second, Bloc leader Gilles Duceppe put crime on the agenda, arguing in favour of a tough anti-gang legislation and against the toughening of the Young Offenders Act. This is an unusual strategy for a center-left party.

The English debate was a more powerful event. First, Jean Chrétien was the object of relentless, and sometimes ferocious, attacks from all sides. The Liberals were way ahead in the polls, and apparently all the other leaders had come to the conclusion that the best way to win the debate was to knock out the Prime Minister and to entice these numerous Liberal supporters to revisit their vote intentions.

The most dramatic moment of the evening was probably Stockwell Day's attempt to respond to Liberal accusations regarding the Alliance's acceptance of a two-tiered health system in Canada. Violating the rules of the debate, Day held up a little cardboard sign with the inscription "No 2-Tier Health Care" before leaving his podium to approach Jean Chrétien and demanding that either he calls him a liar or that he retracts Liberal televised spots accusing the Canadian Alliance of favouring a two-tiered health care system. The fact that this was the most intense moment of the debate shows that Stockwell Day was painfully aware that health was an extremely important issue and that many Canadians had doubts about the Alliance's credibility on this question.

Another noteworthy exchange was the one between Jean Chrétien and Joe Clark, the latter accusing the Prime Minster of having called the election for purely opportunistic reasons: "Mr. Chrétien," asserted a defiant Clark, "let's face it. The only reason you called this federal election is to prevent Paul Martin from getting your job .... It is not because you have a plan for the country, it is because you have a plan for yourself."

The leader debates confirmed the central role of health care in the election campaign and the problems that this created for the party (the Alliance) which tended to be the most critical, in general, of state intervention. They also confirmed that all the opposition leaders were targeting first and foremost all those who were intending to vote Liberal, or who were leaning in that direction. There were clearly many of them, and they were the ones to convert. Finally, the debates raised still another issue, that is, whether it was appropriate for the Prime Minister to have called the election so early.

Discussion

All the parties, in this election as in previous ones, were *not* saying the same thing. They were staking different positions, and these positions presented well-defined contours. On most issues, the basic opposition was between the parties of the right, the Alliance and the Conservatives, and those of center or left, the Bloc, the NDP, and the Liberals. Furthermore, the NDP showed its leftist orientation by committing itself to major improvements to health care, and the Conservatives tried to distinguish themselves from the Alliance on issues such as abortion.

The two issues that the parties talked most about were health care and fiscal matters. Health care is a leftist issue and it was appropriately the Liberals and the NDP that emphasized it. The Alliance would have liked to avoid the issue as much as possible, but this proved to be an impossible task, because this was the voters' top concern. The party was on the defensive, its credibility on the issue being tarred by its anti-statist orientation.

Public finances is a right-wing issue and it was appropriated by the Alliance. But the Liberals were not really on the defensive, thanks to the large tax cuts announced just before the election was called. This induced the Alliance to focus on ethics, and on the integrity of the Prime Minister.

There were two sleeper issues. The first was abortion. The Alliance was attacked for its willingness to have a referendum on such a divisive issue. The second was the timing of the election, the Prime Minister being criticized for calling an unnecessary early election. And crime, which was voters' second priority, right after health, was relatively low on the parties' agenda.

Many of the party messages were pointing to weaknesses and inconsistencies in their adversaries' positions. But different parties had different targets. The Liberals and the Alliance were attacking each other, largely ignoring the others (except in Quebec where the Bloc was also a Liberal target). The NDP and the Bloc were entirely focused on the incumbent Liberals. Only the Conservatives were aiming at two parties at once, the Liberals and the Alliance, a sign of its particular position in the Canadian party system.

Finally, party ads were quite revealing of the very different roles by the leaders of the two right-wing parties. Stockwell Day was extremely important in the Alliance ads, presumably because he was thought to appear well on television. At the other end, Joe Clark was completely absent from the Conservative ads, which were the most negative in their overall orientation.

Notes

1 For all aspects of our content analysis (party programs, press releases, TV ads), we proceeded to reliability tests in which two different coders independently coded a sample of the items. The reliability tests proved to be quite satisfactory, the convergence between the two coders being systematically above 90 per cent, that is, the two coders coded the same item in the same way at least 90 per cent of the time. See the Canadian Election Study Web site <www.fas.umontreal.ca/pol/ces-eec> for full information on the coding scheme.

2 This does not appear in Figure 1.1 because abortion constituted less than 1 per cent of all issue mentions.

3 The press releases could be found on the party Web sites.

4 The Auberge Grand-Mère "scandal" was about a loan that was given by the Business Development Bank of Canada, a federal public corporation, to a local businessman for the renovation of a hotel, which was located in the Prime Minister's constituency. The Bank had initially declined to offer a loan, but it revised its decision after the Prime Minister directly intervened in favour of the businessman with the chairman of the Bank.

5 Note that Table 1.1 deals only with the "attack" segment of the press releases. This leaves out more than half the Liberal messages and about 40 per cent of the opposition parties' messages, which were of a promotional character.

6 The ads were provided by the party organizations. We thank them for their collaboration.

CHAPTER 2

The Media: Getting Out the Messages

Modern election campaigns are media campaigns (Farrell, 1996; Semetko, 1996) with television constituting the voters' primary source of information (Fletcher and Everett, 1991; Ansolabehere et al., 1993). And indeed 52 per cent of the Canadian Election Study respondents said that their main source of information about the 2000 election was television, while only 23 per cent mentioned the newspapers and 11 per cent radio.

The parties were able to communicate directly with the voters through their ads and the leader debates. This is not enough, however. Voters get their daily account of how the campaign is going on the TV news broadcasts, and the parties are keen to have their messages carried to the voters on these broadcasts.

We examine what messages did and did not get out on the principal English-language and French-language nightly networks' newscasts: *The National* (CBC), *CTV National Edition* (CTV), *Le Téléjournal* (SRC), and *Le TVA, Édition réseau* (TVA). We address two main questions. First, which parties and leaders were most and least visible on TV news? Second, which issues were most and least covered? With respect to the latter question, we compare the agendas of the parties with the media's coverage and we determine which parties were more successful, or lucky enough, in having the media focus on the issues that were on top of their own agendas.

The chapter also examines how the media covered the most important event of the campaign: the leader debates. We determine, in particular, whether they were prone to declare a winner and/or a loser. And, finally, we look at how they treated one unusual issue that emerged in the 2000 election, that is, the religious beliefs of one of the party leaders, Stockwell Day.

Party Visibility

Media visibility is an important political resource. Government parties have a significant advantage on this front outside electoral campaigns (Monière and Fortier, 2000). During campaigns, this advantage diminishes, though it is still present (Crête, 1984). By contrast,

Table 2.1   Coverage of Major Political Parties and Leaders in TV News

	TV News		Headlines only	
	English	*French*	*English*	*French*
A. *Parties*				
Liberal	25	29	38	52
Alliance	22	18	37	13
Conservative	12	8	12	2
NDP	12	5	8	2
Bloc	9	23	5	32
(N)	(499)	(326)	(168)	(95)
B. *Leaders*				
Chrétien	27	35	40	63
Day	23	17	33	16
Clark	14	8	15	3
McDonough	11	5	6	2
Duceppe	10	17	6	17
(N)	(499)	(326)	(174)	(96)

Note: The table shows the percentage of stories for which a party or a leader was the main topic. N is the total number of electoral stories in the newscasts. Columns do not add to 100 per cent because of stories that were not about the major parties or their leaders.

weaker parties receive less media attention (Robinson and Sheehan, 1983: 76). These patterns were present in the 1997 election. The Liberal Party was the most widely visible on the television news while the NDP often seemed to be "off the radar screen" (Nevitte et al., 2000). Was the pattern any different in the 2000 election?

Table 2.1 shows the percentage of TV news stories for which a party or leader was the main topic.[1] Two very different patterns emerge in the French and English news. In the former, the Liberals and Jean Chrétien enjoyed a clear visibility bonus over the Alliance and the Bloc Québécois, while the Conservatives and the NDP trailed far behind. In English, the Alliance and Stockwell Day got almost as much coverage as the Liberals, the three other parties receiving only about half the attention paid to the two front-runners.

These results indicate that the Liberals were again the most visible party in the television news in 2000, though their lead over the Alliance on CBC and CTV was quite thin. At the other end of the spectrum were the Conservatives and the NDP, who were much less visible. For the Conservatives, this was quite a change from 1997, when they were as intensively covered as the Reform Party (the predecessor of the Alliance) (Nevitte et al., 2000).

The frequency of appearances in the news is only one indicator of visibility, and that indicator can be misleading depending on when in the broadcast the items featuring the party or the leader are positioned, as, for example, when they are relegated to the end of the newscast. It is also important to consider the order of appearance in the newscast. Making the headlines and/or making the first or second story confers much greater visibility than appearing at the very end of the program.

Table 2.1 also indicates who was most and least visible in the headlines. The dominance of the Liberal party in the French news was even more overwhelming, as was the absence of the Conservatives and the NDP. We can also see that Gilles Duceppe was much less prominent than the Bloc. In the English news, Chrétien still enjoyed a small lead over Day. But the Conservatives and Joe Clark made the headlines much more often than the NDP and Alexa McDonough. The Conservatives were not more often in the news than the NDP, but they were there more often in the "big" news.

A similar story emerges when we look at the order of appearance in the newscasts (Table 2.2). Viewers of the French newscast were very likely to have a report on the Liberals and/or Jean Chrétien, and they were very unlikely to hear about the Conservatives or the NDP, among the first three stories of the program. They were also unlikely to see the Bloc leader, Gilles Duceppe, at the top of the newscast. On the English networks, the Alliance was almost as visible as the Liberals, while the Conservatives, the NDP and the Bloc were much less present. The fact that each and every day of the campaign the NDP and Alexa McDonough failed to make the first story is yet another indication that it was difficult for the party to have voters focus their attention on them.

The content analysis of nightly television news indicates that the NDP was the least visible party of all in the media in 2000, as in 1997. Not surprisingly, the Liberal party and Jean Chrétien were the most visible, especially in the French media. The English networks paid almost as much attention to the Alliance and Stockwell Day, who were quite present throughout the campaign. The Conservative party, for its part, was clearly perceived to be a small party, and it got much smaller coverage. Unlike the NDP, however, the party did succeed in being on "the radar screen." The Bloc Québécois, finally,

Table 2.2   Order of Appearance of Parties and Leaders in TV News

	English-speaking networks				French-speaking networks			
	1st	2nd	3rd	(N)	1st	2nd	3rd	(N)
A. Parties								
Liberal	17	16	12	(124)	13	19	16	(93)
Alliance	14	16	18	(110)	0	11	23	(57)
Conservative	7	5	18	(61)	0	0	4	(25)
NDP	0	10	9	(60)	0	6	6	(17)
Bloc	0	2	9	(47)	12	12	15	(76)
B. Leaders								
Chrétien	19	16	13	(136)	13	21	17	(115)
Day	13	18	13	(114)	0	15	23	(56)
Clark	6	10	18	(68)	0	0	4	(25)
McDonough	0	11	7	(57)	0	0	13	(16)
Duceppe	0	2	9	(48)	8	9	16	(55)

Note: The table shows the percentage of stories about each party or leader that appeared first, second or third in the newscasts. N is the total number of stories about each party or leader in the newscasts.

received substantial coverage in the French news (though much less than the Liberals), but its leader was not very visible.

The nightly newscasts were not the only source of information about the election that was available on television. A number of public affairs programs often had representatives from all the parties. The pattern that we have documented here holds only on the news. Elsewhere, the rule of equal treatment for all the parties tended to prevail. Unfortunately for the small parties, however, the news clearly had a much greater audience.

It should also be stressed that the news coverage of the campaign was very much focused on the party leaders. In fact, party leaders were present in 85 per cent of all the news stories presented in the four networks and in 92 per cent of the stories that were at the front end (among the first three stories) of the program.[2] It was through their leader that the parties were, or were not, visible.

The Issues

The parties not only want the media to talk about them, but also to talk about the "winning" issues, the issues that they think will win them votes. What were the issues that the media focused upon? Was the media agenda particularly beneficial to any party?

Figure 2.1 shows the relative coverage devoted to the various issues on the English and French television networks. Three issues dominated the English news: health, public finances, and ethics. Health also came on top of the French news, followed by crime and ethics.

We may surmise that the Liberals hoped that the newscasts would focus as much as possible on health care, which was a difficult issue for their main adversary, the Alliance. Their hope was largely fulfilled, since health care was at the top of the media agenda. They were less lucky on another front, however. Ethics, which was their weakest theme, emerged as the third most frequent issue in the television news. And the media talked very little about the economy, which was in pretty good shape and which could possibly help them (see Chapter 9).

The reverse holds for the Alliance. The party would certainly have liked the campaign to deal primarily with public finances. The media focused rather on health care, which was the Alliance's least desirable issue. Things were even "worse" for them in the "big" news: there were four times as many Alliance headlines about health care (32 per cent) as about public finances (8 per cent). And the party's second "winning" issue, crime, did not get a lot of attention. The sole consolation for the Alliance was that the media did talk much about ethics, which was their main line of attack against the Liberals.

It is not clear that the Conservatives really had an issue that they wanted to put on the top of the agenda. As we saw in Chapter 1, the most striking aspect of the Conservative message, especially in the TV ads, was its negative character, and the most negative ad focused intensely on the integrity of the Prime Minister. The fact that ethics made the media agenda was perhaps good news for the party.

The NDP may have suffered from low visibility, but its issues were well-covered. They emphasized health throughout the campaign and this was the most frequent issue in the news. They and the Bloc were the only parties to talk to any significant extent about social programs, and that was covered at least modestly.[3] And crime, a right-wing issue, just did not make it on English news.

The Bloc's two priorities were public finances and social programs. The latter was adequately covered, but the party's messages on public finances were not relayed on the evening news.[4] The media focused rather on the constitution, probably more than the party desired.[5]

Figure 2.1   Issue Coverage in TV News

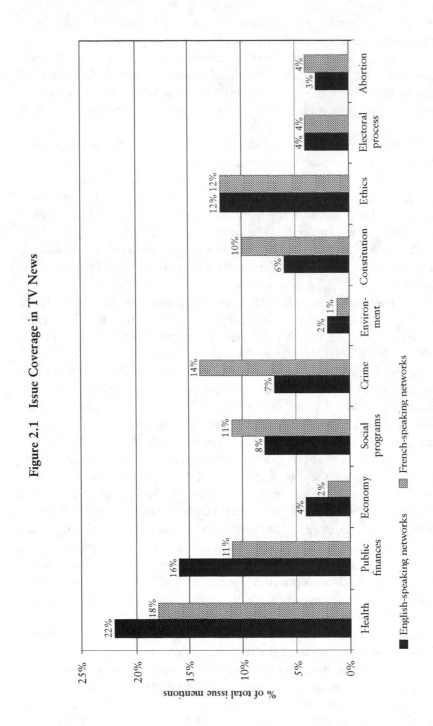

The party whose own priorities were best reflected in media coverage was the NDP, a small consolation for the very thin coverage the party received overall. The two parties worst off were the Alliance and the Bloc, the two parties that tried to avoid talking about the issue voters were most concerned with, that is, health care—an indication that the parties cannot entirely control the agenda.

The Leader Debates

Media coverage of leader debates, and particularly the ritual of crowning a winner, can sometimes have a significant impact on voters. This seems to be particularly the case when the media come to a clear decision about the winners and losers of a debate (Lanoue, 1996). In this respect, the televised debates in November 2000 stood in contrast to those of 1997, where a fairly clear media consensus emerged about Jean Charest's dominance (Nevitte et al., 2000). Journalists and invited experts were extremely prudent in their evaluations of the leaders' performance.

The dominant line in journalistic commentary on the French debate was that it had been a dull one. Without proclaiming a winner, the media underlined Jean Chrétien's good performance given his status as leader of the incumbent government (particularly on SRC). They also indicated that Joe Clark had done well and that Gilles Duceppe had significantly improved compared to his performance in 1997. In the eyes of the journalists, Stockwell Day lost the most ground in the debate due to his inability to be a true participant in a French debate. This damaged his image of becoming a genuine national leader, as journalist Michel Vastel pointed out on TVA.

The English-language debate stirred up more interest and sharper commentary. The media noted that Jean Chrétien appeared shaken by the relentless attacks from the four other leaders. Both Stockwell Day and Joe Clark were said to have delivered a good performance, though the reports stressed that no "knockout" blow had occurred. It is nevertheless revealing that the emblematic sequence of the English debate, which was replayed frequently in the media, was that of Stockwell Day brandishing his "No Two-Tier Health Care" sign. The CTV network reported an "instant" Internet survey suggesting that Stockwell Day had done the best overall, followed by Joe Clark. The bottom line, however, is that the media proclaimed no clear winner.

Stockwell Day's Religious Beliefs

If there was one peculiarity of the 2000 election, it was the presence of a party leader with strong and non-mainstream personal religious convictions. Stockwell Day is a Christian fundamentalist, whose religious beliefs became even more public when he announced his decision not to campaign on Sundays. This decision, as well as its religious basis, was widely covered by the media. Voters who followed the campaign in the television news could not have missed that piece of information.

The issue of Day's religious creed was also raised by the other parties, especially the Liberals. Jean Chrétien, in particular, reiterated that it was crucial for him to maintain a strict separation between religion and politics, implicitly suggesting that this might not be the case with the Alliance. The media widely reported such innuendos. Day himself refrained from talking about his beliefs, simply stating that he had personal beliefs, but that he would not impose them if he were elected.

Then, there was the CBC's documentary on the political past and religious beliefs of Stockwell Day, particularly his views on "creationism," aired on 15 November. The title of the documentary says it all: "The Fundamental Day." The piece raised passionate reactions, both positive and negative. The Alliance was outraged and denounced it as unfair and biased. Whatever the case, once again, the media did contribute to the visibility of Day's religious beliefs.

Discussion

Parties pursue two main objectives in their relations with the media during a campaign. They hope to be visible and to have the media focus on the "right" issues, those that can win them votes. In the 2000 election, no party really achieved both objectives.

The Conservative Party and the NDP had the common misfortune to lack competitiveness both in Quebec and in the rest of Canada. They both entered the campaign trailing so badly in the polls that many observers doubted their ability to conserve their official party status in the House of Commons. This inability to compete may explain their low visibility.

The Conservatives and the NDP adopted different strategies to overcome media indifference. The NDP chose to focus its communications activities on health and public finances, while the

Conservative Party chose to follow the crowd by commenting on most questions and mounted a negative attack on the Prime Minister.

The Bloc Québécois's strategy also ran into its share of difficulties. By neglecting the health issue, the party was placed on the sidelines of the campaign's most important debate from the very start. If the Bloc Québécois's insistence on the question of social programs was taken up by the media, its positions on public finances and economic questions were, by contrast, scarcely picked up. The Bloc Québécois's visibility on the issues of employment insurance, crime, and ethical questions appears to have allowed the party to be heard on issues other than the Constitution. Given the limited interest in this question during the last election, this is perhaps a victory in itself for a party almost entirely associated with the question of Quebec sovereignty.

The Canadian Alliance's greatest success was to impose itself as the main contender to the Liberals, which allowed it to receive as much coverage as the Liberals on English news and almost as much as the Bloc on French TV. The Alliance was also able to raise the ethical practices of the Liberal government and its leader as one of the campaign's principal issues. But these successes hide more important defeats. The Canadian Alliance hoped to promote itself and attack the Liberals first and foremost on the theme of public finances. The media did talk about public finances, but they talked even more about health care, which was precisely the issue the party hoped to avoid. The party also failed to have the media focus much on the other right-wing issue, crime. Finally, the party did not succeed in eschewing all the publicity around Stockwell Day's personal religious beliefs.

The Liberal Party, finally, must have been quite pleased to see the media put health at the top of its agenda, because this was clearly the worst issue for its most serious adversary. Other aspects of media coverage were much less positive, however. It must have been frustrating to see the media say so little about the sound economic situation and so much about ethical issues.

Notes

1 As for party messages, we performed reliability tests in which two different coders independently coded a sample of the news stories. Here again, the reliability tests were quite satisfactory, the convergence

between the two coders being above 90 per cent. See the Canadian Election Study website <www.fas.umontreal.ca/pol/ces-eec> for full information on the coding scheme. We present the findings combining the two English-speaking and the two French-speaking networks; differences between the two English and the two French networks were relatively small.

2 *Le TVA, Édition réseau* was the least focused on the leaders, with "only" 83 per cent of the first three stories mentioning a party leader. The percentages were 93 per cent on *The National,* 94 per cent on *CTV National Edition,* and 95 per cent on *Le Téléjournal.*

3 Twenty-one per cent of issue coverage of the NDP on English news was about social programs.

4 Fifteen per cent of issue coverage of the Bloc on French news concerned social programs, and only 7 per cent was about public finances.

5 In fact, 22 per cent of issue coverage of the Bloc on French news dealt with the constitution; this was the most widely covered issue for the party.

CHAPTER 3

Why Was Turnout So Low?

Turnout in the 2000 federal election was a record low. Only 61 per cent of registered voters went to the polls. This is the lowest recorded turnout in a federal election since Confederation. We have to go back to the end of the nineteenth century to find a turnout that was almost as low.[1] And actual turnout in 2000 may have been lower even than the recorded figure. This is because turnout in Canada is calculated on the basis of the number of *registered* voters and not, as in the United States, on the basis of the number of *eligible* voters.

Turnout has been falling steadily since the 1988 federal election (see Figure 3.1). Turnout was not unusually high in that election. In fact, at 75 per cent, the turnout rate corresponded to the average of the 15 elections held between 1945 and 1988. Since 1988, turnout has plummeted 14 points. Such a precipitous decline is serious cause for concern. Our purpose in this chapter is to identify the reasons for the low turnout in 2000.

Figure 3.1   Turnout in Federal Elections, 1945 to 2000

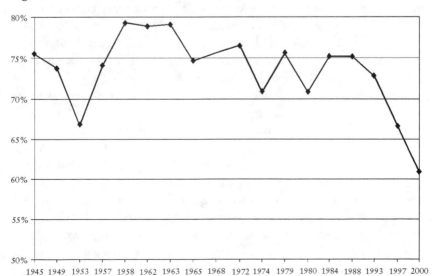

Only three provinces and one territory bucked the trend of declining turnout between the 1997 and 2000 federal elections: Newfoundland, Prince Edward Island, Alberta, and Yukon (see Figure 3.2). Newfoundland and Alberta actually registered small increases. These were the two provinces that had had the lowest turnout in the 1997 election. In that election, turnout had been highest in Prince Edward Island, Quebec, and New Brunswick. The largest declines occurred in Canada's two most populous provinces, Quebec and Ontario, as well as in the Northwest Territories. The other two provinces to experience a significant drop-off in voting levels between 1997 and 2000 were Nova Scotia and New Brunswick.

Who is Not Voting?

The single most important point to grasp about the decline in turnout since 1988 is that turnout has not declined in the electorate at large, but is largely confined to Canadians born after 1970. In Figure 3.3, we track rates of non-voting[2] for four cohorts: the pre-baby boomers (born before 1945), the baby boomers (born between 1945 and 1959), generation X (born between 1960 and 1969), and post-generation X (born since 1970).[3] The rates are tracked relative to the rate of non-voting among the oldest cohort in 1988. Since only those born in 1970 or earlier had reached voting age in 1988, we start the tracking for the youngest generation in 1993. The contrast between the post-generation-X cohort and the three older cohorts is striking. Rates of non-voting do not show any clear trend among the three older cohorts. Non-voting did increase a little among all three cohorts between 1993 and 1997, but by 2000 rates had fallen back to close to their 1988 levels. In the post-generation X cohort, by contrast, non-voting increased by 14 points between 1993 and 2000. The implication is clear: if we want to understand why turnout is declining in Canada, we need to focus on the generation that was born after 1970.

The first question that has to be addressed is whether this is really a generational effect or simply a life-cycle effect. In other words, is there something about this generation of Canadians that makes them less likely to vote than younger voters of generations past? Or are younger voters less likely to vote just because they *are* younger? Answering this question is important. If it is only a life-cycle effect, then we can expect turnout to increase as these younger voters age, but if it is a true generational effect, then their rates of non-voting will remain higher than those of previous generations.

Figure 3.2   Turnout in the 1997 and 2000 Federal Elections

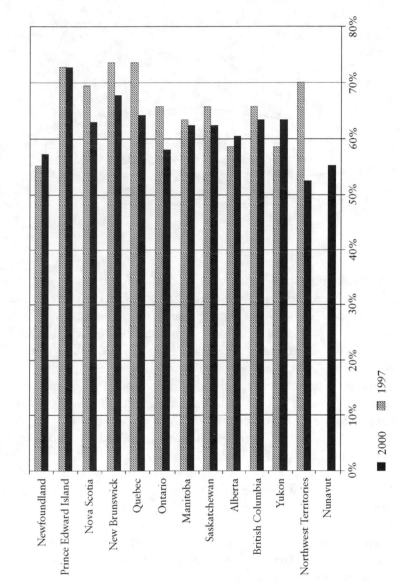

Figure 3.3   Trends in Non-voting by Age Cohort

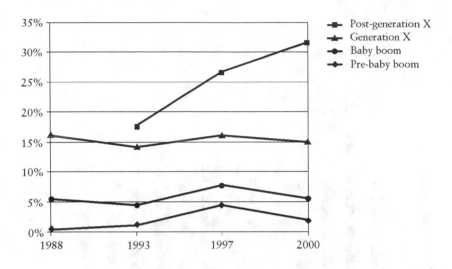

Disentangling these effects requires a comparison of the turnout rates of different cohorts at different stages of their life cycle, and this can only be done by analyzing non-voting across time. Detailed analyses of non-voting in nine federal elections going back to 1968 reveal a mix of life-cycle, generational, and period effects (Blais et al., 2001b). The life-cycle effect is substantial, amounting to an increase of about 15 points between the ages of 20 and 50. The propensity to vote increases by 7 or 8 points from age 20 to age 30, by 4 to 6 points from age 30 to age 40, and by 2 or 3 points from age 40 to age 50. From age 50 to age 70, the propensity to vote remains stable, but then starts to decline from age 70.

The generational effect is even larger. At the same age, turnout is 3 or 4 points lower among baby boomers than it was among pre-baby boomers, 10 points lower among generation X than it was among baby boomers, and another 10 points lower among the most recent generation than it was among generation X at the same age. This translates into a total generational effect of over 20 points.

Finally, there is a period effect of about 3 points, meaning that turnout declined by about 3 points in all age and cohort groups after 1988, compared with the earlier period. This implies that much of the post-1988 drop *cannot* be attributed to the times through which young and old generations alike have recently lived. Nor can it be attributed to life-cycle effects since the age composition of the electorate has not changed substantially since 1988.

That leaves generational replacement. Where post-baby boomers made up a quarter (28 per cent) of the electorate in 1988, they accounted for one-half (49 per cent) in 2000. Meanwhile, where the pre-baby boomers made up 35 per cent of the electorate in 1988, they represent only 22 per cent in 2000. If the relative weight of the four cohorts had remained unchanged, turnout would have been 71 per cent in 2000 instead 61 per cent.[4] In short, most of the decline in turnout is attributable to the fact that post-baby boomers have gradually been replacing pre-baby boomers.

Social Background Characteristics and Voting

This presents a puzzle. After all, the literature on non-voting suggests that education is one of the strongest correlates of voting: the more schooling people have, the more likely they are to vote. This association holds across numerous countries (Blais, 2000; Dalton, 1996; Franklin, 1996; Oppenhuis, 1995; Teixeira, 1992; Topf, 1995; Verba et al., 1995). It is easy to explain. Education socializes citizens into norms of civic engagement and equips them with the cognitive skills that active engagement requires. It is much harder to explain why turnout rates have declined even as education levels rise. With record numbers of Canadians completing their post-secondary education, we would have expected the very reverse.

Looking at the sample as a whole, the impact of education on turnout seems surprisingly modest: turnout was barely 8 points higher among university graduates than it was among those who had not completed high school. However, this masks the massive impact of education on the youngest cohort. Turnout was almost 50 points higher among university graduates in the youngest age cohort than it was among those who did not complete their high school education. And while turnout remained at the same level among university graduates in the youngest cohort as it had been in 1993, it plummeted over 30 points among those with the least formal schooling. Meanwhile turnout in the youngest cohort dropped about 15 points among those who had received their high school diploma and about 18 points among those who had some post-secondary education. Clearly, higher education has served to dampen the decline in turnout amongst the youngest generation of eligible Canadian voters. The rate of non-voting among the least-educated members of that generation is alarmingly low.[5] There may be some reassurance, though, if we look at the generation that had reached their thirties by the time of the 2000 election: turnout in this group actually increased by almost 15 points between 1993 and 2000 among those with the least formal schooling.

The period of our lives between our twenties and our thirties is typically one of considerable change. This is the time when people are most likely to settle into a job, to marry, to purchase a home and to put down roots in their community. All of these changes may enhance people's sense of having a stake in the political process and may also expose them to social pressures that reinforce their sense of civic duty (Wolfinger and Rosenstone, 1980). This is precisely why we observe such strong life-cycle effects on turnout.

We need to see, then, how much impact generation has, once we have taken these and other possible correlates of turnout into account. The results are shown in Table 3.1. Income proves to be an important determinant of turnout: the higher people's income, the greater their propensity to vote. This is an association that turns up regularly in cross-national studies of turnout (Blais, 2000; Kleppner, 1982; Teixeira, 1992; Wolfinger and Rosenstone, 1980). This is not surprising. The more preoccupied people are with providing for their basic needs, the less time and energy they have to pay attention to politics (Wolfinger and Rosenstone, 1980). Moreover, the less affluent may quite possibly perceive that the political system is not particularly responsive to their needs and concerns. The more affluent, in contrast, have both the resources and the perceived stake to become involved politically. Another factor that enhances the likelihood of voting is having a university education. Meanwhile, being a recent immigrant is associated with a lower probability of voting.

It is also worth noting some non-effects. Religiosity has been found to boost turnout, both in Canada (Blais et al., 2001b) and elsewhere (Blais, 2000; Miller and Wattenberg, 1984; Oppenhuis, 1995; Verba et al., 1995), most likely by encouraging a sense of duty to vote. However, religiosity had only a weak impact on propensity to vote in 2000, net of other social background characteristics, and the effect failed to approach conventional levels of statistical significance.[6] There is also evidence in other settings that union membership can mobilize voters (Dalton, 1996; Franklin, 1996), but it had virtually no role whatsoever in encouraging turnout in the 2000 election. This may well be due to the diminishing impact of NDP affiliation on union members (see Nevitte et

Table 3.1 The Determinants of Turnout (Logistic Regressions)

	Column 1	*Column 2*
Baby boom	-.87 (.26)[a]	-.64 (.33)[b]
Generation X	-1.46 (.26)[a]	-1.23 (.34)[a]
Post-generation X	-1.99 (.25)[a]	-1.49 (.33)[a]
High income	.49 (.17)[a]	.59 (.21)[a]
Low income	-.55 (.17)[a]	-.34 (.23)
University	.37 (.18)[b]	-.26 (.23)
Below high school	-.17 (.19)	.05 (.27)
Immigrated within last 10 years	-1.19 (.36)[a]	-.75 (.52)
Religiosity	.18 (.22)	.45 (.28)
Union household	.00 (.16)	-.14 (.19)
Public sector worker	.20 (.20)	.35 (.26)
Working full time	-.01 (.17)	.12 (.21)
Rural	.11 (.16)	.29 (.22)
Married	.29 (.15)	.05 (.19)
Children under age 18 at home	-.18 (.16)	-.25 (.20)
Female	-.03 (.14)	.43 (.19)[b]
Atlantic	.62 (.26)[b]	.42 (.32)
Quebec	.42 (.17)[b]	.48 (.23)[b]
West	.07 (.17)	-.16 (.22)
Political interest		.85 (.37)[b]
Political information		2.00 (.32)[a]
Cynicism		-.50 (.56)
Party identification		.35 (.18)[b]
Negative party sentiment		-.95 (.32)[a]
No race		-.45 (.30)
Contacted during the campaign		.54 (.19)[a]
Constant	2.29 (.31)[a]	.12 (.68)
N	2373	1692
Pseudo R^2	.13	.20
Log likelihood	-938.68	-556.45

a: significant $\alpha \le .01$; b: significant $\alpha \le .05$

Note: Cell entries are unstandardized regression coefficients and standard errors are in parentheses.

al., 2000, and Chapter 5). The effects were similarly weak for pub-lic-sector employment and being in the full-time paid work force, both of which have been found to enhance turnout in the United States (Verba et al., 1995; Wolfinger and Rosenstone, 1980). Finally, there is no evidence that rural citizens, or those who are married, were more likely to vote.[7]

Clearly, the most important socio-demographic influences on propensity to vote in 2000 were income, education, recentness of arrival in Canada, and, above all, generation cohort. What is important for our purposes is that the generational effects[8] persist, despite a host of controls. This is not to say that other social background characteristics are irrelevant to explaining the impact of generation. On the contrary, according to our estimates, taking account of these characteristics reduces the turnout gap between the oldest and the youngest generations from 30 points to 24 points and the gap between the two youngest generations from 17 points to 9. Half of the difference in the turnout rates of generation X and generation post-X is thus accounted for by socio-demographic characteristics, but most of the turnout gap between the two younger and the two older generations remains unexplained.

A Disengaged Generation?

These findings suggest that we should turn to attitudinal factors in order to gain more insight into the reasons for the low—and declining—turnout among the youngest generation of eligible Canadian voters. The two most important correlates of turnout are the level of political interest and the level of information about politics (see Table 3.1). The more interest people express in politics and the better informed they are, the more likely they are to vote.

This is not surprising. On the one hand, interest and information are both important indicators of motivation to vote. Political interest represents a person's *affective* engagement with politics, while political information indicates his or her *cognitive* engagement. On the other hand, the act of voting requires cognitive resources, and the fact that a person has been able to acquire some politically relevant information is an indication that he or she possesses those resources. And, unless we assume that the choice of party is entirely random, some minimal level of information is required in order to choose not just to vote but which party to vote for. So where cognitive engagement helps to motivate the act of voting, cognitive resources facilitate it.

Differing levels of interest and of information are clearly part of the explanation for generational differences in turnout. When asked to rate their interest in politics generally on a 0 to 10 scale, respondents born before the post-second world war baby boom had an average rating of 6.2, compared with only 4.4 for those born since 1970.[9]

Given their low level of interest, it is not surprising to find that members of the youngest generation are more poorly informed than those of older generations. This is the case whether we look at general knowledge about politics or campaign-specific knowledge. The gap was widest when respondents were asked to name the leader of the Conservative party: barely half (51 per cent) of those born since 1970 came up with Joe Clark, compared with 85 per cent of those born before 1945. The skeptical might be tempted to attribute this gap to Mr. Clark's political longevity, but the generational gaps also appear for the newer leaders. Only 65 per cent of those born since 1970 could name Stockwell Day as Alliance leader and only 44 per cent were able to name Alexa McDonough as leader of the NDP. For the oldest cohort, the figures were 83 per cent and 63 per cent, respectively. At 12 points and 10 points respectively, the gaps were narrower for the leader of the Liberal party and for the leader of the Bloc in Quebec, but only 81 per cent of the youngest age group could come up with Jean Chrétien's name and only 69 per cent of young adults in Quebec could name Gilles Duceppe. Finally, only two in five (40 per cent) of younger respondents could name Paul Martin as federal Finance Minister, compared with three in four (77 per cent) of their elders. This low level of knowledge of political figures is not confined to federal politics: only 69 per cent in the youngest age group could name their provincial premier, compared with 87 per cent in the oldest cohort.

While knowledge of political leaders increases from the youngest to the oldest cohort, the gap is widest between those born since the 1970s and those born in the 1960s. Only 39 per cent of those born since the 1970s could name four party leaders, compared with 63 per cent of those born in the 1960s, 56 per cent of the baby-boom generation, and 60 per cent of those born before 1945. At the other end of the scale, 17 per cent of those born since the 1970s could not name a single one of the party leaders, compared with only 6 per cent, 5 per cent, and 3 per cent, respectively, in the three older generations.

The gaps were generally narrower when respondents were asked to associate political parties with their campaign promises, but this was because knowledge of campaign promises tended to be low among all cohorts. Forty-six per cent of those in the youngest cohort could not identify a single promise with the correct party, compared with 21 per cent of those in the oldest. Conversely, 52 per cent of the latter had at least two correct answers, compared with only 30 per cent of the youngest age group. The only factual question on which younger Canadians (81 per cent) fared nearly as well as their elders (85 per cent) was being able to name the capital of the United States.

In order to gauge the impact of political information on turnout, we used a simple scale based on the number of correct answers to four factual questions about the names of the premier in the respondent's province, Canada's Finance Minister, the Prime Minister of Canada at the time of the Free Trade Agreement with the United States, and the capital of the United States. The overall percentage of correct answers ranged from 59 per cent among the most recent generation to 77 per cent among those born before 1945.

The low level of interest and information of those born after 1970 is clearly a crucial source of their high level of abstention. If the youngest generation had been as interested and informed as the older generation, its turnout rate would have been a hefty 14 points higher[10] and the generation gap would have been substantially reduced. Thus, the largest portion of the generation gap in turnout flows from differences in interest and information.

The decline in turnout is often linked in political commentary with the overall rise in political cynicism that has taken place in most countries, and it has been hypothesized that this has particularly affected younger voters. In other words, younger generations may be less inclined to vote because they are more likely to have lost confidence in politics and politicians generally. In order to examine this possibility, we have created a cynicism scale (see Appendix E), which allows us to identify those who believe that the government does not care much what people like them think and that all parties are basically the same, and who give low ratings to politicians and political parties in general. Not surprisingly, we find widespread cynicism in the electorate; 64 per cent, for instance, agree with the statement that "the government does not care much what people like me think." We find, however, that once we control for interest and information, political cynicism is not independently correlated with non-voting. Furthermore, we find very little difference across cohort groups in the overall level of cynicism. In fact, the youngest generation appears to be slightly *less* cynical than the others.[11] So cynicism as such does not seem to be the cause of declining turnout nor of the generation gap in turnout.

Indeed, the timing of the trends is quite different. It is only in the 1990s that turnout started to decline in Canada, as in many other countries (Blais, 2000), while cynicism rose in the 1970s and 1980s

(Blais and Gidengil, 1992). Moreover, cynicism has declined slightly over the last 10 years: the percentage of Canadians who agree with the statement that the government does not care much what people think was 76 per cent in 1993, 67 per cent in 1997, and 64 per cent in 2000. Second, as we have seen, while abstention has a strong generation component, cynicism is not any higher among the younger generation.

Perhaps what really matters is not how people feel about politics and politicians in general but how they view the *parties*. Dennis and Owen (2001), in particular, have argued that support for the political regime hinges first and foremost on citizens' orientations towards the party system, because parties remain the most crucial linkage between the people and the government in a representative democracy. If people think that no party really represents their views, they will feel that the political system is fatally flawed.

It is useful, in this respect, to distinguish positive and negative feelings about the parties. On the positive side, some people develop a feeling of attachment to a party and come to think of themselves as Liberals, Conservatives, Alliance, NDP, or Bloc supporters. We would expect those who identify with a party to vote most of the time. As the proportion of partisans is lower among the most recent generation,[12] this could be another reason for the generation gap in turnout. Table 3.1 confirms that expectation. Party attachment does have an independent impact, even after controlling for overall levels of interest and information and other attitudes. The direct effect of party identification is not very strong, however. The overall propensity to vote increases by only five points when someone identifies with a party. But party identification may also have indirect effects on turnout: perhaps the younger generation is less interested in politics because it is less prone to identify with a political party. The low level of party identification among those born after 1970 suggests a possible breakdown of processes of inter-generational transmission of partisanship within the family (Martinez, 1984).

As important as the absence of a positive attachment to a particular party is the general feeling that no party really represents one's views. This is what we might call negative party sentiment.[13] To examine its effects, we created a dummy variable that equals 1 for those who gave negative ratings to *each* of the parties.[14] We expected that those who feel negative about all of the parties will be more prone to abstain, for want of any positive reason to vote. Table 3.1 supports the hypothesis. Everything else being equal, the probability of voting was 12 points lower among those who were disenchanted with all the parties.

However, this does *not* explain the low turnout observed in 2000 nor the generation gap. Only 6 per cent of our respondents expressed negative feelings about every single party. Many people were negative about one or two parties, but very few voiced dissatisfaction with all of them. Furthermore, the percentage expressing systematic negative party sentiment was the same as it had been in 1988 and was lower than it was in 1997.[15] And the percentage of respondents who reported "across the board" negative feelings among the most recent generation was 6 per cent, exactly the same percentage as among those born before 1945.

Another hypothesis is that turnout was particularly low in this election because many electors perceived there to be no real race. To that effect we created a No Race variable that equals the perceived difference in the chances of the two front-runners in the respondents' constituency. Respondents were asked to estimate each party's chances of winning in their constituency on a scale from 0 to 100, where 0 means no chance at all and 100 certain victory. We standardized the responses so that the perceived chances of the parties add up to 1.[16] The "no race" variable corresponds to the difference between the two front-runners' (standardized) chances of winning. If a respondent gave a score of 100 to a party and 0 to all others, the variable equals 1, indicating absolutely no race at all; if the two front-runners were perceived to have identical chances, the variable equals 0, indicating an extremely close contest. If the front runner was thought to have a 50 per cent chance of winning and the top contender a 30 per cent chance, the variable takes the value of .2 (.5 - .3).

Table 3.1 indicates that the propensity to abstain did increase slightly when someone thought there was no race in his or her constituency. The relationship is quite weak, however, and is not significant at the conventional .05 level. There is some support for the view that those who believed that there was "no race" in their constituency were more tempted not to bother going to the polls, but we should not overestimate the impact of that perception. Furthermore, few people thought that there was "no race" in their constituency; only 19 per cent of our sample scored above .5 on the No Race variable. And Canadians were only slightly more inclined to see No Race in 2000 than in 1997 or 1993.[17] Finally, the younger generation was *less*, not more, likely to think that there was "no race" in their constituency.

So it will not do to explain the low turnout in the 2000 election by appealing to the particularities of that election. As Figure 3.3 shows, turnout did not decrease among three of the four cohorts. It decreased only among the youngest cohort, which is much less interested in politics in general. The election might not have been very close but the closeness of the race is not a major determinant of turnout (see Blais, 2000). There were some voters who felt negative about all the parties but there were no more of them than in previous elections. The low turnout was essentially the outcome of generational replacement. If the relative weight of the four cohorts had been the same as in 1988, turnout would have been 71 per cent. A more "interesting" election could have increased turnout by two or three points. The point is that what is or is not interesting is a subjective call. And the young generations just find most elections not very interesting.[18]

A final factor that can affect turnout is political mobilization. Rosenstone and Hansen (1993) in particular, have shown that one reason some people vote is simply that they are asked to by the parties and candidates who want to get out their vote. We asked our respondents whether they had been contacted by a political party or a candidate during the election campaign; 44 per cent said "yes." People who had been contacted were more likely to vote, and that relationship remains statistically significant, even after controlling for all the prior attitudes that make people inclined or disinclined to vote. Everything else being equal, the likelihood of voting increased by five percentage points when someone had been contacted by a political party. Furthermore, this is clearly one factor that helps to account for the lower turnout in the younger generation. Only 30 per cent of those born after 1970 said they had been contacted, compared with 43 per cent of those born in the 1960s and 50 per cent of those born earlier. Some of this difference can probably be explained by the fact that young people are more likely to have moved recently or may simply be harder to reach. Still, it may pay parties and candidates to make more efforts to contact younger voters.

We have seen previously that social background characteristics account for half of the turnout gap between the two youngest cohorts. There remained, however, a nine-point difference. That difference dwindles to three points when the attitudes examined above are considered. As for the initial 30-point gap between the youngest and oldest cohort, it was slightly reduced to 24 points after controls for social background characteristics, and now it declines to 16 points when attitudes are also taken into account. This still leaves an important difference between the oldest and the youngest.

One plausible explanation is that the younger generation has a weaker sense of voting duty. Sense of duty is a powerful motivating factor when it comes to voting (see Blais, 2000). We may detect something of its impact in the pattern of gender effects. Once we allow for the fact that women tend not to follow electoral politics as closely as men, women are actually a little more likely than men to vote. This may well reflect a stronger sense of obligation to vote: in the mail-back survey, women (29 per cent) were more likely than men (23 per cent) to agree strongly with the statement "If I did not vote, I would feel guilty." The differences between cohorts were even greater. Only 18 per cent of respondents in the youngest age cohort expressed this strong sense of moral obligation to vote, compared with 34 per cent of those in the oldest cohort, and fully 38 per cent said that they would not feel guilty at all, compared with only 15 per cent of those born before 1945.[19] Why this should be so is not clear. One possible explanation is that the most recent generations reached maturity during a period of declining deference (Nevitte, 1996).

Do the Younger Generations Choose Other Forms of Political Engagement?

Voting is only one form of political activity and a very traditional form at that. As Verba and Nie (1972) observed, citizens will act politically in ways that they expect will be most effective in producing a desired outcome. If they perceive the traditional vehicles of political participation to be unresponsive, they will be more likely to turn to non-partisan forms of political action (Dalton, 1988). The cognitive mobilization thesis suggests that this may be particularly true of younger citizens. Rising education levels mean that they are more capable of autonomous political action and have less need to rely on political parties to mediate their involvement.

Simpson (2001: 172), in particular, suggests that there may be a link between the rise of interest-group politics and the decline of voting:

There are too many variables to trace a direct cause and effect, but the rise of interest-group politics roughly coincided with the years of declining respect for government and politicians. Interest groups target specific issues, and these may be of more importance to particular sets of citizens than the broad range of issues with which parties must grapple.

This raises the question: Is the younger generation more involved when we look beyond the conventional institutions of electoral politics? It is not clear that they are. When asked whether they had ever been "a member of an interest group that worked for change on a particular social or political issue," those born since 1970 were the least likely to answer in the affirmative (7 per cent). This figure was only slightly higher than that for having ever been a member of a political party (5 per cent). The corresponding figures for those born before 1945 are 13 per cent and 28 per cent. This is hardly surprising: the older people are, the more opportunities they have had for involvement. It may be telling, though, that party membership outstrips interest-group membership among the older cohorts, but not the youngest. In all four cohorts, interest groups (61 per cent) won out over political parties (20 per cent) when respondents were asked which is "the more effective way to work for change nowadays: joining a political party or joining an interest group," though those born before 1945 were a little more skeptical (54 per cent). Where the youngest cohort differed was in the impact of views about the relative efficacy of political parties and interest groups: turnout was about 9 points lower among those who thought that joining an interest group was more effective than joining a political party.[20] Focusing on those who have actually been a member of an interest group, though, turnout was uniformly high and varied by only about 6 points from the youngest cohort to the oldest. Clearly, this form of involvement complements rather than supplants participation in conventional electoral politics.

Interest-group activity could still be seen as a fairly conventional mode of political involvement. Even when we look at involvement in community groups and other voluntary associations, though, there is little to suggest that the younger generation is turning from conventional politics to other forms of political engagement. Those born since 1970 were the least likely (40 per cent) to indicate that they had been active in a community service group during the past five years and they were no more likely to report involvement in an environmental group (9 per cent) than respondents of older generations.[21] A similar pattern holds for unconventional forms of political activity such as signing a petition or joining a boycott. Interestingly, though, people in the youngest cohort were the most likely to say that they might join an illegal strike (44 per cent) or occupy a building or factory (28 per cent).

Much more research is required to determine whether the younger generation is turning to more unconventional forms of political involvement. It would be particularly important to disentangle generational and life-cycle effects, something that would entail pooling studies conducted at different points in time.

Nonetheless, these findings clearly raise an important practical question: Are there ways to encourage a higher level of turnout in this cohort? One possibility might be to allow more flexibility in how people vote. Interestingly, support for methods of voting from home, such as voting by mail, voting by telephone, or voting by Internet, is highest among the younger generation. The other facet of voting that may need to be looked at is the permanent voters' list. That list was not as fully updated as it should ideally be. Voter information cards were mailed to people at their addresses as indicated on the list. Fully one-third of those born since 1970 in our study reported that they had not received a voter information card showing that their name was on the voters' list, compared with only 18 per cent of those born in the 1960s and 9 per cent of those born earlier. And among those who did not receive a card, it was members of the youngest age cohort who were the most likely (50 per cent) to say that it was difficult to get their name on the list.

Conclusion

The decline in turnout since the 1988 election does not bode well for the country's democratic health. It is important, though, to recognize that this is not a generalized trend. On the contrary, turnout has remained fairly stable among those who were born before 1970. The decline is largely confined to the generation of young adults that has come of voting age since 1988. And within that generation, the decline is largely confined to those who have not completed a university education.

To the extent that low turnout among the young reflects a life-cycle effect, we can expect their turnout to rise as they move from their twenties into their thirties. As we have shown, though, life-cycle related factors are only a part of the story. The bigger story, and the one that promises less well for the future, is the low level of political engagement in this generation. They are less interested in electoral politics than their elders, they pay less attention, and they are less well-informed. And it is not clear at this point that they are turning to other forms of political involvement instead. On a more positive note, the younger generation is no more disaffected with politics than the older cohorts. The problem seems to be one of disengagement rather than of active discontent.

In short, the answer to why turnout was so low in 2000 is that turnout is being dragged down by the increasing weight of the younger generations who are just less interested in politics than the older generations. The implication is that explanations that stress the particularities of the election, like the fact that there was no "real" reason for it, are not compelling. A more "interesting" election could have produced a turnout of 64 per cent instead of 61 per cent. But the bottom line is that what is and is not interesting is in the eye of the beholder. And many young Canadians find politics in general quite boring.

Notes

1 Turnout in 1896 was 63 per cent.

2 Non-voting is underestimated in the Canadian Election Studies, as it is in all surveys, in part because those who are less interested in politics and less inclined to vote are less prone to answer surveys, in part because participating in a campaign survey makes people more likely to vote (Blais and Young, 1999; Granberg and Holmberg, 1992), and in part because of mis-reporting due to social desirability. It seems, however, that social desirability does not substantially affect the findings (Brady et al., 1995: 292).

3 The term "generation X" originates with the book of the same name, written by Douglas Copeland in 1991. It is typically taken to denote the generation that followed the baby boomers. While some would use the term to encompass all of those who have been born since 1960 and who have now reached adulthood, we have chosen to divide the post-baby boomers into two distinct cohorts, distinguishing between those who were already 20 or older when *Generation X* was published and those who followed.

4 These estimations are derived from the logit estimations presented in Blais et al. (2001b), Table 1.

5 Our simulations suggest that a 30-year-old had only a 34-per-cent probability of voting in the 2000 election if he or she had not completed high school (Blais et al., 2001b).

6 In an uncontrolled setup, religiosity does increase the odds of voting. There is a gap of 8 or 9 points between those who say that religion is very important in their lives and those who say it is not important at all. We also tried representing religious involvement by a dummy variable for those who gave a religious affiliation and those who did not, but it had no independent effect at all on the propensity to vote.

7 Furthermore, having children under 18 at home does not appear to have any effect.

8 Because it pertains to a single point in time (2000), Table 3.1 does not allow us to separate generation and life-cycle effects. However, it does include controls for a number of variables that might plausibly account for life-cycle effects like income, employment, and marital status. Still, it would be unwise to attribute all of the observed cohort effects to generational differences.

9 The average scores for generation X and baby boomers were 5.8 and 6.0, respectively.

10 We re-estimated for each individual his/her probability of voting, on the basis of the logit regression presented in Table 3.1, after giving each individual the mean interest and information level observed in the whole sample. The mean predicted probability of voting for those born after 1970 increases by 14 points and the gap between the predicted turnout of those born after 1970 and those before 1945 is reduced to 16 points.

11 The mean level of cynicism is .51 among those born after 1970 and .53 in the three other cohorts.

12 Fifty-three per cent of those born after 1970 think of themselves as partisan, against 73 per cent among those born before 1945.

13 The literature distinguishes "generalized" and "specific" anti-party sentiment (Poguntke, 1996; Gidengil et al., 2001). The former is tapped through questions about the parties in general and the latter through questions about specific parties. Negative party sentiment is conceptually closer to the latter.

14 Respondents were asked to rate each of the parties on a scale from 0 to 100 where 0 means that someone really dislikes the party and 100 means that he or she really likes it. We interpret all scores below 50 as negative. In previous work, we have used the number of negative ratings given to the established parties as a measure of specific anti-party sentiment. Here, we employ a stricter indicator: someone is construed as disenchanted with the party system only if she or he feels negative about each of the parties.

15 The percentages with no positive ratings were 6 per cent in 1988, 4 per cent in 1993, and 8 per cent in 1997.

16 This is obtained by dividing each party's score by the total scores given to all the parties.

17 The average value of No Race was .27 in 1988, .17 in 1993, .20 in 1997, and .28 in 2000.

18 Pammett (2001) notes that more people were unable to name the most important issue in the election campaign in 1997 and 2000 than in 1988 and 1993. But the 1988 and 1993 figures were themselves exceptional; the 1997 and 2000 figures are similar to those observed from 1974 to 1984 inclusively (see Clarke et al., 1996: 29).

19 These figures are the more telling in that the mail-back under-represents non-voters in the youngest cohort.

20 The difference was only about 3 points in each of the three older cohorts.

21 These data are taken from the mail-back survey. The mail-back under-represents non-voters, especially in the youngest age cohort, so some caution is warranted in interpreting these numbers.

CHAPTER 4

The Vote: Stability and Change

Even though turnout was extremely low, a majority of Canadians did go to the polls on 27 November 2000 and expressed a preference for a party or a candidate. The remainder of the book is devoted to explaining, at the individual level, why voters voted the way they did, and, at the aggregate level, why some parties were more successful than others. Before providing such explanations, we need to have a good sense of what is to be explained. A first step is to put the outcome of the election into proper context, and to determine, in particular, how similar or different it was from that of the 1997 election.

Table 4.1 presents vote shares in the country as a whole, and in the provinces and regions in 1997 and 2000. The 2000 election has been widely construed as a great victory for the Liberals and for Prime Minister Jean Chrétien. Meanwhile, the Alliance has come to be seen as the great loser with Stockwell Day held squarely to blame. The numbers in Table 4.1 help us to put the outcome of the election in a rather different perspective.

The Liberals increased their vote share from 38.5 per cent to 40.8 per cent, very close to the percentage (41.3 per cent) they had obtained in 1993. But it was the Alliance that progressed most, going from 19.4 per cent to 25.5 per cent. The Bloc remained at 10.7 per cent. The "losers" were the Conservatives, who slipped from 18.8 per cent to 12.2 per cent, and the NDP, who declined from 11 per cent to 8.5 per cent.

It is true that the Liberals increased their share of the vote. Outside Quebec, though, the Liberals made minimal gain, and they actually lost two points west of Ontario. Within the West, they did particularly poorly in Saskatchewan and Alberta, though they managed to get 33 per cent of the vote in Manitoba. It was only east of the Ottawa River that the outcome could be declared a great Liberal victory: with 44 per cent of the vote in Quebec and 41 per cent in Atlantic Canada, the Liberals gained eight points over 1997. Within Atlantic Canada, they did particularly well in Newfoundland and Prince Edward Island, though they were significantly weaker in Nova Scotia.

It is also true that the Alliance failed to win a significant number of seats in Ontario, but the Alliance did manage to register advances

Table 4.1   Vote Shares, 1997 and 2000

	Liberal		Alliance (Reform)		Conservative		NDP		Bloc		Other	
	2000	(1997)	2000	(1997)	2000	(1997)	2000	(1997)	2000	(1997)	2000	(1997)
Atlantic	**40.7**	**(32.8)**	**10.2**	**(9.0)**	**31.3**	**(33.8)**	**16.5**	**(23.7)**			**1.2**	**(0.7)**
Newfoundland	44.9	(37.9)	3.9	(2.5)	34.5	(36.8)	13.0	(24.8)			3.7	(0.9)
P.E.I.	47.0	(44.8)	5.0	(1.5)	38.4	(38.3)	9.0	(15.1)			0.5	(0.3)
Nova Scotia	36.5	(28.4)	9.6	(9.7)	29.1	(30.8)	24.0	(30.4)			0.9	(0.8)
New Brunswick	41.7	(32.9)	15.7	(13.1)	30.5	(35.0)	11.7	(18.4)			0.3	(0.6)
Quebec	**44.2**	**(36.7)**	**6.2**	**(0.3)**	**5.6**	**(22.2)**	**1.8**	**(2.0)**	**39.9**	**(37.9)**	**2.3**	**(1.0)**
Ontario	**51.5**	**(49.5)**	**23.6**	**(19.1)**	**14.4**	**(18.8)**	**8.3**	**(10.7)**			**2.2**	**(1.8)**
West	**25.3**	**(27.6)**	**49.9**	**(43.0)**	**10.0**	**(10.5)**	**12.3**	**(16.7)**			**2.6**	**(2.2)**
Manitoba	32.5	(34.3)	30.4	(23.7)	14.5	(17.8)	20.9	(23.2)			1.7	(1.1)
Saskatchewan	20.7	(24.7)	47.7	(36.0)	4.8	(7.8)	26.2	(30.9)			0.6	(0.6)
Alberta	20.9	(24.0)	58.9	(54.6)	13.5	(14.4)	5.4	(5.7)			1.3	(1.2)
British Columbia	27.7	(28.8)	49.4	(43.1)	7.3	(6.2)	11.3	(18.2)			4.3	(3.7)
Outside Quebec	**39.6**	**(39.2)**	**32.6**	**(26.9)**	**14.6**	**(17.5)**	**11.0**	**(14.6)**			**2.2**	**(1.8)**
Canada	**40.8**	**(38.5)**	**25.5**	**(19.4)**	**12.2**	**(18.8)**	**8.5**	**(11.0)**	**10.7**	**(10.7)**	**2.3**	**(1.6)**

Source: Elections Canada

Note: Cell entries are percentages.

over the 1997 Reform results in all but one of the provinces. And it was the Alliance that registered the largest net gain of any of the parties. The Alliance got 6 per cent of the vote in Quebec and 33 per cent outside Quebec. While the party won only 10 per cent in Atlantic Canada as a whole, it managed to obtain 16 per cent in New Brunswick. It received 24 per cent in Ontario and 50 per cent in the West. In Alberta, three voters out of five (59 per cent) voted Alliance, twice as many as in Manitoba (30 per cent), where the party trailed the Liberals. Compared to the performance of Reform in 1997, the Alliance made some gain in all four regions, a little more in the West and a little less in Atlantic Canada. The most substantial gain came in Saskatchewan (+12 points). Nova Scotia was the only province where the Alliance made no advance on the Reform 1997 result.

It is true that Joe Clark ran a good campaign, but the Conservatives saw their vote share slip in almost every province. In Quebec, they lost a disastrous 17 percentage points, finishing fourth behind the Alliance. With only 6 per cent of the Quebec vote, the party's share of the vote in 2000 was barely one-fourth of what it had been in 1997 in that province. Outside Quebec, the party lost three points, and those losses were more or less uniformly distributed across the provinces. The party obtained 15 per cent of the vote outside Quebec: 10 per cent in the West, 14 per cent in Ontario, and 31 per cent in Atlantic Canada. In the West, they got 14 per cent of support in Alberta (the only Western province where they came third in overall vote support) and 15 per cent in Manitoba, but a dismal 5 per cent in Saskatchewan.

The NDP was the other loser. The outcome must have been disappointing to the party: the NDP's vote share was only slightly better than its disastrous 1993 election result. The party lost almost four points outside Quebec, a relative decline of 25 per cent, with the sharpest drops occurring in Atlantic Canada and British Columbia. The NDP obtained less than 2 per cent of the vote in Quebec, 12 per cent in the West, and 17 per cent in Atlantic Canada. Its support was concentrated in Nova Scotia, leader Alexa McDonough's home province. In the West, the NDP did well in Manitoba and Saskatchewan.

The Bloc saw its share of the vote in Quebec slightly increase in 2000, edging up from 38 per cent to 40 per cent, but for the first time in its history the Bloc failed to win the plurality of the vote in Quebec. Finally, "other" candidates were somewhat more successful at the two ends of Canadian geography: "independent" candidates took 4 per cent of the vote in Newfoundland and the Green party obtained 3 per cent support in British Columbia.

The Inter-Election Period

These numbers tell us how much better or worse the parties did in 2000, but they do not indicate anything about *when* party fortunes shifted. Were the gains and losses registered before the campaign even began, or did the campaign prove decisive? Between 1997 and 2000, the Reform Party had reconstituted itself as the Alliance and two new leaders had come on board: Joe Clark for the Conservatives and Stockwell Day for the Alliance. Did the the creation of the new party and the advent of these new leaders affect party popularity?

Figure 4.1 shows the evolution of vote intentions over the period starting after the 1997 election and ending at the beginning of the campaign.[1] The figure confirms the high level of Liberal popularity throughout the inter-election period. By the spring of 1998, the Liberals were at about 50 per cent in vote intentions, much higher than the 38 per cent they received in the 1997 election. The Reform party and the Conservatives had declined to about 15 per cent each and the NDP to 10 per cent. The Liberals managed to maintain themselves around the 50-per-cent mark right through to the spring of 2000. While there is evidence of a small surge in Conservative Party support in the summer of 1999, that turned out to be just a temporary blip. By the beginning of 2000, the Conservatives and Reform were still tied at about 15 per cent.

Then we see a substantial surge in support for Reform/Alliance in 2000. The surge seems to have started with the beginning of the contest to nominate the new leader of the Alliance and continued through July, when Stockwell Day was elected. The Alliance gained about 10 points over a period of five months, at the expense of both the Liberals and the Conservatives.[2] By September, on the eve of the election, the Liberals stood at 45 per cent, the Alliance at 25 per cent, and the Conservatives and the NDP at 10 per cent.

Figure 4.1 establishes the dominance of the Liberals throughout the period. They managed to maintain themselves above 45 per cent in bad times as well as in good times. The figure conveys the image of considerable solidity. Until the summer of 2000, the Liberal lead over its nearest rival was typically 35 percentage points, and it was never less than 25 points. Of course, that lead had shrunk to a

Figure 4.1   Evolution of Vote Intentions, Canada, 1997-2000

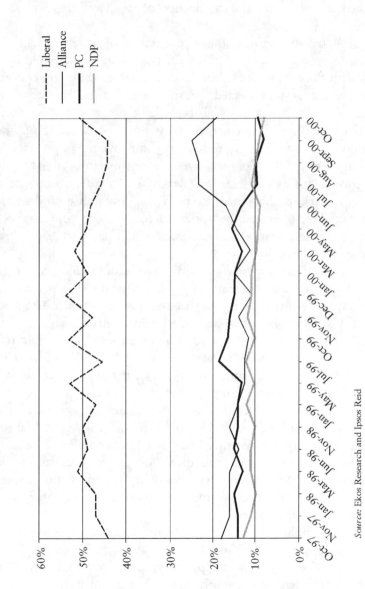

Source: Ekos Research and Ipsos Reid

"mere" 20 points by September 2000, but the Liberals could afford to lose a few points and still easily form a majority government. And they could hope that some of the boost to the Alliance associated with the leadership race and the election of Stockwell Day would dissipate.

Figure 4.1 also confirms that the election of a new leader does make a difference. Vote intentions for the Alliance increased by 10 points with the election of a new leader. Some of that gain occurred before the leader was elected, presumably because the leadership contest enhanced the party's visibility, but most of the gain took place after Stockwell Day emerged the winner. The election of a new leader does not, of course, automatically improve the popularity of a party. Support for the Conservatives did not increase after the election of Joe Clark as party leader. Clearly, Day made a bigger difference than Clark, perhaps because he was a new figure on the federal scene, perhaps because he appeared to be more charismatic, or perhaps because it is more difficult for a small party to benefit from a new leadership boost.[3]

The observation that parties with new leaders enjoy a surge in popularity is not new. Nadeau (1987) has shown that a party's popularity typically increases by four or five points when it gets a new leader.[4] A similar boost has been observed in Britain (Nadeau and Mendelsohn, 1994). But it is also clear that these boosts tend to be short-lived. One of the big questions of the 2000 election, therefore, was whether the recent surge of support for the Alliance could be sustained through election day.

There was some indication that the Alliance surge was in the process of dissipating in early October. The Liberals were then back at 50 per cent, and the Alliance back at 20 per cent. The most plausible interpretation is that the death of Pierre Trudeau, in late September, gave the Liberals a temporary lift. Our data, though, indicate that by the time the election was called that temporary boost had completely disappeared.

In Quebec, finally, there appears to have been little movement in vote intentions between the spring of 1998 and October 2000.[5] Throughout this period, Bloc support typically stood at about 40 per cent of vote intentions, slightly above the 38 per cent they had obtained in the 1997 election. The drop in Conservative support that occurred in late 1997 and early 1998 seems to have benefited the Liberals, who maintained themselves at about 45 per cent throughout the period.[6]

The Election Campaign

Moving on from the inter-election shifts we turn to the campaign itself.[7] Figure 4.2 shows the (five-day) moving averages of vote intentions during the course of the campaign.[8] The first full day of interview was Wednesday 25 October,[9] three days after the election had been called. Because we use five-day moving averages, the figure starts on Friday 27 October. By that time, the Liberals were at 46 per cent, the Alliance at 27 per cent, the Conservatives at 8 per cent and the NDP at 6 per cent. The Alliance seemed to have gained a couple of points since September.

Our data suggest that the Alliance continued to gain some ground in the first week of the campaign. By 29 October, they were at 30 per cent, "only" 17 points behind the Liberals. But these gains evaporated in the next 10 days. By the time of the debates, the Alliance was back at 25 per cent, just where they had been at the beginning of the campaign.

The five-point decline that took place between 28 October and 9 November could be due to the attack that the party was in favour of two-tier health care, which was the headline of the *Globe and Mail* on 31 October. Alternatively it could simply reflect a decay of the boost to the party at the beginning of the campaign. Our data suggest the latter interpretation. The percentage of voters who thought that the Alliance was the best party for improving health care did decline slightly in early November,[10] but fewer voters chose the Alliance on almost every dimension and the most substantial change concerned the Alliance's ability to cut taxes,[11] not its competence on health. It was at this time in the campaign that Day's ratings started to decline, from about 49 to about 46 (on a 0 to 100 scale).

Then there were the debates. The winner of the English debate was Joe Clark. Forty-four per cent of those interviewed after the English debate and who had seen the debate[12] thought that Clark had performed the best, 17 per cent chose Day, 10 per cent Chrétien, and 19 per cent could not name a winner. Ratings of Joe Clark increased by four points, and by six points among those who watched the English debate.[13] At the same time, vote intentions for the Conservatives went from six to eight per cent. The Conservatives gained about four points during the campaign and these gains can be imputed to Clark's performance in the debates.[14]

Who lost the debates?[15] It seems to have been Jean Chrétien. Among those who saw the English debate, 37 per cent said that

Figure 4.2   Evolution of Vote Intentions, Canada, Campaign 2000 (Five-Day Moving Averages)

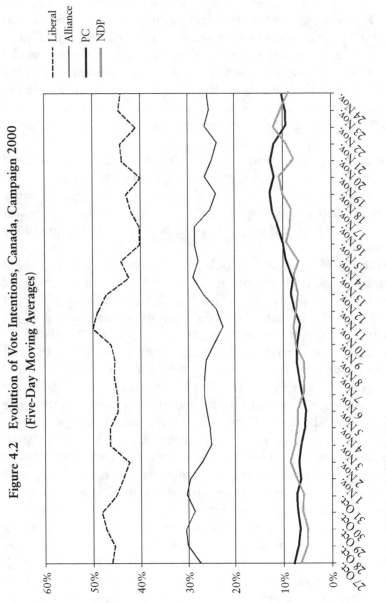

Source: 2000 Canadian Election Study

Chrétien had performed the worst, 18 per cent chose Day, and 18 per cent could not name a loser. Chrétien's own ratings went down by three points, from about 52 to 49 in the five days following the English debate,[16] and remained there for the rest of the campaign. The impact of the debate on Liberal vote intentions appears to have been felt only some days later.[17] The implication is that the three-point drop in Liberal support between the first and last 10 days of the campaign is attributable to the debates. Our data also indicate that the so-called Grand-Mère scandal, which erupted on 16 November, had no impact on the vote. Chrétien's personal ratings and Liberal vote intentions hardly moved in the aftermath of the scandal.[18]

As for the Alliance, they ended up with 25 per cent of vote intentions, exactly what it had at the time of the debates. The Alliance's campaign experienced some difficulties after the debates. The first such difficulty occurred when the issue of a possible referendum on abortion came up, following information that the Alliance would hold a referendum if 3 per cent of the voters petitioned for it. This was the headline of CBC's *The National* on 6 November and of the *Globe and Mail* on the 7th. But this abortion referendum issue did not seem to affect voters. Overall evaluations of Day did not move at all[19] and vote intention for the Alliance remained at 25 per cent.

The following week, the Alliance and its leader faced some tough attacks. On the 14th, the Immigration Minister Elinor Caplan charged some of Day's supporters with being racist, anti-immigrant, and anti-Semitic. These accusations, as well as Day's denunciations, figured prominently on CBC and CTV news broadcasts on the 15th. That very same evening, the CBC carried its infamous report on "Fundamental Day," which focused on the religious beliefs of the Alliance's leader. This set of events appears to have had some effect. Ratings of Day went down by six points and Alliance vote intentions declined by five points.[20] The effect, however, seems to have been temporary. Day's ratings increased by five points in the last days of the campaign and vote intentions rose by two points.

The Alliance finished the campaign where it started, at 26 per cent of the vote. It gained some ground at the very beginning of the campaign but those gains dissipated in early November. They suffered slightly from allegations of racism and/or the media report on Day's religious beliefs, but the effect had also disappeared by election day. No single event seems to have had a lasting impact on the party's overall popularity.

Finally, the NDP appears to have gained some support during the campaign. It moved up from about 6 per cent to about 9 per cent. But these gains do not seem to be related to any single specific event. Neither vote intentions for the party nor evaluations of Alexa McDonough moved in the aftermath of the debates. Rather, what seems to have occurred is a slow and gradual increase in the overall evaluation of the party throughout the campaign.[21] At the beginning of the campaign, the mean NDP rating (on a 0 to 100 scale) was a mere 36, five points lower than the Conservatives and nine points below the Alliance. By the end of the campaign, the NDP mean score had risen to 40, just two points below that of the PC and four points less than that of the Alliance. Exactly how and why these gains were made is unclear.

One word, finally, about "other" parties and candidates. Support for them did go down during the campaign. They had about 3 per cent at the beginning and only 1 per cent at the end. The decline appears to be related to the debates, as support for "others" had maintained itself at around 3 or 4 per cent until 9 November, and then dropped to around 1 per cent.

So the election campaign did matter. If vote intentions had not moved during the campaign, there would have been a Liberal landslide, and the Conservatives and the NDP would not have obtained official status in the House of Commons. At the same time, however, things moved less during this particular campaign than in previous ones. There was a debate effect, and vote intentions moved two or three points, but the dynamics were more muted in 2000 than in 1988, 1993, or 1997.

The two parties that gained ground were the two weakest parties at the beginning of the campaign, the Conservatives and the NDP. The fact that Joe Clark won the debate confirms the "rule" that debates are almost always won by the leaders of weaker parties. The 2000 election also confirmed the rule that the party that is ahead at the beginning of the campaign typically loses ground during the campaign.

We have looked at how vote intentions moved, or did not move, in the aggregate. It is also important to see what happens at the micro or individual level. Table 4.2 focuses on those individuals who were initially interviewed before the debates and compares how they were intending to vote before the debates with how they actually voted on election day. We examine the situation outside Quebec.

Table 4.2   Vote Intentions and Reported Vote Among Respondents
Interviewed Before the English Debate (Outside Quebec)

	Vote intentions					
Vote	Liberal	Alliance	PC	NDP	Other	Undecided
Liberal	84	6	8	10	40	24
Alliance	4	84	10	0	0	28
PC	7	8	72	4	19	32
NDP	5	1	5	83	8	17
Other	0	1	6	3	32	0
N=	217	191	38	44	15	44

Source: 2000 Canadian Election Study
Note: Cell entries are percentages.

A number of interesting patterns emerge from Table 4.2. First, among those who indicated a vote intention, 20 per cent changed their mind after the debates and actually voted for a party other than the one they initially intended to support. About one voter out of five changed his/her mind during the campaign.[22] And another 10 per cent made up their mind after the debates (the percentage of voters who made up their mind after the first week is 13 per cent; the percentage who made up their mind after the debates is 8 per cent). For all these voters, about one out of three, the campaign mattered.

Second, all kinds of vote shifts took place. As we would expect, the most frequent shifts were from the Liberals or the Alliance to the Conservatives, but the Conservatives also lost some supporters. Because the shifts were not unidirectional, their net impact was relatively small. The parties gained or lost a couple of points overall but many voters did move during the campaign.

Third, movements of opinion tend to help the small parties and hurt the strong ones. The Conservatives lost almost 30 per cent of their supporters, but that entailed a lost of only two points (29 per cent × 7 per cent); the Liberals lost less than 20 per cent of their voters but that entailed a loss of seven points (16 per cent × 42 per cent). Campaign events that lead voters to reconsider their vote decision are likely to hurt the party that is ahead.

Fourth, "truly" undecided voters were not very numerous. They represented only about 10 per cent of those who actually voted.[23] And many of those who said they were undecided held opinions that made them lean in a particular direction. For instance, three-fifths of the "undecided" gave one party a higher rating than all the other parties and two-thirds of them ended up voting for that party. The Conservatives did particularly well among those who said they were undecided before the debates, but many of them were already giving the party the highest rating before the debates. Joe Clark's performance appears to have reinforced their initial inclination.

First and Second Choices

The fact that about one voter out of three changes his/her mind during the campaign suggests that many people have a first and a second choice and are willing to reconsider their choice order. But what were Canadians' first and second choices? Were there some clear patterns? The attempt to unite the right, for instance, is based on the view that there are people on the left, in the centre, and on the right, and that the right is handicapped by vote-splitting between the Conservatives and the Alliance. The assumption seems to be that most of the Conservative voters have the Alliance as their second choice and vice-versa.

Table 4.3 shows the second choices of Canadians.[24] The table indicates that the Liberals are the most frequent second choice of Conservative and NDP voters and the Conservatives the most frequent second choice of Liberal and Alliance voters. As for Bloc voters, 40 per cent are unable to name a second choice. A similar pattern holds across the regions. The only exceptions are that in the West Liberal voters split between the Conservatives and the NDP, while in Ontario and Atlantic Canada Alliance voters split between the Conservatives and the Liberals.

The most striking finding from Table 4.3 is that the Alliance is the second choice of very few people, 9 per cent in the country as a whole and 8 per cent outside Quebec. This is a clear signal that the growth potential of the Alliance is limited. Outside Quebec, the Alliance got 33 per cent of the vote. Our data suggest that the most they could have hoped for was about 40 per cent. At the other end, the Conservatives were the second choice of many Canadians. Even though they received only 15 per cent of the vote, the percentage who found the party acceptable was about the same, around 40 per cent. The problem confronting the Alliance was that so many voters deemed the party completely unacceptable. The best indication of that is that 29 per cent of Canadians (outside Quebec) named the

Table 4.3 Voters' Second Choice

Outside Quebec	Vote				
	Liberal	Alliance	Conservative	NDP	Other
Liberal	—	27	45	48	3
Alliance	13	—	17	3	6
Conservative	34	38	—	17	0
NDP	24	7	14	—	0
Other	2	3	3	6	0
DK/None	27	26	23	26	91
N=	559	455	169	160	19

Quebec	Liberal	Bloc	Alliance	Conservative	NDP	Other
Liberal	—	14	34	29	29	13
Bloc	16	—	19	21	16	21
Alliance	16	16	—	4	5	3
PC	26	17	4	—	5	5
NDP	4	11	12	2	—	10
Other	1	3	0	4	32	0
DK/None	38	40	32	41	13	49
N=	254	280	45	30	20	21

Note: Cell entries are percentages.

Alliance as *the* party that is too extreme in their view. These data highlight the problems facing the "unite the right" strategy. Only 17 per cent of Conservative voters have the Alliance as their second choice; almost half chose the Liberals.

These patterns are very similar to those observed in the 1997 election (Nevitte et al., 2000: 16, Table 2.3). In 1997, 18 per cent of Conservative voters chose Reform as their second choice outside Quebec; in 2000, the percentage stood at 17 per cent. Outside Quebec, 24 per cent spontaneously referred to Reform in 1997 as an extremist party; the percentage was 28 per cent in 2000. In voters' minds, the Alliance party was very much a continuation of the "old" Reform party.[25]

It is important to specify what these data do and do not tell. They do tell us that there is no guarantee that a new party resulting from the merger of the Conservatives and the Alliance would get the support of those who voted for either party in 2000; they also tell us that many Conservatives could be tempted to go to the Liberals. These data do *not* tell us, however, that the left/right cleavage is irrelevant. Quite the contrary. The fact that Liberal and Alliance voters have the Conservatives as their second choice and that NDP voters' second choice is the Liberals is entirely consistent with a left/right perspective. And so is the propensity of Conservative voters to choose the Liberals, if we assume that the Conservative party is a centre-right party. The implication could be that the Conservative party (or at least its electorate) is closer to the centre than to the right (Blais et al., 2002). In short, the pattern of second choices indicates that between the two parties on the right, one—the Alliance—is perceived to be more "extreme" than the other, and that the reaction of Conservative voters to the creation of a new right-wing party would depend on how "moderate" or "extremist" the new party will be perceived to be.

Discussion

The 2000 election confirmed the dominance of the Liberal party in Canadian politics. Having managed to come up ahead in every poll conducted in Canada since they were elected in 1993, the Liberals won their third successive majority election. The election also seemed to confirm the status of the Alliance as the official opposition, with twice as many votes as the Conservatives. In that sense, there appears to have been more stability than change.

But change there was, as well. Only after the election of a new leader was the Alliance able to re-establish itself as the second-strongest party. And change there was also during the campaign. Only thanks to the gains realized during the campaign were the Conservatives and the NDP able to maintain their status as official parties in the House of Commons.

Our analysis also confirms the central role of leaders' televised debates in Canadian election campaigns. The English debate was critical in the small Conservative surge that took place during the campaign. None of the other campaign events seems to have had a lasting effect on the parties.

This raises the question of what would happen if there were no debates. The question is particularly perplexing considering the evidence that the debates typically hurt the party that is ahead at the time they take place. For the medium term, the Liberals look to be the leading party, and it is easy to imagine that the leader of the Liberal Party might reason that he/she would be better off without debates. The problem, of course, is that Canadians now expect to have televised leader debates. Would there be an outcry if the Liberals were to refuse to participate in this most democratic exercise? The risk, of course, is that the refusal to participate in a debate could hurt the party even more. Perhaps the optimal scenario from the Liberal perspective would be to modify the format of the debates in such a way that their potential impact will be reduced. An interesting strategic game to watch in 2004.

Judgement about who did well, or badly, in any election depends very much on the criteria one adopts. The election was hailed as a major victory for the Liberals and, above all, for Prime Minister Chrétien. After all, the Liberals did manage to increase their vote share. On the other hand, the Liberals hardly increased their vote share outside Quebec, they lost some ground during the campaign, and they ended up with only 41 per cent of the vote, well below the 50 per cent or so support they had enjoyed until early 2000. Of course, it could also be argued that campaigns are usually particularly tough for the leading party and that it was a significant achievement for the Liberals to lose only a few points during the campaign.

The same pattern applies to the Alliance. With the benefit of hindsight, it is easy to believe that the Alliance was the great loser in the election and that Stockwell Day was to blame. But the Alliance did make substantial progress compared to 1997. It should be kept in mind that the party was tied with the Conservatives at around 15 per cent before Day was elected. The real failure, of course, was that the party did not get the 30 per cent of the vote, or the 10 seats, that it needed in Ontario.

The ultimate irony, perhaps, is that Joe Clark emerged as the "moral" winner in the election. Clark won the English debate and that performance enabled his party to retain its status as an official party in the House of Commons. At the same time, however, his election as the leader of the party failed to bring any boost to the party, and his performance in the debates brought the party only two or three points in terms of vote support. This was a small effect, but it was *not* too little, too late.

Notes

1 The Bloc, which is confined to one province, is considered separately.

2 More specifically vote intentions for the Alliance went from 14.5 per cent in May to 17 per cent in June, before the first ballot (June 24), to 23.5 per cent in July and August, after the second ballot (July 8), and 25 per cent in September.

3 Nadeau (1987) has shown that vote intentions for the NDP have not been enhanced substantially by the election of a new leader.

4 Nadeau's results suggest that the boost to a party that forms the government may be higher than for opposition parties and that the one for smaller parties like the NDP may be even smaller. This could be another reason why the boost for the Conservatives was smaller than that for the Alliance.

5 Our analysis of the pattern in Quebec is based on polls conducted by Léger and Léger.

6 The election of a new Alliance leader seems to have had some effect on Liberal support but very little on vote intentions for the Bloc.

7 The small sample size in Quebec does not allow us to examine the evolution of support for the Bloc in Quebec. The public polls do not indicate any substantial shift in vote intentions in Quebec, except perhaps a small Conservative gain after the debates.

8 For all the analyses that compare vote intentions, or opinions and attitudes, at different times in the campaign, we use a special weighting procedure so that the weighted percentage of respondents is the same in every region for every day of the campaign. Consequently, differences between sub-periods cannot be imputed to variations in the regional makeup of daily samples.

9 Interviews outside Quebec started Tuesday 24 October; 25 October was the first day with interviews in all regions.

10 The percentage choosing the Alliance as the best party for improving health care dropped from 19 per cent in the last five days of October to 16 per cent in the first five days of November.

11 The percentage choosing the Alliance as the best party for cutting taxes dropped from 43 per cent to 35 per cent.

12 Thirty-six percent said they had watched the debate, 18 per cent in Quebec and 43 per cent outside Quebec.

13 The average rating for Clark (on a 0 to 100 scale) went from 42.5 in the five days preceding the debates to 46.5 in the five days following them. The numbers were 45.0 and 51.5 for those who had viewed at least one debate.

14 There is a four-point difference between vote intentions for the Conservatives in the first and last ten days of the campaign. Seven per cent of those interviewed before the debates indicated they intended to vote Conservative. When these same people were reinterviewed after the election, 10 per cent said they had voted Conservative.

15 Here again, we are focusing on the English debate. Only 21 per cent of our respondents said they had watched the French debate, 40 per cent in Quebec. There was no clear winner. Among those who watched it, 25 per cent chose Chrétien as the winner, 25 per cent Clark, 23 per cent Duceppe, and 24 per cent could not name anyone. As already indicated, there is no evidence of significant campaign dynamics in Quebec.

16 There was a five-point drop among those who saw the debate.

17 The data suggest that the drop in Liberal vote intentions might have started only four days after the English debate (around 13 November) and was followed by a small recovery. The 13th of November was also the day that Health Minister Allan Rock admitted that the two-tier health system already existed. There is no indication, however, that this hurt the Liberals. The percentage of voters who thought that the Liberals were the best party for improving health care did not decline after that date.

18 The average Chrétien rating was 48.4 in the five days following the news that Chrétien had intervened with the head of the Federal Development Bank, compared to 49.6 in the five previous days. There is a four point drop (from 43.9 per cent to 40.2 per cent) in Liberal vote intentions if we compare the five days before and after the event but that drop is only two points if we use six days rather then five. In fact, Liberal vote intentions had reached their lowest level by November 16.

19 Mean ratings of Day were 46.2 from November 2 to 6 and 46.5 from November 7 to 11.

20 We compare the five days before (and including) and after November 15. Mean Day ratings slipped from 47 to 41 and Alliance vote intentions from 29 per cent to 24 per cent.

21 There is indeed a significant linear trend in daily ratings of the NDP.

22 Twenty-one percent indicated they voted differently from what they initially intended among those who were interviewed in the first week of the campaign. We are not considering here those who changed their mind during the campaign but came back to their initial choice by election day.

23 They constituted a larger proportion of the whole electorate but the propensity to abstain was higher among those who were undecided during the campaign.

24 After asking our respondents which party they voted for, we inquired whether this was the party they liked the most and, when appropriate, which party they liked the most. For those who indicated they voted for a party other than the one they liked the most, we took the party they liked the most as their second choice.

25 Indeed, among those with an opinion, 59 per cent thought that there was hardly any difference between the Alliance and Reform.

CHAPTER 5

A Multi-Stage Model of Vote Choice

Our attention now shifts to understanding why Canadians voted the way they did. There are many different reasons why a voter decides to vote for a given party and these reasons are likely to vary from voter to voter. So any account of vote choice must necessarily simplify what is inherently a very complex decision process. The goal is to identify factors that are important for substantial numbers of voters.

We use a multi-stage explanatory model. The basic idea is that some of the factors that affect vote choice, such as how people feel about the party leaders, are closer in time to the vote decision, while others, such as their ideological orientations, are more distant from actual vote choice. These longer-term predispositions can affect the vote directly, but they can also affect the vote indirectly by influencing more proximate factors, like leader evaluations and issue positions.

Figure 5.1 illustrates the model. It is inspired by the "bloc recursive" approach developed by Miller and Shanks (1996). The model incorporates eight blocs of variables. These blocs are similar to the ones we utilized in our analysis of the 1997 Canadian election (Nevitte et al., 2000) and also to those retained by Miller and Shanks.[1] Each bloc corresponds to a set of considerations that can affect vote choice.

At the farthest remove are a variety of social background characteristics that can shape voters' fundamental beliefs and political values and influence their party loyalties. Conventional wisdom has tended to be that Canadians' vote choices are only weakly rooted in the social structure, that relatively few Canadians have any sort of durable psychological attachment to a political party, and that relatively few Canadians have coherent ideological beliefs. Accordingly, attention has focused on the short-term factors that are specific to a given election.

The first of these proximate influences is the economy. How voters feel about the economy may well affect their evaluations both of the parties and of their leaders. A voter who was generally inclined to vote Liberal, for example, may have been tempted to vote for

Figure 5.1   The Multi-Stage Explanatory Model

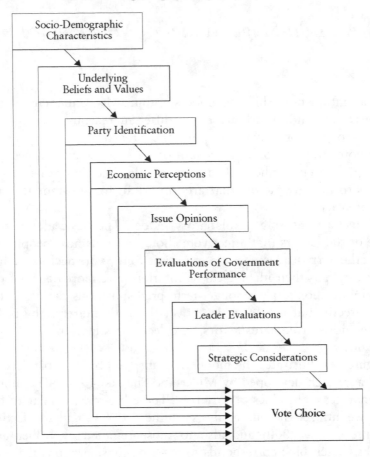

another party if the economy was perceived to be doing poorly. Economic perceptions may also have affected where voters stood on the fiscal issues that were so prominent in the 2000 election (Clarke and Kornberg, 1992).

Like economic voting, issue voting potentially has both a *prospective* dimension and a *retrospective* dimension. Voters can look at the parties' positions and decide to support the party that seems to share their views on the issues. Voters who want tax cuts, say, will be more inclined to support parties that favour cutting taxes, while those who want more spending on health care will support parties that promise increased spending in that area. This might seem to be almost a truism, but the notion of prospective issue voting is actually quite problematic. It assumes that voters are well-informed about where the parties stand on the issues, and there is ample evidence to suggest that this may not be the case. This is where the retrospective dimension comes in. Voters may decide to vote based not on what should be done about taxes or health, but on their evaluations of what the incumbent party has actually done about them (or not) during its mandate. Voters who are satisfied with the incumbent party's performance in a given area will be more likely to vote for the party, while those who are dissatisfied will vote for one of the opposition parties.

Then there are the leaders. Given the leader-centred nature of television coverage, it would be truly stunning if we were to find that leaders did not figure prominently in voters' decision calculations. We need to understand, though, *why* leaders mattered, and whether they had an impact over and above any social, ideological, or partisan predispositions that may have shaped voters' reactions to them.

The final factor to consider is qualitatively different from the previous ones. The factors discussed so far are all assumed to affect voters' *preferences* among the parties. But in a "first past the post" system, such as Canada's, some voters may cast a *strategic* vote. In other words, they may decide to vote for their second choice rather than their most preferred party, because they feel that the latter has no chance of winning in their constituency. If strategic voting does occur, it is likely to hurt the least-competitive parties.

We are not claiming that all voters go through each of these stages in exactly the same order. Nor are we claiming that all voters engage in such lengthy reasoning chains. Indeed, some voters may rely on simple socio-demographic cues when it comes to figuring out how to vote, such as the degree of social similarity between themselves and the party leaders (Cutler, forthcoming). Nonetheless, this explanatory schema does capture a sequence in which many voters participate, if only incompletely, and it represents a useful simplification of a complex and heterogeneous decision process. It also has the advantage of forcing us to think in terms of causal processes and to pay careful attention to the temporal sequence of these processes. The bloc recursive model explicitly retains all exogenous factors as explanatory variables at each stage of the analysis and this makes it possible to sort out spurious relationships. The multi-stage approach is particularly appropriate if there are likely to be significant projection effects (Miller and Shanks, 1996: 209). Projection occurs when proximate variables are strongly affected by more distant ones. Evaluations of government performance, for example, are likely to be shaped by voters' social background characteristics, values and beliefs, and partisan loyalties, as well as by their opinions on the issues, and so we need to ascertain whether they have an independent influence on the vote over and above these various predispositions.

The dependent variable is vote choice. Fortunately, there is a good fit between reported vote in the post-election survey and the actual outcome of the election, both for the country as a whole and for the various regions (Blais et al., 2001c). There is only one instance where the deviation is greater than three percentage points, and that is the under-estimation of the Liberal vote in Quebec. This bias is typical of surveys conducted in Quebec: support for federalist parties is systematically under-estimated.[2]

We analyze vote choice separately inside and outside Quebec. The presence of the Bloc Québécois means that Quebec voters were not offered the same choice as voters in other provinces. Outside Quebec, of course, the vote was strongly regionalized, and there is evidence from the 1997 election that regionalization can extend to the determinants of the vote itself (Gidengil et al., 1999). Accordingly, we estimated separate models of vote choice within each region, and we report these results where appropriate.[3]

There were not enough voters who supported smaller parties to be able to offer reliable generalizations about them. Accordingly, our analysis is confined to those who voted Liberal, Alliance, Conservative, or NDP outside Quebec and to those who voted Liberal, Bloc Québécois, Alliance, or Conservative in Quebec.[4]

The estimations are based on multinomial logit. The results are reported in Appendices A and B. These estimations allow us to look at each pair of parties and to determine which explanatory factors significantly enhanced (or reduced) the odds of voters choosing the first party over the second, controlling for other factors. Explanatory factors were retained in the model only if their effects were statistically significant at the .05 level or higher when they were first entered in the equations.[5]

The meaning of the logit coefficients depends on the values of the other variables in the model and so the coefficients themselves are not easy to interpret. However, they enable us to estimate the independent impact of a variable on the propensity to vote for each party. Take the urban/rural cleavage, for example. Appendix A.1 shows that rural voters were more likely to vote Alliance while urbanites were more prone to vote Liberal. On the basis of the multinomial estimations, we can compute the mean probability of voting Alliance, first, if everyone were rural and, second, if everyone were urban, keeping the effects of the other social background characteristics unchanged. The results indicate that, everything else being equal, the average probability of voting Alliance is 10 points higher when everyone is assumed to be rural than when everyone is assumed to be urban (Appendix C.2). The impact of being rural depends on other factors, but its average overall effect across the whole sample is to enhance the propensity to vote Alliance by 10 percentage points. The estimated average impact of each variable on the propensity to vote for the different parties is presented in Appendices C and D.

It is quite possible for a factor to have a substantial effect on how people vote, but to have no net impact on the outcome of the election. In order to estimate the net overall effect of each factor on the parties' vote shares, we determine how different the outcome would have been if a given factor had had no effect on the vote. This involves comparing the mean estimated probability, for all voters, of voting for each party based on the multinomial estimations presented in Appendices A and B, with the mean estimated probability when the coefficient for a given factor is set to 0 (which corresponds to no impact on vote choice) and all the other coefficients are kept constant. To use the urban/rural cleavage again, we can compare the mean probability of a person's voting for the Alliance when all the social background characteristics (including rural/urban), are considered and when the coefficient for rural/urban is set at 0 (all other coefficients being equal). The results indicate that if the rural/urban variable had had no effect on vote choice, the mean probability of voting Alliance would have declined from 33 per cent to 30 per cent. This implies that the Alliance gained three points overall, thanks to its rural support. We report the results of these estimations, as appropriate, throughout the text. They indicate how many fewer—or more—votes the various parties would have received if a given factor had had no impact on vote choice.

When assessing the *total* impact of a variable on vote choice or on the parties' share of the vote, it is important *not* to control for more proximate variables that may mediate that impact. Suppose that we found (as we did) a relationship between living in a rural area and voting Alliance, but suppose that this relationship completely vanished when we controlled for social conservatism. This would tell us that the reason why rural residents vote Alliance is that they are more socially conservative. Under such a scenario, the rural/urban cleavage remains a very real, though distant, factor in the vote equation, and we would miss something very important if we did not incorporate this variable into our explanation. In order to understand why some people are more socially conservative than others, it is essential to take into account whether they live in a rural or an urban setting. More proximate factors can *explicate* the impact of more distant factors on vote choice, but they cannot explain it away, and so we should not control for their effects when estimating the *total* impact of more distant factors.

On the other hand, it *is* crucial that we control for the effects of more distant factors when estimating the total impact of more proximate ones. This is because the more distant factors could explain away the apparent impact on vote choice. Suppose that we found that more socially conservative people were more likely to vote for the Alliance, but that this relationship vanished when we controlled for rural/urban residence. This would indicate that the relationship between social conservatism and Alliance voting was spurious. In other words, the only reason that social conservatism appeared to be related to Alliance voting was because they had a common cause: rural residents were more likely *both* to vote Alliance *and* to be socially conservative. Take away this common cause and the apparent relationship would evaporate. In this scenario, social conservatism *per se* would have no effect: what really mattered was whether the voter resided in a rural or an urban setting.

Accordingly, our assessments of the total independent impact of a given factor are based on the multinomial estimations in which that factor was first entered. In this way, we are only controlling for more distant factors and not for more proximate ones. This does not mean that the only relevant column (in Appendices A, B, C, and D) is the one showing the coefficient when the factor was initially entered. On the contrary, we can compare the coefficients across the subsequent columns to determine how much of that factor's effect is "explicated" by more proximate factors. For instance, by comparing columns 1 and 2, we can see how much of the impact of rural residence is mediated by values and beliefs. If the effect of the rural variable vanishes in the second column, we can conclude that it is because of values and beliefs—and only because of them—that rural voters vote differently from urban ones. If the effect of the variable is left completely intact, we can infer that values and beliefs do not explain any of the impact of the urban/rural cleavage. If (as is often the case), the effect decreases slightly in the second column, the implication would be that values and beliefs are part of the explanation, but only a part.

Our multi-stage model is necessarily an over-simplification of a complex and heterogeneous process whereby voters arrive at their final decision. It is nonetheless a powerful way of modelling vote choice. It enables us to take both a bottom-up and a top-down approach to making sense of the 2000 election. We can identify which factors mattered most to Canadians on election day, and we can also identify which of those factors actually affected the outcome. Finally, we can gain some insight into *why* those factors mattered, and avoid the pitfall of attributing too much influence to factors whose root causes lie elsewhere.

Notes

1 In both cases, social background characteristics and party identification figure among the most distant factors, and leader evaluations among the most proximate ones, but there are some slight differences. We see values and beliefs as being prior to party identification, and economic evaluations as being prior to issue opinions. Changing these assumptions does not greatly affect the conclusions.

2 For an analysis of the sources of that bias, see Durand et al., (2001).

3 Unfortunately, we did not have enough cases to examine provincial variations within the West or Atlantic Canada.

4 The NDP received less than 2 per cent of the vote in Quebec.

5 When a coefficient is significant at the .05 level, the chances are at least 95 per cent that the relationship observed in our sample holds for the whole population (or, put differently, the chances are less than 5 per cent that the relationship does not hold in the whole population).

CHAPTER 6

The Social Bases of Party Support

There is an old tradition in political science of relating voting behaviour to a host of socio-demographic variables (see, especially, Rose, 1974). That tradition has weakened over time, as researchers have come to emphasize the attitudinal components of vote choice and as evidence accumulates that some social background characteristics, notably class, may have become less important (Franklin et al., 1992). In Canada, the conventional wisdom has been that the effects of these characteristics were rather weak to begin with (Clarke et al., 1979; LeDuc, 1984). While this is certainly true of social class (Gidengil, 2002), the role of other factors like region and gender is actually more important now than it was 30 years ago.

The depth of the regional divide is readily appreciated. The Liberals obtained 52 per cent of the vote in Ontario, but only 25 per cent in the West.[1] Meanwhile, the Alliance received 50 per cent in the West, but a mere 10 per cent in Atlantic Canada. Conversely, the Conservatives won 31 per cent of the vote in the Atlantic provinces, but only 10 per cent in the West. Finally, the NDP won twice as many votes (17 per cent) in Atlantic Canada as they did in Ontario (8 per cent). These regional differences are not simply a matter of differences in the socio-demographic make-up of the regions (Gidengil et al., 1999). The Liberals, for example, are strongest in Ontario but this is not the region with the highest concentration of such voters as Catholics or Canadians of non-European origin, who are predisposed to vote Liberal.[2] Even controlling for a host of other social-background characteristics, the effects of region remain substantial (see Appendix C).

A significant gender gap has also emerged in Canada over the years (Erickson and O'Neill, forthcoming; Gidengil et al., forthcoming). The most striking aspect of this gap in the 2000 election was the greater propensity of men to vote for the Alliance (Table 6.1). Outside Quebec, the Alliance received 38 per cent of the vote among men, but only 27 per cent among women. The equivalent figures for the NDP were 9 per cent and 15 per cent. These differences are unaffected by region, religion, or ethnicity. Indeed, the estimated total impact of sex on vote choice when other social background

Table 6.1   Vote Choice by Socio-Demographic Characteristics

A. *Outside Quebec*

	Liberal	Alliance	Conservative	NDP
All	40	33	15	11
Sex				
Men	41	38	11	9
Women	41	27	15	15
Residence				
Rural	30	45	13	10
Urban	43	31	12	13
Religion				
Catholic	54	24	10	11
Other religion	34	41	15	9
No religion	40	25	10	22
Origin				
North European	31	50	7	10
Non-European	72	14	5	9
Other origin	39	33	15	13
Language				
English	36	36	14	12
French	58	20	8	15
Other language	58	27	6	8
Marital Status				
Married	40	37	13	10
Not married	43	25	12	18
Education				
Below high school	39	38	9	14
Middle	40	35	13	10
University	43	28	14	13

B. *Quebec*

	Liberal	Bloc	Alliance	Conservative
All	44	40	6	6
Age				
18-54	34	45	9	4
55 +	51	37	3	5
Language				
French	33	48	8	5
Other language	70	15	6	1

Note: Cell entries are percentages. The percentages do not add up to 100 per cent because they include those who voted for other parties.

characteristics are taken into account is 12 points for Alliance and just over 6 points for the NDP. The Alliance's inability to obtain the support of more women is one crucial reason for its lack of success in Ontario. Thirty per cent of men in that province voted Alliance. If the party had been able to do as well among Ontario women, it would have managed to make the inroad it was aiming for at the beginning of the campaign.

Rural voters were significantly more likely to vote Alliance. Indeed, rural areas proved to be the party's strongest supporters. Outside Quebec, 45 per cent of rural voters voted for the Alliance, while only 30 per cent opted for the Liberals. In Ontario, the party did as well (42 per cent) as the Liberals (39 per cent) in rural settings. The problem for the Alliance is that rural voters account for only a relatively small proportion of the total electorate (21 per cent of our sample) and very few constituencies are controlled by rural voters. And the rural/urban cleavage failed to emerge in Atlantic Canada, Canada's most rural region. Still, the rural vote was very important for the Alliance. If rural voters had voted like their urban counterparts, the Alliance would have trailed the Liberals by 12 points outside Quebec instead of seven. But the larger point remains that the party received little support from urban voters outside the West and this was a significant factor in its inability to win a larger share of the vote. The Liberals, on the other hand, did better among urban voters than among rural voters.

Religion has been one of the most enduring sources of cleavage in federal elections (Irvine, 1974; Johnston, 1985; Mendelsohn and Nadeau, 1997). Since the very earliest studies of voting behaviour in Canada, Catholic voters have been significantly more likely to vote for the Liberal Party. Meanwhile, voters with no religious affiliation have traditionally been more likely than other voters to opt for the NDP. In 2000, 54 per cent of Catholics outside Quebec voted Liberal (Table 6.1); everything else being equal, the probability of voting Liberal was 14 percentage points higher among Catholics (Appendix C). In contrast, 22 per cent of those with no religious affiliation voted NDP; the party got only 10 per cent among those with a religious affiliation. All in all, the probability of voting NDP was 16 points higher among those with no religion, even taking into account other salient social-background characteristics like region and ethnicity. Protestants, for their part, were more likely to support the Alliance. Our simulations indicate that the Liberal vote share would have dropped by four points and the Alliance share would have increased by three points if Catholics (who made up 29 per cent of our sample outside Quebec) had voted like Canadians of other religious denominations.[3]

The support of Canadians of non-European origin was also a crucial component of Liberal success. As many as 72 per cent of them voted Liberal (Table 6.1). According to our simulations, if voters of non-European origin had voted like those of other origins, the Liberal vote would have been three percentage points lower and the Alliance vote two points higher. The propensity to vote Liberal was a hefty 31 points higher among voters of non-European origin, while the propensity to vote Alliance was 11 points higher among those of Northern European (excluding Britain and Ireland) origin (Appendix C). Likewise those whose first language is neither French nor English were more inclined to vote Liberal. The probability of a Liberal vote was 44 points higher among voters of non-European origin whose first language is neither French nor English.

The only other social background characteristic that had a significant impact on vote choice outside Quebec was marital status. The Alliance did significantly better among voters who are married, whereas the NDP fared better among those who are not. However, the impact of marital status was not of much consequence for the parties' vote shares.

Finally, it is important to highlight some social background characteristics that did not have a significant effect on vote choice. Union membership used to be associated (albeit not very strongly) with support for the NDP (Archer, 1985), but that is no longer the case. Outside Quebec, only 14 per cent of union members voted NDP in 2000, compared with 11 per cent of non-union members, and union members were much more likely to vote Alliance (30 per cent) than they were to vote NDP. Income also failed to have any significant independent impact on vote choice, confirming the lack of class-based voting in Canada. Indeed, the only socio-economic characteristic that affected vote choice was education: the NDP did slightly better, and the Conservatives did slightly worse, among less-educated voters. Education was one of the few social background characteristics that had a significant independent effect on the propensity to vote Conservative. Finally, in striking contrast to the generational cleavage in turnout, there was no sign of an association between age and vote choice outside Quebec.

Social background characteristics played out quite differently in Quebec. First, age mattered. The Liberals were clearly ahead among those over 55 and the Bloc led among younger voters (Table 6.1). The propensity to vote for the Bloc was 11 points lower among those aged 55 and over (Appendix D). This is consistent with the familiar finding that older voters in Quebec are significantly more likely to be federalists. But the effect of age pales beside that of language. The impact of language is huge: the probability of a Liberal vote is 42 points higher among non-francophones. Language and age are the only two socio-demographic variables that really count in Quebec.[4]

In Quebec, then, the situation is relatively simple. There are three major groups: non-francophones, francophones under the age of 55, and francophones 55 years and older. Seventy per cent of non-francophones voted Liberal, 55 per cent of francophones under the age of 55 voted for the Bloc, and the two parties were more or less tied (with a slight Liberal edge) among francophones aged 55 and over.[5]

Models of vote choice in Canada have traditionally downplayed the importance of social background characteristics. One reason has been a perception that characteristics that change slowly, if at all, across time cannot account for electoral change (Kanji and Archer, 2002). However, even within the short time frame of an election campaign the social bases of party support can sometimes shift in consequential ways.

Is there any evidence that some groups became more or less supportive of some party as the campaign progressed? We can check whether the various groups that we have identified had different vote intentions at the beginning and end of the campaign. The test that we have performed and that will be repeated in the following chapters is whether things were different before and after the English debate, that is, before and after November 9. The debates occurred at midpoint in the campaign and they provide the logical divide between the first and the second halves of the campaign.[6]

Do the CES data indicate that vote intentions were substantially different within some groups in the first and second halves of the campaign? The short answer is No, with one exception. For about every group, vote intentions in the second half of the campaign looked very similar to vote intentions in the first half. There is one exception. There is evidence of a substantial shift among voters whose first language was neither French nor English. Outside Quebec, the Alliance managed to obtain 33 per cent of the vote among those interviewed during the first half of the campaign, but the percentage fell to 18 per cent in the second half.[7] This raises the possibility that allegations of racism within the Alliance made members of minority ethnic groups more reluctant to support the party. It also drives home the point that social groups need to be treated as live social forces, not static categories.

Our data confirm that social cleavages matter in Canada. In Quebec, only two socio-demographic characteristics—language and age—were electorally relevant, but their effects were powerful. Outside Quebec, there were multiple lines of cleavage, the most important being region, religion, ethnicity, gender, and type of community.

It would be impossible to understand the Liberals' victory in the 2000 election without recognizing the extent to which their strength outside Quebec hinges on the support of Catholics and Canadians of non-European origin. These two groups constitute the core of Liberal support outside Quebec. Fifty-four percent of Catholics and 72 per cent of Canadians of non-European origin voted Liberal. The Liberal lead outside Quebec is heavily dependent on the strong support of these two groups. Without them, the seven-point lead obtained by the Liberals over the Alliance outside Quebec would translate into a five-point edge for the Alliance. In Ontario, the huge 28-point Liberal lead would shrink by almost half.

Support for the Alliance was concentrated among rural Protestant men of Northern European origin. Those who shared at least two of these characteristics had about a 50 per cent chance of voting Alliance if they lived in Ontario, a 70 per cent probability if they resided in the West, and a 30 per cent chance if they were from Atlantic Canada. The best predictor of NDP vote was having no religious denomination, followed by being a woman and being non-married. As in 1997 (Nevitte et al., 2000), the Conservative vote appeared particularly unstructured, apart from its regional dimension. So, in a way, is support for the Bloc in Quebec, leaving aside the dominant linguistic cleavage.

The next challenge is to explain how and why these social cleavages affect vote choice.

Notes

1 There are important differences among the Western provinces in how the parties fared. The same is true of the Atlantic provinces. However, the provincial samples are too small to allow for the modelling of vote choice within the individual provinces in these regions.

2 There are proportionally more Catholics in Atlantic Canada and the percentage of Canadians of non-European origin is the same in the West and in Ontario.

3 According to the multinomial logit regressions reported in column 1 of Appendix A , the average probability of a Liberal vote outside Quebec was 42 per cent. We can also estimate the average probability of a Liberal vote if the coefficient of the Catholic variable were set to 0, which would be the case if Catholics had voted like non-Catholics (and all voters kept their other socio-demographic characteristics); that average probability is 38 per cent. Thus, we can make the inference that the Liberals would have had four percentage point less in the absence of stronger Catholic support or, in other words, that the Catholic support gave the Liberals an additional boost of four percentage points in the whole electorate. The same procedure was applied to estimate the impact on the Alliance vote. See Chapter 5 for a full description and justification of the approach. Unless otherwise indicated, all the simulations reported in this study proceed with the same logic. We determine whether the average overall probability of a vote for a given party, in our sample, changes if a specific variable were to have had no effect, keeping all other factors constant. The difference between the initial overall average probability and the same probability under a scenario of no effect provides an estimate of the impact of the variable on the parties' vote share.

4 There are also signs of a gender gap in Quebec. Women were more prone to vote Liberal, while men were more inclined to support the Bloc; but the gap did not quite reach statistical significance.

5 It should be kept in mind that the CES, like most surveys in Quebec, underestimate support for the Liberal party.

6 We performed these tests for the "outside Quebec" sample. The small numbers in Quebec make such comparisons fragile. There is the possibility that some groups shifted only at the very end of the campaign, which our pre/post debate comparison would not pick up. But given what we know about the relatively small net effect of the campaign and the central role of the debates, such late shifts are not very likely to have occurred.

7 The difference is statistically significant at the .05 level.

CHAPTER 7

Values and Beliefs

When Prime Minister Chrétien called the election on October 22, he immediately launched into a forceful appeal to voters to think about their values and beliefs. The election call was framed as an opportunity for Canadians to choose between different visions and different values: "This election," Chrétien declared, "offers two very different visions of Canada, two crystal clear alternatives. The nature of that choice is clear and the right time to choose is now" (CBC, *The National*, 22 October). And if there was ever any ambiguity about which parties spoke for each of the "two visions," clarity on the matter was supplied by the Liberal Minister of Finance at the end of the first week of the campaign. "Never has there been an election in the history of this country," claimed Paul Martin, "where the line in the sand has been drawn as clearly as it has been between the Liberal vision and the Alliance vision" (CBC, *The National*, 29 October). The Liberals portrayed the Alliance as a party appealing to "narrow interests" and as a party that would "Americanize Canada" (*Globe and Mail*, 28 October, A8). Meanwhile, the Liberals presented themselves as the champions of "the values that made Canada what it is today" (*Globe and Mail*, 26 October, A10) and they argued that it was important to "keep working on that because we never know when there will not be a force who will come and appeal to the dark side that exists in human beings"(*Globe and Mail*, 31 October, A4). A more direct appeal to citizens to look to their values when making their vote decision would be hard to imagine. The question is: did Canadians respond?

There are at least two reasons to expect that they would. First, fundamental value commitments can help people to reason about politics (Sniderman et al., 1991). Encapsulating as they do conceptions of what is desirable, values potentially enable citizens to simplify complex choices by serving as a template for evaluating their political worlds. Thus, leaders and parties will be rated positively or negatively depending on whether they are perceived as likely to advance or impede the realization of those values. Similarly, the kinds of issue positions that people take may owe more to their values than to their assessments of policy alternatives (Butler and

Stokes, 1971: 230). Second, there is evidence from a variety of advanced industrial states that values can have a larger impact on vote choice than voters' social background characteristics (Van Deth and Scarbrough, 1995).

The Visions and Values Theme

Which values are likely to have mattered to voters in the 2000 election? Religiosity and social conservatism are two obvious candidates. Stockwell Day's religious fundamentalism drew attention to religious convictions in a way that is highly unusual in contemporary Canadian election campaigns. The Alliance portrayed Day's religious beliefs as an asset. Alliance campaign co-director Jason Kenney argued that because of these "strong personal convictions," people will know that "Stockwell Day is somebody that will stick to his commitments" (*Globe and Mail*, 23 October, A8). The implication was that the Alliance leader would be more likely to "keep promises." This was a pointed reference to what Reform in the previous election campaign had called the Liberal record of "broken promises."

The Liberal counterattack was swift and vigorous, and it touched on several themes at the same time. One was that Canadians who were not fundamentalists of the Stockwell Day variety might have something to worry about. "It's not for me," Chrétien re-assured Canadians, "to impose my morality on others in a diverse society with many religions like the one we have" (CBC, *The National*, 10 November). Chrétien also seized the opportunity to muse out loud about whether the Alliance wanted religion to play a larger role in shaping public policy while expressing thinly veiled skepticism about Day's views about "creationism." "In my family," Chrétien told *The National*, "separation of Church and the separation of state is important. Church is private but now there is a debate about evolution and creation and I'm not getting involved with that" (CBC, *The National*, 17 November). "I believe in the 'creation' of jobs," Chrétien quipped (*Globe and Mail*, 17 November, A6).

The issue of race also emerged during the campaign, albeit briefly. Alliance candidate Betty Granger's views about "the Asian invasion" were broadcast across the country by English network TV in the third week of the campaign. This controversy handed the Liberals an opportunity to take the high ground and to cast the Alliance as a haven for the intolerant. "That kind of anti-immigrant, racist, bigoted opinion is not something the Liberal Party would tolerate and it says a lot about Stockwell Day and his supporters," Liberal immigration minister Elinor Caplan charged (CBC, *The National*, 17 November). Gender issues, by contrast, received hardly any campaign attention although the NDP's Alexa McDonough raised concerns about them from time to time.

The economic policy issue that featured most prominently throughout the campaign concerned how much taxes should be cut and how the surplus should be used—to cut taxes, to pay down the federal debt or to increase spending on social programs. Every party expressed a position on the matter and often in ways that invoked more general beliefs about free enterprise and the role of the state. Both the Alliance and the Liberals reminded voters about where they stood on the basic question of the role of the government in the economy. "Anytime you have a strong economy," argued Stockwell Day, "you have to look to the private sector for creating that economy" (CBC, *The National*, 23 October). The Liberals responded that governments have an important role to play in managing the economy. "Eliminating the role of the national government in developing high skills jobs is the Reform-Alliance's concept of a new idea," countered Chrétien. "It is not a new idea but a bad idea, and it's no way to run a country" (Jean Chrétien. CBC, *The National*, 24 October). Two weeks later, Finance Minister Martin acidly remarked, "the Alliance believes that the only role for government is to sit back and watch the world go around" (*Globe and Mail*, 13 November, A9). The Alliance, meanwhile, emphasized the virtues of the private sector and the need to end "corporate welfare."

Where did voters stand?

Just because the parties chose to make direct appeals to values it does not follow that Canadians responded to those appeals or that they divided over those value appeals in partisan ways. If we want to sort out whether values mattered—and which values mattered—the place to begin is with an examination of where the electorate's centre of gravity was on these dimensions.

Beliefs about *free enterprise* and how much of a role governments should have in directing the economy have been a primary value cleavage mobilizing and dividing publics in most states for generations and Canada is no exception. In the post-war era, social democratic parties promoting expansive welfare states enjoyed electoral success by arguing that unfettered free enterprise had unfair consequences for have-nots in society. The role of governments was to put in place social safety nets. By the 1980s that Keynesian welfare state orthodoxy was in retreat, and in Canada, the United States, Britain, and elsewhere, political parties wanting less state intervention in the economy rode to power. They charged that welfare states stifled individual initiative and hobbled governments with unacceptably large public debts. Their solution was to "roll back the state."

Canadians turn out to be quite ambivalent about the virtues and vices of the free-enterprise system. Two in three (68 per cent) agree that "people who don't get ahead should blame themselves, not the system," but almost as many (65 per cent) reject the view that "when businesses make a lot of money, everyone benefits, including the poor" and only one in four (24 per cent) say that business should have more power (and 29 per cent say it should have less). Still, Canadians seem more positive about business than about unions: only 13 per cent think that unions should have more power and as many as 44 per cent would like them to have less. And, close to half (43 per cent) are ready to endorse the idea that "the government should leave it entirely to the private sector to create jobs." When responses to these questions are combined to form a scale, just over a quarter (27 per cent) have a basically favourable view of the free-enterprise system (scoring above +.25 on a -1 to +1 scale) and just under a quarter (22 per cent) have a basically unfavourable view (scoring below -.25). The typical position, though, is one of ambivalence (scoring between -.25 and +.25).[1]

Opposing beliefs about the free enterprise system and about the appropriate balance between government and the market are at the core of the so-called "old" left-right cleavage. The "new" left-right distinction, by contrast, revolves around social rather than economic questions. Most publics can be differentiated according to how conservative or progressive they are when it comes to a variety of matters that relate to so-called "family values," such as alternative lifestyles and the role of women in the household and the workplace, and again Canada is no exception. Canadian society used to be based on a traditional model in which the man worked outside the home and the woman stayed home to take care of the children. That traditional family is no longer the dominant norm. Half of our respondents (52 per cent) rejected the notion that "society would be better off if more women stayed home with their children," while 44 per cent agreed. The traditional family also has been challenged by the advent of same-sex partnerships. Canadians are quite divided about whether "gays and lesbians should be allowed to get married." Fifty-one per cent think so, but 42 per cent are opposed. Combining responses to these two questions into a *social conservatism* scale reveals that social liberals (35 per cent) outnumber social conservatives (27 per cent), but that many Canadians remain ambivalent (39 per cent).

Traditionally, beliefs about these kinds of issues have been profoundly shaped by organized religion. Canadian society is far more secular than it once was, but these social orientations might nonetheless still be influenced by people's personal *religiosity*. As many as 31 per cent indicated that religion is very important in their lives and another 41 per cent said it is somewhat important. On the other hand, only 16 per cent replied that it is not very important and a mere 11 per cent said that religion is not at all important in their lives. A clear majority thus expressed some degree of religiosity. While there is little doubt that higher figures would have been obtained 30 or 40 years ago, religion still appears to be an important dimension for most Canadians.

Increasing secularism is not the only trend that has characterized Canada in recent decades. We have also been witnessing the growing salience of—and sensitivity to—groups that have stood at the margins of the political mainstream. These include racial minorities and women. Significant changes in the character of the Canadian population, and most particularly the shifting pattern of immigration over the last 30 years, mean that Canada is now a far more culturally diverse society. As a result, the question of how much should be done for *racial minorities* could well have been salient to voters. Respondents were asked how much they thought should be done for racial minorities: 41 per cent said "more" and 40 per cent "about the same as now." Only 13 per cent said "less," but social desirability effects suggest that this antipathy towards racial minorities might be understated. Still, the question does help us to distinguish groups with different views about racial minorities. Views about feminism also have the potential to mobilize voters, particularly on matters of gender equality. Like other publics, Canadians are divided when it comes to their *sympathies towards feminism*.[2] When we asked people how sympathetic they were, 62 per cent of our sample indicated that they were very or quite sympathetic,[3] though again social desirability biases could mean that antipathy is understated.

Finally, there is the perennial question of the place of Quebec in the Canadian federation. In Quebec, the debate about whether

Quebec should become a sovereign country has been at the very top of the political agenda for the last 30 years. That debate raises deep questions about Quebecers' political identities (Blais and Nadeau, 1992). The emergence of the Bloc Québécois virtually guarantees that Quebecers' positions on the *sovereignty* question will strongly affect both their political perceptions and their federal vote. According to our survey, there were 40 per cent sovereignists and 57 per cent federalists at the time of the election.[4] Outside Quebec, the question of what should be done to accommodate Quebecers' aspirations has also been a central source of frustration, and *orientations towards Quebec* have proven to be a crucial dividing line. When Canadians outside Quebec were asked how much should be done for Quebec, only 9 per cent said "more," while 39 per cent opted for "less" and 43 per cent for "status quo." There is thus a strong element of hostility and this was also apparent when respondents were asked to indicate their general feeling towards Quebec on a 0 to 100 scale; 30 per cent indicated a negative feeling (under 50). Still, close to half (47 per cent) did respond positively (over 50). When these two questions are combined, 24 per cent of respondents outside Quebec emerge as quite sympathetic towards Quebec (scoring above +.25 on the scale), 28 per cent as quite antipathetic (scoring below −.25) and 48 per cent as ambivalent.[5]

Table 7.1 shows how these various values are related to social background characteristics. Differences between men and women prove to be quite modest. Women feel slightly more sympathetic towards racial minorities, they are more ambivalent about free enterprise, and, perhaps surprisingly, they express slightly less sympathy for feminism. There is one large difference, though: women are much more religious than men.

Westerners are more socially conservative, more supportive of free enterprise, and less sympathetic towards racial minorities and feminism. The differences, however, are quite modest: the average Ontario/West gap on these four values is only .07 on a −1 to +1 scale. As for Quebec, it is distinguished by the high level of sympathy for feminism and the relatively low degree of religiosity. Rural/urban differences are generally small, and are smaller than the regional differences

Differences between religious groups also tend to be small. There is one striking exception: those with no religion are clearly less socially conservative. As for ethnicity and language, not surprisingly, Canadians of non-European origin and those whose first language is

Table 7.1   Political Attitudes by Socio-Demographic Characteristics

	Social conservatism	Free enterprise	Racial minorities	Feminism	Religiosity	Quebec (outside Quebec)	Sovereignty (Quebec)
All	-.04	.04	.19	.19	.33	-.08	-.20
Sex							
Men	-.01	.07	.16	.22	.23	-.10	-.10
Women	-.08	.00	.22	.16	.43	-.06	-.28
Region							
Atlantic	-.06	-.03	.27	.21	.52	-.02	
Quebec	-.07	.10	.25	.31	.20		-.20
Ontario	-.08	-.01	.19	.16	.38	-.06	
West	.02	.06	.12	.13	.31	-.13	
Outside Quebec	-.04	.02	.17	.15	.37	-.08	
Residence							
Rural	.08	.03	.14	.14	.38	-.11	-.14
Urban	-.08	.03	.21	.20	.31	-.07	-.22
Religion							
Catholic	-.03	.06	.21	.25	.40	-.08	-.17
Other religion	.05	.04	.18	.11	.52	-.08	-.85
No religion	-.32	-.03	.16	.24	-.40	-.07	.11
Origin							
North European	.12	.05	.08	.09	.45	-.10	-.61
Non-European	.00	.09	.41	.16	.40	-.01	-.71
Other origin	-.07	.03	.19	.20	.30	-.08	-.19
Language							
English	-.08	.00	.16	.16	.34	-.09	-.60
French	-.07	.08	.23	.31	.22	.02	-.13
Other language	.15	.09	.25	.11	.47	-.08	-.65
Marital Status							
Married	.01	.05	.16	.18	.37	-.09	-.22
Not married	-.17	.00	.25	.22	.23	-.06	-.15
Education							
Below high school	.21	.08	.24	.17	.49	-.16	-.33
Middle	-.06	.03	.16	.16	.31	-.10	-.19
University	-.23	.00	.21	.27	.23	.02	-.07

Note: Cell entries are mean scales scores. The scales range from -1 to 1.

neither French nor English are more supportive of racial minorities.[6] Those of north European origin and those whose first language is neither French nor English tend to be more socially conservative. So, too, are married people. Marital status is also associated with differences in religiosity.

Finally, education shows some interesting patterns. Those with less formal education are more socially conservative and more religious and, in Quebec, they are less supportive of sovereignty. Outside Quebec, they are somewhat more hostile to Quebec.

Values and the Vote

It turns out that sympathy/antipathy towards Quebec was simply unrelated to voting for the Alliance in 2000. This is perhaps the most striking change that took place between 1997 and 2000. The Reform Party broke through in the 1993 election by politicizing this cleavage, and antipathy towards Quebec continued to be a crucial ingredient of support for the party in 1997 (Nevitte et al., 2000). However, it also became clear that its perceived stance on Quebec was hurting the party, contributing to a perception that it was just too extreme and preventing Reform from making significant inroads in Ontario. The desire to distance itself from this image was part of the motivation for the party's reinventing itself as the Alliance. Its success in this regard is evident from the fact that the debate about what should or should not be done for Quebec was no longer on the political agenda in 2000 and had no effect on vote choice outside Quebec.

The most powerful value dimension, at least outside Quebec, appears to be the classic left/right cleavage about the place of free enterprise in our society (Appendices A and C). "Left" and "right" may not be part of many Canadians' political vocabulary, but the reality is that the traditional left/right opposition is central when it comes to making sense of the vote outside Quebec. Indeed, this was the most important value motivating both the Conservative and the NDP vote. The NDP does particularly well among those who are highly sceptical of the virtues of free enterprise, while support for free enterprise seems to be the only value that matters for the Conservative vote. People who supported free enterprise, though, were even more likely to vote Alliance. Views about free enterprise were also important for the Liberal vote. Everything else being equal, the propensity to vote Liberal was 11 points lower outside Quebec when someone was very positive about free enterprise, compared with someone who was neutral or ambivalent.

Social conservatism also mattered and so did views about feminism and racial minorities. Outside Quebec, the propensity to vote Liberal decreased by 6 points for social conservatives and increased by 5 points for those sympathetic to feminism and racial minorities. The NDP vote was also partly driven by a rejection of social conservatism. The Alliance vote was even more strongly affected by people's positions on these normative dimensions. People who are socially conservative were much more likely to vote for the Alliance, while those who expressed sympathy for feminism and racial minorities were less prone to vote for the party.

Religiosity as such does not appear to be as powerful a factor as these other value dimensions, though it did have an impact on the vote, especially when it came to the choice between the NDP and the Alliance. What mattered was not religiosity but rather Christian fundamentalist beliefs. These had been made salient by the infamous *CBC* report on Stockwell Day, "Fundamental Day," that focused on the Alliance leader's personal beliefs about the Bible and creationism. Based on their agreement with the statement that "the Bible is the actual word of God and is to be taken literally word for word," almost one mail-back respondent in five (19 per cent) could be considered a Christian fundamentalist. When we added this variable to the multinomial estimations, it was clear that Christian fundamentalism was indeed associated with support for the Alliance and that religiosity per se was no longer significant.[7] Still, the effect of fundamentalism was hardly huge: everything else being equal, the propensity to vote Alliance was only 8 points higher among those who believe that the Bible should be taken literally. This is smaller than the effect of views about free enterprise and social conservatism. It remains to be seen how much evaluations of Day himself were affected. This is a question that will be taken up in Chapter 12.

In Quebec, meanwhile, only two values emerged as significant: support for sovereignty and social conservatism (Appendices B and D). The most powerful factor was clearly people's views about sovereignty. Everything else being equal, the propensity to vote for the Bloc Québécois was 34 percentage points higher when a voter was strongly in favour of sovereignty, compared with a voter who was neutral or ambivalent. No other consideration, inside or outside Quebec, was as consequential for vote choice as this one. Because it was so dominant a consideration, there was little room left for other value cleavages. The only other electorally relevant cleavage was social conservatism, and then only for the choice between the Bloc and the Alliance.

Beliefs about Politics and the Political System

Not only did values matter but so did underlying beliefs about politics and the operation of the political system.[8] Since the early 1980s, most advanced industrial states have experienced an erosion in the levels of trust in public officials (Dalton, 1988; Nevitte, 1996). Citizens have increasingly come to believe that governments are unresponsive and this *cynicism* finds expression in anti-party sentiment (Gidengil et al., 2001). Perhaps the most telling indicator of popular cynicism is that almost two-thirds (64 per cent) of Canadians agree with the statement that the government does not care much what people like them think. Likewise, about political parties and politicians in general only 31 per cent and 37 per cent, respectively, of the respondents felt positively.[9] And as many as 45 per cent were willing to agree with the rather strong statement (given the presence of parties such as the Bloc and the Alliance) that all parties are basically the same.

In a similar vein, a number of Canadians have come to perceive the federal government as largely insensitive to the needs and concerns of their province or region. A straightforward question measured this sense of *regional alienation*: "In general, does the federal government treat your province better, worse, or about the same as other provinces?". Thirty-one per cent said "worse."

Predictably, there is a huge gap between the West (.50 on a 0 to 1 scale) and Ontario (.11) with respect to regional alienation. We should note, however, that the level of regional alienation is only slightly higher in the West than it is in Atlantic Canada (.43). As for Quebec, the high level of cynicism (.18 on a −1 to +1 scale) is notable compared with the rest of the country (.02). Canadians of non-European origin (.15) and those whose first language is neither French nor English (.19) seem to feel less regionally alienated than Canadians at large (.31). Women (.27) are also somewhat less likely than men (.35) to express a sense of regional alienation.

We can expect these beliefs to colour how Canadians viewed the choices that they were offered in the 2000 election. From the very first day of the campaign, every single opposition party tried to capitalize on the perception that public cynicism was high and that the

Liberals had been in power too long. The Alliance opened with a sharp volley: "This is a government which is obsessed with perpetuating itself and keeping power for its own sake," pronounced Jason Kenny, the party's campaign co-chair. "We think that is a record of arrogance not moderation" (CBC, *The National*, 22 October). NDP leader Alexa McDonough took the same line. "Jean Chrétien," she charged, "is extremely arrogant and completely out of touch with ordinary people" (*Globe and Mail*, 23 October, A9). The Alliance leader echoed the very same sentiments in almost exactly the same words the very next day (CBC, *The National*, 24 October). And Progressive Conservative leader Joe Clark chimed in with a similar attack on the Liberal government two days after that (*Globe and Mail*, 27 October).

These attacks hit home. Voters who felt cynical about politics and who believed that their province was not being treated fairly by the federal government were less inclined to vote Liberal. Our estimations indicate that, other things being equal, the probability of voting Liberal outside Quebec was 18 points lower among voters who were highly cynical, compared with those who were neutral. The effect was similar in Quebec. Though not quite as consequential, feelings of regional alienation were also important. There is one interesting difference, however. Whereas cynicism fueled support for all of the opposition parties, regional alienation tended to produce a vote only for the Alliance, outside Quebec, or for the Bloc, in Quebec. The perception that one's province is treated unfairly in Ottawa was clearly an important consideration in voting Alliance. Meanwhile, in Quebec, a substantial minority (22 per cent) of *non*-sovereignists thought that Quebec is less well-treated than other provinces: 29 per cent of them voted Bloc, and a not negligible 18 per cent voted Alliance. So support for the Bloc did not depend solely on support for sovereignty.

How Much Did Values and Beliefs Matter?

Core values and beliefs were clearly an important ingredient of vote choice in the 2000 election. According to our results, socio-demographic characteristics account for 12 per cent of the variance in vote choice outside Quebec (Appendix A). Adding values and beliefs contributes an additional 10 percentage points, increasing the explained variance to 22 per cent. In Quebec, the effect of adding values and beliefs is huge, increasing the variance explained from 6 per cent to

40 per cent. However, this is largely because of the powerful impact of attitudes about sovereignty.

Values and beliefs explain part, but only part, of the observed relationships between social-background characteristics and the vote. By comparing columns 1 and 2 in Appendix C, we can see that the strong support for the NDP among those with no religion flows in good part from the fact that most of them reject social conservatism. Likewise, support for the Liberals in Quebec among non-francophones and older voters is very much the result of these two groups' widespread opposition to sovereignty. Meanwhile, the success of the Alliance in the West has much to do with the strong sense of regional alienation in the region. However, the Alliance's lack of success in Atlantic Canada remains unexplained. And values and beliefs do not account for Conservative success in Atlantic Canada nor for strong Liberal support among Catholics.

One way to gauge how much of the impact is mediated through values and beliefs is to compare the median impact of social background characteristics before and after taking values and beliefs into account. For example, the median estimated impact of social background characteristics on the Alliance vote before incorporating values and beliefs is 11.3 points (column 1 of Appendix C.2); once values and beliefs are introduced, the median estimated impact drops to 7.6 points (column 2 of Appendix C.2). So, typically, about a third of the socio-demographic variation in Alliance support is mediated by values and beliefs.

While underlying values and beliefs are clearly important for understanding why individual voters vote the way they do, it is not clear that they are so crucial when it comes to making sense of the *outcome* of the election. The reason is simple. An attitude will only affect the outcome if it influences vote choice *and* if it is skewed in one direction. Take views about free enterprise. These views are relatively strongly related to vote choice, but many Canadians are ambivalent about free enterprise and the government's role in the economy, and opinion among the rest is more or less evenly divided. So Alliance gains among those who are favourable to free enterprise were washed out by its losses among those who are opposed. A similar pattern applies to social conservatism.

Feelings about racial minorities and feminism were skewed in a positive direction and could have had a net impact on the outcome by helping the Liberals and the NDP at the expense of the Alliance. It is important, though, to take account of a possible social desirability bias in some of these positive responses. Fundamentalism also had some impact on the outcome of the election. According to our estimates, if fundamentalism had had no effect on voters, the Alliance would have obtained 34 per cent of the vote outside Quebec instead of 33 per cent. So it hurt the Alliance, but the impact was small.

The situation is somewhat different with respect to beliefs about politics and the operation of the political system. In Canada, as elsewhere, there is a strong dose of cynicism about politics and politicians and this cynicism fuels support for the opposition parties. This hurt the Liberals. The same can be said about the sense of regional alienation that prevails outside Ontario. And it clearly contributed to the success of the Alliance and the Bloc.

Values and beliefs play a greater role in the outcome of the election in Quebec. At the time of the election, there were more federalists than sovereignists in Quebec, and that is the main reason why the Liberals won more votes than the Bloc. According to our estimates, if views about sovereignty had had no effect on vote choice (or if everyone in Quebec had been at the neutral point on the sovereignty scale), the Liberals would have had 31 per cent of the vote instead of 44 per cent and the Bloc 52 per cent instead of 40 per cent. These Liberal gains were partly offset by losses related to cynicism and the sense of regional alienation, both of which benefited the Bloc at the Liberals' expense.

Our analysis has focused on the impact of values and beliefs on actual vote choice. But we also examined whether their influence changed over the course of the campaign, with voters coming to pay greater attention to some dimensions to the detriment of others. To do this, we looked at the relationship between each of the dimensions examined in this chapter and vote intentions before and after the leader debates, which marked the midpoint of the campaign. We found no evidence that one particular value or belief became markedly more—or less—salient as the campaign progressed.

Discussion

We began this chapter by arguing that there were good reasons to expect that values would matter to vote choice in the 2000 election. The governing Liberals opened the campaign with two clear messages: they wanted the campaign to be about values and they wanted the battle lines to be drawn between the Liberal vision and the

Alliance vision. In Quebec, the cleavage between sovereignists and federalists is so powerful that there is little room for other values to play a significant role. Outside Quebec, though, voters clearly did respond to the Liberal strategy. The most powerful division pitted those who were basically favourable to the free enterprise system against those who were more sceptical. The former were inclined to vote Alliance or Conservative, while the latter were prone to support the Liberals or the NDP. The second most important dimension concerned social conservatism: social conservatives were particularly inclined to vote for the Alliance.

We also began this chapter by arguing that there were more general reasons to expect values to matter. The 1997 election campaign did not revolve around the theme of visions and values, and yet values were still important to vote choice (Nevitte et al., 2000). This point bears emphasis. Models of vote choice in Canada have traditionally focused on short-term factors like the economy, leaders, and issues. Values have been notably absent (see, for example, Clarke et al., 1979; 1984; 1991; 1996). Our results suggest that we cannot understand vote choice in Canada (in recent elections, at least) unless we take voters' fundamental value commitments into account.

There is a second implication of our findings that needs to be underlined and that is the relevance of the "old" left-right cleavage in Canadian elections. Many Canadians undoubtedly feel uncomfortable using terms like "left" and "right" and some may very well be confused about what these terms really mean (see Lambert et al., 1986). But most Canadians do have views about the virtues and the vices of the free market economy. And, while "class voting" (as conventionally conceived) may be almost non-existent in Canada, views about free enterprise do have a significant impact on how many Canadians decide to vote.

At the same time, it is important to emphasize how misleading it is to refer to *the* right in Canada. Recognizing that there are two rights—an *economic* right and a *social* right—is critical to understanding the so-called "fight for the right." Alliance and Conservative voters converged in their views about the market, but they parted company when it came to social conservatism. On the latter dimension, Conservative voters were much closer to Liberal voters than to Alliance voters. There is a second difference between the two parties: the strongest relationships between values and vote choice appeared for the Alliance, while the weakest relationships appeared for the Conservatives. In that sense, the former appears the most ideologically oriented party and the latter the least ideologically oriented. This is yet another indication that the two parties, despite both being "to the right" of the Liberals, had different clienteles.

Even though values affected individual vote choice, their impact on the overall outcome of the election was relatively small. The main reason is that on questions such as free enterprise and social conservatism, Canadians seem to be about evenly divided. There is one important exception. Views about sovereignty were critical to the Liberal victory in Quebec: the Liberals won in that province because there are many more federalists than sovereignists. Beliefs about politics and the operation of the political system also affected vote choice. Many Canadians expressed deep cynicism and these people were less inclined to vote for the incumbent Liberals. Meanwhile, quite a few believed that their own province or region is not being fairly treated in Ottawa and that perception fueled support for the Alliance and the Bloc. Cynicism and regional alienation hurt the Liberals and they are clearly part of the explanation of why the Liberal victory was a small one.

Notes

1 See Appendix E for a description of the scales utilized for values and beliefs.

2 Social conservatism, views about racial minorities and feminist sympathies are relatively independent of one another. There is a greater propensity for social conservatives to express less sympathy for racial minorities and feminism, and for those who feel more should be done for racial minorities to have greater sympathy for feminism, but the correlations are all under .25.

3 The great majority of them opted for "quite sympathetic."

4 Opposition to sovereignty was more intense than support for it. As many as 39 per cent were very opposed, and only 17 per cent were very favourable.

5 Again, the degree of antipathy is likely to be understated.

6 The differences between French- and English-speaking Canadians largely reflect the differences between Quebec and the rest of Canada.

7 Because the mail-back has a lower response rate, the number of cases drops from 1221 to 755.

8 The correlations between the various values and beliefs were generally

less than .25. The exceptions were the correlations between views about sovereignty and regional alienation in Quebec (.40), and between attitude about Quebec and sympathy for racial minorities (.34) and cynicism (-.27) outside Quebec.

9 Positive ratings are those above 50 on a 0 to 100 scale. Note that the percentage of negative (below 50) feelings is "only" 30 per cent for politicians and 40 per cent for parties. People seem to find it easier to agree with negative (and sometimes strongly negative) statements about politicians' behaviour and/or attitudes than to express directly negative feelings about them.

CHAPTER 8

Partisan Loyalties

Few concepts have generated as much debate in the study of voting behaviour in Canada—or elsewhere—as party identification. Originally developed by the Michigan school in the United States, party identification involves a feeling of closeness or psychological attachment to a political party (Campbell et al., 1960). The concept was central to the socio-psychological model of voting elaborated by Campbell and his colleagues.[1] In their model, party identification affected vote choice both directly *and* indirectly via its influence on more proximate factors like leader evaluations and issue positions. Party identifiers would vote for "their" party unless there were powerful short-term forces in the immediate election that induced them to defect temporarily and to vote for another party. The key point was that party identification remain unchanged in the face of these temporary defections.

There has been a vigorous debate in the United States about the meaning and measurement of party identification, as well as its origins and its consequences. The dominant view there remains that it is "the most enduring of political attitudes, responsible for shaping a wide variety of values and perceptions, and, therefore, an appropriate starting point for an analysis of partisan political preference, such as the choice between presidential candidates." (Miller and Shanks, 1996: 117).

In Canada, on the other hand, the prevailing view has been that the concept of party identification is "almost inapplicable" (Meisel, 1975: 67).[2] The problem in Canada was that the concept seemed to predict vote choice *too* well. Party identification appeared to be "as volatile as the vote itself" (Meisel, 1975: 67): when people changed their vote, their party identification changed along with it. Rather than abandoning the notion of partisanship altogether, though, Clarke and his colleagues (Clarke et al., 1979; 1984; 1991; 1996) introduced a distinction between "durable partisans" and "flexible partisans." To qualify as a durable partisan, voters had to identify fairly or very strongly with their party, identify with the same party at both the federal and provincial levels, and report identifying with the same party across time. Voters who failed to satisfy one or more of these criteria were classified as flexible partisans.

In this chapter, we will argue that this approach underestimates the number of durable partisans and overstates the flexibility of Canadians' partisan ties. We will go on to argue that it is impossible to make sense of the outcome of the 2000 election and the Liberals' continued dominance, unless we take party identification into account.

Measuring Party Identification

The evidence that party identification tends to be quite unstable in Canada appears to be rather compelling, resting as it does on panel data (LeDuc et al., 1984). However, there are reasons to believe that some of this observed instability is an artifact of the question used to measure party identification. The traditional party identification question in Canada asked: "Generally speaking, in federal politics, do you usually think of yourself as Liberal, Conservative, NDP, or what?" The problem with this wording is that respondents were not explicitly offered the option of saying that they did not identify with any of the parties (Johnston, 1992; Blais et al., 2001a). As a result, some people were induced to indicate an attachment even if they did not really have one. It is not surprising, then, that there was a good deal of instability in their responses across time. The problem was not so much fickle partisans as a seriously flawed question. Accordingly, since 1988, the Canadian election studies have used the following question to measure party identification: "In federal politics, do you usually think of yourself as a Liberal, Alliance (Bloc), Conservative, NDP, or none of these?" This question has the advantage of explicitly offering a no-identification option ("none of these").[3]

Meanwhile, the requirement that people have the same identification at both the provincial and the federal levels understated the number of durable partisans. Blake (1982) has argued persuasively that there is nothing inherently inconsistent about identifying with one party at the federal level and another (or none at all) at the provincial level. He concluded that what did matter was the intensity of party identification.

Our approach is to count only those who think of themselves as fairly strong or very strong partisans.[4] Many of those who say that they feel "not very strongly" Liberal (or whatever) may lack a meaningful sense of attachment to the party. For instance, they are apt to give "their" party lower ratings than non-identifiers who say

Figure 8.1   The Distribution of Party Identification

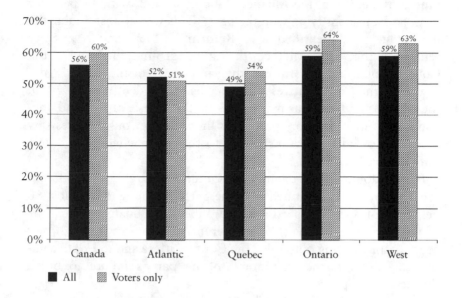

only that they feel a little closer to the party (see Blais et al., 2001a). Counting only those who identify very strongly or fairly strongly with their chosen party suggests that party identifiers made up 56 per cent of eligible voters at the time of the 2000 election, and 60 per cent of those who actually voted (see Figure 8.1). The proportion of partisans was slightly higher in Ontario and the West, and slightly lower in Quebec and Atlantic Canada. That leaves 44 per cent who cannot be considered to have a genuine partisan tie. Clarke and his colleagues were quite correct, then, in their assessment that there is the potential for considerable electoral volatility in Canada. At the time same, though, it is important to recognize that party identifiers supply an important inertia component. Their vote is not *predetermined*, but they are certainly *predisposed* to vote for "their" party.

The Liberal Advantage

When we look at the distribution of partisans among the parties, it is clear that the Liberal Party starts any election with a natural advantage over the others (see Figure 8.2). Fully one quarter of Canadians think of themselves as Liberals. This means that over half of those who identify with a party identify with the Liberals, giving the party a substantial edge among loyal partisans. At the time of the election, the Alliance came in second, with 11 per cent of Canadians identifying with the party. This was almost double the percentage who identified with Reform in 1997 and is another reminder that the Alliance did gain ground. In 1997, the Conservatives and Reform had the same share of the vote (19 per cent), but the Conservatives had twice as many identifiers. In 2000, the Alliance had twice as many votes as the Conservatives and one-and-a-half times as many partisans. Indeed, the Conservatives saw their core of loyal partisans shrink to the point where they barely outnumbered the NDP.

Liberal dominance is daunting in Ontario. Fully one-third (35 per cent) of Ontarians identified with the party, meaning that almost 60 per cent of Ontario partisans are Liberals. Equally telling, the Alliance share (8 per cent) lagged behind the Conservatives (10 per cent), despite having out-polled the Conservatives and the NDP combined. This is further testimony to the party's failure to break through in the province.

The Liberals also dominate in Atlantic Canada, though not as single-handedly. They benefited from a five-point drop between 1997 and 2000 in the per centage of Conservative identifiers and from the Alliance's inability to establish any base of support in the region. As a result, there were twice as many Liberal partisans as Conservative ones at the time of the election, giving the Liberals a substantial lead in the region with respect to core supporters.

In the West, not surprisingly, the Alliance succeeded in becoming the party with the greatest number of partisans. At the time of the election, one-quarter of Westerners thought of themselves as Alliance supporters. More surprising is the fact that the Alliance edge over the Liberals was so modest. The Alliance had twice as many votes as the Liberals in the region, but their lead in terms of core supporters was a modest four points. Finally, the per centage of Conservative identifiers declined from 12 per cent in 1997 to 7 per cent in 2000, confirming the difficult plight of the party in the West.

In Quebec, there are clearly only two parties with any significant number of core supporters, the Liberals and the Bloc. These two parties are on a more or less equal footing in terms of loyal partisans.[5] The weakness of the Conservatives in Quebec is striking. Hardly any voters in Quebec still think of themselves as Conservatives. The fact that Conservative identifiers in Quebec amount to only 1 per cent, the same percentage as NDP identifiers, is truly staggering.

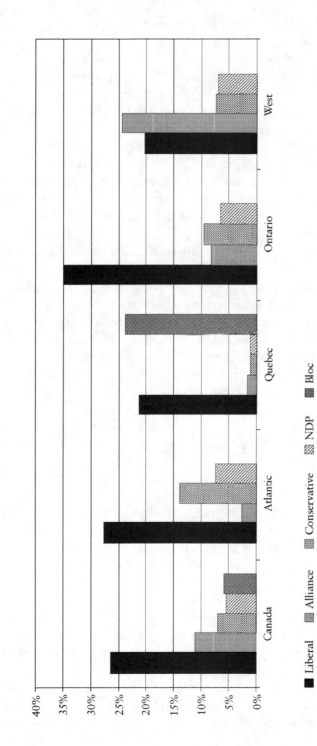

Figure 8.2 The Liberal Advantage

Party Identification and Vote Choice

Party identification is strongly correlated with vote choice (see Figure 8.3). All in all, 85 per cent of those with a party attachment voted for "their" party. But one partisan out of seven also decided to switch to another party. The most interesting story here concerns the behaviour of Conservative identifiers. As many as two Conservative partisans out of five voted for another party, and that party was typically the Alliance. Indeed, in the West, the Alliance had as many votes as the Conservatives among Conservative partisans, and in Ontario, 30 per cent of Conservative identifiers ended up voting Alliance. Tellingly, though, these defectors did still think of themselves as Conservatives.

Our multinomial logit estimations indicate that the probability of voting for a party was typically 40 points higher when voters identified with the party (as opposed to having no attachment), even after controlling for social background characteristics and ideological orientations (see Appendices C and D). For instance, the estimated mean probability of voting NDP (outside Quebec) is 49 per cent when people are assumed to identify with the NDP, but only 8 per cent when they are assumed to have no party attachment. The 41-point difference gives us the independent effect of New Democratic Party identification. The impact of party identification is particularly strong in the case of the Alliance; this reflects the fact that almost all of those who identified with the Alliance reported having voted for the party.

It should also be noted that a substantial fraction of the impact on vote choice of both social background characteristics and core beliefs and values is mediated by party loyalties (see Appendices A to D). For example, party identification explains much of the Liberal support found among Catholics and among voters of non-European origin. Similarly, views about free enterprise influence the vote indirectly via their effect on party identification.

Partisan loyalties appear to play a weaker mediating role in Quebec. Opinion about sovereignty remains powerfully linked to vote choice, even after controlling for party identification. This reflects the fact that even among those with no party identification the link between opinion about sovereignty and vote choice is strong. Eighty-six per cent of non-partisans who strongly favoured sovereignty voted for the Bloc, while 64 per cent of those who were strongly opposed voted Liberal. As a consequence, partisan loyalties

Figure 8.3 Party Identification and Vote Choice

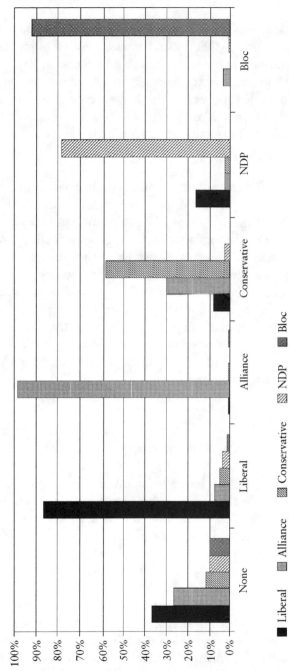

as such make a smaller contribution to explaining vote choice in Quebec.[6]

Indeed, it is important not to overplay the effect of party identification on vote choice. Once social background characteristics and core values and beliefs have been taken into account, partisan loyalties explain 15 per cent of the variance in vote choice in Quebec and 24 per cent outside Quebec. The link with vote choice is not automatic for partisans, and almost half of all voters do not identify with any of the parties. That said, any factor that can account for more than 10 per cent of the variance has to be considered important in the vote decision.

For many non-partisans, the campaign proved decisive. As we would expect, their vote intentions were much more likely to move over the course of the campaign. Vote shifts among non-partisans are an essential part of the explanation for the Conservative surge in the wake of the leaders' debates. Most of the ground gained by the Conservatives was among those who lacked a party identification. Outside Quebec, only 8 per cent of those without a party identification indicated that they intended to vote Conservative before the debates; that percentage increased to 14 after the English debate. Thus, the bulk of the Conservative surge that took place after the English debate appears to have come from non-partisans. And those Conservative gains came at the expense of the Liberals, whose share of vote intentions among non-partisans declined from 46 per cent to 39 per cent.[7]

Party Identification and Vote Shares

Still, party identification had a substantial impact on the *outcome* of the election. On the basis of the regression estimates presented in Appendices A and B, we simulated how many more—or fewer—votes each party would have obtained if party identification had had no effect on vote choice.[8] These simulations indicate that the Liberal vote share outside Quebec would have dropped from 40 per cent to 37 per cent, while the Alliance share would have increased from 33 per cent to 36 per cent. In other words, almost all the seven-point Liberal lead over the Alliance is attributable to Liberal dominance among partisans. Meanwhile, the Conservatives would have won 16 per cent instead of 15 per cent, and the NDP would have dropped from 11 per cent to 9 per cent. That two-point difference may seem trivial, but it suggests that the NDP was saved from losing its official status in Parliament by its small core of loyal supporters.

The impact of party identification was particularly important in Ontario. If party identification had not mattered, the 28-point gap between the Liberals and the Alliance would have been reduced to 16 points.[9] In the West, the Conservative vote share would have increased from 10 per cent to 14 per cent, while the Alliance and NDP vote shares would have fallen by one point (from 50 per cent to 49 per cent) and two points (from 12 per cent to 10 per cent), respectively. In Atlantic Canada, on the other hand, the Alliance would have increased its share of the vote from 10 per cent to 13 per cent and the NDP would have dropped from 17 per cent to 15 per cent. Finally, the Bloc vote would have fallen by three points from 40 per cent to 37 per cent if party identification had not mattered. This would have given the Liberals a much larger lead over the Bloc in Quebec.[10]

These regional variations point to two important conclusions. First, partisan loyalties benefit the dominant party in a given region and, second, much of the regionalization of the vote flows from long-term differences in partisan climate (Gidengil et al., 1999). When values and beliefs (especially the latter) are added to the estimations, the 21-point gap in the Liberal vote between Ontario and the West is reduced to 13 points (see Appendix C.1). When party identification is added as well, the gap is cut in half, narrowing to only six points. Clearly, the regional divides in vote choice owe much to long-standing differences in political culture and partisan loyalties. There is one noteworthy exception to this pattern: neither the Conservatives' success in Atlantic Canada nor the Alliance's poor showing in the region can be attributed to partisan traditions (or to political culture).

Discussion

Party identification is clearly an important part of the explanation for the Liberals' success in recent elections. Almost 30 per cent of voters outside Quebec think of themselves as Liberals. Assuming that about 85 per cent of them will normally vote Liberal, the Liberals can count on a core of about 25 per cent. That is more than twice as much as any other party, and it means that the Liberals start an election with a lead of at least 10 points over their nearest rival.[11] The challenge for them is to do as well as any other party among non-partisans. And this is precisely what they did in the 2000 election.

Indeed, the Liberals (38 per cent) actually managed to out-poll the Alliance (33 per cent) among non-partisans outside Quebec. Added to their core of loyal voters, this assured them a seven-point lead, enough to win a clear majority of the seats.[12]

There are almost as many loyal Liberal supporters in Quebec, but the Bloc has as many partisans as the Liberals. And the concentration of Liberal identifiers in ridings where non-francophones predominate means that the Liberal vote share has to be at least six or seven percentage points more than the Bloc in order to win a majority of the seats (Louis Massicotte and André Blais, *La Presse*, January 7, 1999). Among non-partisans, the two parties were tied at 37 per cent in our sample. Given the underestimation of Liberal support, it is plausible to assume that the Liberals had a small edge among non-partisans, enough to give them a plurality of the vote in Quebec, but not enough to win a majority of the seats.

The fact that over half the party identifiers in Canada are Liberals provides the party with a huge advantage. It is what enables them to remain the "natural" party of government. This is not to imply that the Liberals are certain to win any election, but it does mean that the other parties start with a serious handicap. It is possible for the Liberals to lose an election, but only if short-term factors are strongly against them.

Notes

1 "Few factors are of greater importance for our national elections than the lasting attachment of ten of millions of Americans to one of the parties. These loyalties establish a basic division of electoral strength within which the composition of particular campaigns takes place." (Campbell et al., 1960)

2 For dissenting views, see Sniderman et al., (1974); Jenson (1975); Elkins (1978); and more recently Johnston (1992).

3 The "none of these" still does not explicitly convey the idea that respondents do not think of themselves as having a general predisposition to support any party. Accordingly, we experimented with a new wording of the question in the campaign survey, in which the final response category corresponds more closely to our conception of what the absence of party identification entails. The new wording is: "Generally speaking, do you usually think of yourself as a Liberal, Alliance, (Bloc), Conservative, NDP, or do you usually think of yourself as not having a

general preference?". That question cannot be used in the present analyses because it was put only to a random half of respondents.

4 We utilized the same approach in our analysis of the 1997 election (see Nevitte et al., 2000).

5 The Bloc has a small edge in our survey but, like all surveys in Quebec, our survey slightly overrepresents sovereignists (see Durand et al., 2001).

6 More specifically, the pseudo r square increases by .24 outside Quebec after introducing party identification; the increase is .15 in Quebec.

7 The Conservative surge is statistically significant (at the .03 level), but not the Liberal drop.

8 For instance, the estimated mean probability of voting Liberal (outside Quebec) in our sample is 42 per cent. The same estimated probability when the coefficients of the four party identification coefficients are set to 0 (keeping everything else constant) is 39 per cent. The implication is that if party identification had had no independent effect on the vote, the Liberal share of the vote would have been reduced by three points, and so the Liberal net gain resulting from their dominance among loyal partisans is three percentage points.

9 The Liberal share would have dropped from 52 per cent to 47 per cent and the Alliance share would have increased from 24 per cent to 31 per cent.

10 We would normally expect supporters of new parties to have weaker attachments, and this is precisely what we observe in the case of the Alliance. The fact that this pattern does not emerge with respect to the Bloc may indicate that the party is not really a new party, but just an extension of the Parti Québécois on the federal scene. Indeed, 88 per cent of respondents who said they would vote for the PQ in a provincial election voted for the Bloc.

11 At the time of the election, 16 per cent of voters outside Quebec identified with the Alliance. This gave them a baseline core of 14 per cent.

12 The lead was reduced by the Alliance's success among Conservative identifiers (see Figure 8.3).

CHAPTER 9

The Economy

In the 2000 election, one key short-term factor was clearly *not* working against the Liberals and that was the economy. The Canadian economy appeared to be performing well in the fall of 2000. The unemployment rate stood at 6.9 per cent in November, much lower than the 9.6 per cent at the time of the 1997 election. Real GDP per capita had increased by an average of 3.5 per cent per year during the Liberal mandate, and real disposable income had risen by 2.3 per cent.[1] In fact, it is tempting to attribute the Liberal success to the good economic times. According to conventional wisdom, the fate of incumbent governments hinges on economic conditions at the time the election is held. An economic downturn can lead to defeat, but when the economy is in good shape, the party in power is likely to be re-elected.[2] The 2000 election seems to support the conventional wisdom: not only were the Liberals re-elected, but they increased their share of the vote.

It is certainly plausible that voters will reward the party in power when the economy is doing well and punish it when there is a recession. After all, voters surely prefer a strong economic performance to a weak one. However, this reward-and-punish calculus is deceptively simple. It assumes that voters will necessarily hold the government responsible for the performance of the economy. This assumption is problematic in a country like Canada where the health of the economy is so tied to the state of the international economy and especially the US economy. To put the point bluntly, is it rational to reward a government for a booming economy if the boom is largely the result of forces beyond its control?

It makes sense to assume that voters will be more inclined to vote for the incumbent party when the economy is doing well, but it also makes sense to assume that many people will think that the government does not deserve the credit. Clarke and Kornberg (1992) provide some telling evidence on this point from the Mulroney era: the more positively Canadians evaluated the state of the Canadian economy (and their own financial circumstances), the *less* likely they were to credit the government. Clearly, the link between the economy and the vote is not an automatic one.

The Economy and Election Outcomes

Conventional wisdom is usually couched at the *aggregate* level: the better the economy is doing, the more votes the incumbent party will receive. While there is undoubtedly a relationship between the state of the economy and the vote at the aggregate level, the relationship is not as strong as conventional wisdom would like us to believe. Consider the international evidence. Perhaps the simplest and most telling piece of evidence comes from Norpoth (1996) in his review essay on the role of the economy in elections. Norpoth looked at election outcomes in 38 countries and found that incumbent parties do seem to do better when the economy is in good shape. However, the correlation between the growth of real GDP and the vote received by the major party in office was quite modest (.36), suggesting that there are quite a few exceptions to the pattern. According to Norpoth's results, an increase of one percentage point in real GDP is associated with a 1.5-point boost in the incumbent party's vote. This means that if economic growth is two points above (below) average, the incumbent party typically gets three points more (less), everything else being equal. This is clearly not a negligible effect, but it is hardly an overwhelming one, either.

The risk of imputing too much weight to the economy was amply illustrated in the 2000 American presidential election. All the forecasting models (in which economic indicators are key variables) predicted an easy Gore victory over Bush, given how strong the economy was at the time (Campbell and Garand, 2000). The predictions were that Gore would win between 53 per cent and 60 per cent of the two-party vote, the mean predicted vote share being 56 per cent. The actual outcome was a dead heat at 50/50 per cent, a very substantial deviation from the models' predictions. There have been ingenious attempts to salvage the forecasting models, usually involving modifications to the economic indicators (see Bartels and Zaller, 2001; Lewis-Beck and Tien, 2001; Holbrook, 2001; Norporth, 2001), but a dose of scepticism is certainly warranted in evaluating such ex post facto explanations. Perhaps the lesson to be drawn is this: there is strong evidence that the economy matters, but it does not follow that it always matters nor that it matters more than other factors.

What is the situation in Canada? When Nadeau and Blais (1993) analyzed election outcomes between 1953 and 1988, they found that the vote for the incumbent was systematically related to one economic indicator, namely, the unemployment rate. They make two important points: first, that voters are likely to assess economic performance in *relative* terms, on the basis of what they are used to and, second, that voters focus on the most recent period rather than on the government's entire term.[3] They found that, everything else being equal, the vote for the incumbent party typically decreases by two points when the relative unemployment rate increases by one point. The 1984 election stood out as the one where the recent relative unemployment rate had increased the most substantially, by three percentage points. According to the model, this "dramatic" three-point increase was associated with a six-point decline in the vote for the incumbent Liberal party.[4] However, the Liberal vote actually dropped by 16 points between 1980 and 1984, meaning that most of the Liberal drop in 1984 should be attributed to factors other than the economy.

If we apply the same measure to the 2000 election, there was a 1.7-point relative decrease in the unemployment rate, compared with a relative decrease of 0.8 points in 1997. This confirms the widespread perception that the mid-1990s were good economic times and that should have helped the Liberals. However, others facts do not square well with such an interpretation. As we saw in Chapter 4, the Liberals actually lost ground in the West, including Alberta where the economy was booming. And the Liberal gains in Quebec can easily be explained by the disappearance of a very popular opposition leader (Jean Charest) and the decline in support for sovereignty.

Economic Perceptions and Vote Choice

What really matters are voters' own perceptions, not the economic realities (Nadeau et al., 2000). Between the 1993 and 1997 elections, for example, the unemployment rate went down from 11.2 per cent to 9.6 per cent, and yet Canadians (37 per cent) were more likely to think that it had increased than decreased (17 per cent). Were voters more sanguine in 2000 and was this a major reason for the Liberal victory?

There are at least two possibilities. The first is that voters look at the state of the national economy, and if they perceive the economy to be doing well, they vote for the party that is in power. This is the *sociotropic* perspective. The second possibility is that voters consider their own economic situation, and only vote for the incumbent

Table 9.1   Economic Perceptions

		Personal past	Personal future	Canada past	Canada future	Unemployment past
Canada	2000	.06	.24	.26	.17	.28
	1997	-.11	.12	.12	.27	-.19
Atlantic	2000	.03	.16	.15	.14	.12
	1997	-.24	-.02	-.10	.16	-.27
Quebec	2000	-.05	.22	.30	.21	.21
	1997	-.21	.07	.05	.22	-.26
Ontario	2000	.15	.29	.39	.15	.43
	1997	-.03	.16	.21	.33	-.14
West	2000	.03	.19	.10	.15	.18
	1997	-.08	.15	.13	.25	-.18

Note: Cell entries are mean scales scores. The scales range from -1 to 1.

party if things are going well for them personally. This is the *ego-centric* perspective. In either case, voters may vote *retrospectively*, on the basis of their evaluations of past economic performance, or *prospectively*, on the basis of their judgments about future economic performance.

Table 9.1 shows average perceptions on each of these dimensions. Positive evaluations were scored +1, negative evaluations were scored –1, and "no change" and "don't knows" were set to 0. The results indicate that Canadians were quite sanguine about the Canadian economy and that their judgments were more positive than they had been in 1997. Close to half of the electorate (42 per cent) thought that the Canadian economy had improved over the past year, and only 15 per cent believed that it had worsened. Similarly, 49 per cent said unemployment had gone down, while only 18 per cent thought that it had increased. This was a major change from 1997, when only 17 per cent thought that unemployment had declined. And the dominant view was that things would basically stay the same in the following 12 months; only 11 per cent were predicting a slowdown, whereas 31 per cent foresaw an even better economy. So, clearly, the Canadian economy was perceived to be in good shape.[5]

Canadians were less sanguine about their own personal situation. The majority (55 per cent) said that they were financially the same as a year before, 26 per cent described themselves as being better off, while 20 per cent said that they were worse off. Still, perceptions were more positive than they had been in 1997. And Canadians felt better about the future than they had in the previous election. While 55 per cent expected no change in the following year, those who did expect a change were much more likely to foresee an improvement (35 per cent) than a downturn (9 per cent).

So, all in all, economic perceptions were moderately positive. The modal response was "the same" and, except for the personal retrospective dimension, there were many more positive than negative evaluations. Tellingly, though, fewer than 13 per cent of respondents gave the same response ("better," "worse," "the same") on each dimension.[6] For instance, only 30 per cent of those who said that their own personal situation had deteriorated perceived the Canadian economy to have worsened.

Given the regional variations in the performance of the economy, it comes as no surprise to discover substantial regional variations in how Canadians saw the economy. Ontarians were more likely to take a rosy view, especially about how the Canadian economy had been doing over the previous year. Differences were more modest with respect to people's evaluations of their personal financial situation (both retrospective and prospective) and there were few regional differences when it came to expectations about the Canadian economy. On this last dimension, Quebecers, interestingly enough, emerged as the most optimistic. Atlantic Canadians were less likely to see a decline in unemployment. Overall, though, the similarities across regions are more striking than the differences.[7]

Women had less positive perceptions than men, especially when it came to retrospective evaluations of the Canadian economy. The mean score was +.16 (on the −1 to 1 scale) among women and +.37 among men.[8] Even so, economic perceptions were still on the positive side among women, and the gender gap was more modest (five to eight points) on the other dimensions. People living in rural settings were also less positive in their retrospective judgments about the Canadian economy, with a mean score of +.16, compared with +.30 in urban settings.[9]

It is important to bear in mind that economic perceptions are affected by partisan predispositions. This was most evident in the case of perceptions of whether the Canadian economy had improved over the previous year. Liberal partisans were more prone to believe that the economy was in good shape The average score among those who thought of themselves as Liberal was +.43, compared with only +.22 among non-partisans. However, identifying with the Alliance, the Conservatives, the NDP or the Bloc did *not* induce people to see the economy in a negative light: the mean score among those who identified with one of the opposition parties was +.23.[10] So the projection effect was modest, and it was smaller still with respect to the other indicators.

The crucial question, of course, concerns the impact of these perceptions on the vote. It turns out to be quite small, once prior dispositions and especially partisan loyalties are taken into account (see Appendices A to D). In Quebec, there is simply no trace of an effect. Outside Quebec, the situation is only slightly different.[11] Among the five economic perception variables included in our study, only one emerged as significant. Everything else being equal, the propensity to vote Liberal increased by three points if a voter thought that his or her financial situation had improved, compared with a voter who saw no change. This is really rather a small effect. Moreover, the mean score on this dimension was very close to 0, implying that its net effect on the outcome of the election was minimal.

These results are surprising. There is no support for the conventional wisdom that the Liberals won the election because the economy was doing well. Many Canadians did feel positive about the economy and relatively few felt negative. The point is, however, that, those who felt positive did not vote differently from those who felt negative or neutral, once their predispositions were taken into account.

One possible explanation for this nil finding is the asymmetry hypothesis: voters punish the governing party for a poor economic performance but they do not necessarily reward it for a good performance (see Bloom and Price, 1975). However, when we examined the impact of negative and positive economic evaluations separately, there was little indication that negative evaluations were more consequential than positive ones.[12] In that form, at least, the asymmetry hypothesis must be discarded. It could be, though, that the economy is simply a less salient consideration in voters' minds when it is doing well, perhaps because the media are less likely to focus on the economy when it is going well than when it is doing badly (Norpoth, 1996).

The Impact of Credit and Blame

Another possible explanation for the weakness of the link between economic perceptions and vote choice in the 2000 election is that many Canadians did not give the government credit for the good economic times. There is some support for this interpretation, at least with respect to personal finances. Only 22 per cent of those whose personal situation had improved said that this was due to the policies of the federal government. People were much more prone to blame the government for any deterioration in their financial lot: 44 per cent blamed the policies of the federal government. As for the state of the national economy, Canadians were almost evenly divided: 45 per cent of those who perceived the economy to have gotten better were willing to credit the Liberal government and 41 per cent of those who thought things had gotten worse blamed the government. The bottom line is that there were only 18 per cent of voters who thought that the economy had improved *and* attributed some responsibility to the Liberal government for that state of affairs. And half of them were Liberal partisans to start with. As a consequence, the Liberals did not benefit much from positive economic perceptions.

This raises the possibility that what really mattered was not economic perceptions per se, but whether one credited or blamed the government for economic change. We tested that hypothesis by regressing vote choice (Liberal or not) on two new "responsibility for economic change" variables, one for retrospective personal evaluations and one for retrospective national evaluations. Each variable equaled +1 if the respondent perceived an improvement *and* credited the federal government and −1 if the respondent saw a deterioration *and* blamed the government for the downturn. Both "economic responsibility" variables had a statistically significant impact on the propensity to vote Liberal, even after controlling for social background characteristics, values and beliefs, and partisan loyalties (see Table 9.2). Everything else being equal, the probability of voting Liberal increased by over 10 points[13] when voters perceived a positive change in the economic situation *and* believed that this was due at least in part to the policies of the federal government.

The impact was limited, however, to a relatively small segment of the electorate, and as a consequence the net effect on the outcome of the election was minimal. According to our estimates, the Liberals

Table 9.2   The Impact of Perceived Governmental Economic Responsibility on Liberal Vote (Logistic Regressions)

	Perceived economic responsibility only	+ SES	+ SES + Values and beliefs	+ SES + Values and beliefs + Party identification
Responsibility – Canada	1.15 (.17)[a]	1.04 (.18)[a]	.95 (.19)[a]	.65 (.21)[a]
Responsibility – personal	1.06 (.20)[a]	.99 (.22)[a]	.74 (.23)[a]	.81 (.27)[a]

a: significant $\alpha \leq .01$

Note: The first column presents results of the regression including only perceived economic responsibility. The following columns include additional variables. In order to save space, the coefficients of those variables are omitted.

made a net gain of one percentage point because there were more people who credited the government for the good economic performance in the country as a whole (18 per cent) than blamed it for a poor record (6 per cent). However, they made no gain at all on the personal finance front, because the evaluations overall were neutral.[14]

Finally, there is little indication that economic perceptions mattered more or less as the campaign progressed. Before the debates, for example, 72 per cent of those (outside Quebec) who perceived an improvement in the national economy and gave some credit to the government said they intended to vote Liberal; after the debates, the percentage was 74 per cent.

Discussion

It would be difficult to claim that the Liberals won the 2000 election because the economy was doing well. Voters' perceptions of the economy were modestly positive and they were more positive than they had been in 1997, but once we take account of prior dispositions, economic perceptions as such simply did not have much effect on vote choice. The effect was largely confined to those who thought that the government was at least partly responsible for the improvement (or perceived deterioration) in the economy. And because this group was so small, the net overall impact on the outcome of the election was minimal.

That said, it would surely be a mistake to assume that the economy played *no* role in the 2000 election. It is hard to believe that things would not have been more difficult for the Liberals if the election had been held during a recession. Clearly, though, the impact of the economy was more limited than conventional wisdom suggests.

Notes

1 Note, though, that the drop in the unemployment rate occurred in the early part of the Liberal mandate. With the unemployment rate already down to 6.8 per cent in January 2000, there was no improvement in 2000. Similarly, real disposable income increased by only 0.6 per cent in 2000.

2 "It is now the accepted wisdom that incumbent parties are virtually impossible to beat during strong economic upturns and extremely vulnerable during recessionary periods" (Dalton and Wattenberg, 1993: 208). That accepted wisdom is still very much with us, as testified by this more recent verdict: "For all democratic nations that have received a reasonable amount of study, plausible economic indicators, objective or subjective, can be shown to account for much of the variance in government support." (Lewis-Beck and Stegmaier, 2000: 211)

3 Their measure of recent relative unemployment was the average difference, over the 10 quarters preceding the election, between the unemployment rate in each quarter and the average rate in the previous five years.

4 Strictly speaking, the model predicts a decline of only four points because the relative unemployment figure was already at 1 per cent in 1980; compared to 1980, the relative unemployment rate had increased by "only" two points.

5 Note, however, that optimism about the future of the Canadian economy was even more widespread in 1997.

6 The correlations between prospective and retrospective evaluations were .26 for personal finances and .25 for the national economy. The correlations between personal finances and the national economy were .24 for retrospective evaluations and .23 for prospective evaluations.

7 In the West, though, it is important to distinguish Saskatchewan and British Columbia, where the economic outlook was pretty dim, from Manitoba and Alberta, where the economy was perceived to be in good shape.

8 The difference remained substantial within income groups. Among low-income voters, 40 per cent of men and only 27 per cent of women said that the Canadian economy had improved. The equivalent percentages were 57 per cent and 39 per cent among high-income men and women.

9 The urban/rural gap was slightly smaller with respect to prospective evaluations.

10 Conservative identifiers, in particular, had rather positive perceptions.

11 Even in the absence of any controls, the impact of economic perceptions is modest. For instance, when vote choice (Liberal versus another party) outside Quebec is regressed against the five economic perceptions variables, only two perceptions emerge as statistically significant at the .05 level: retrospective personal evaluations and retrospective national evaluations. When social background characteristics are included, the effect of retrospective national evaluations does not quite reach the conventional level of statistical significance. And when values and beliefs and party identification are also added, the impact of retrospective personal finances also ceases to be statistically significant. Retrospective evaluations of personal finances remain significant with respect to vote choice between the Liberals and the Alliance or the NDP in the multinomial logit estimates reported in Appendix A because these estimates allow us to pick up subtle differences between pairs of parties.

12 For similar verdicts on this, see Lewis-Beck (1988) and Norporth (1996).

13 More precisely, the probability of a Liberal vote was 13 points higher in the case of personal finances and 11 points higher with respect to perceptions of the national economy.

14 Six per cent scored +1, 9 per cent scored -1, and 85 per cent were at 0 on the economic responsibility variable.

CHAPTER 10

The Issues

The Liberals may not have been vulnerable on the economic front, but issues were another matter. Many Canadians were deeply concerned about the state of the health care system in Canada and believed that the quality of health care had deteriorated in recent years. So this was clearly an issue with the potential to hurt the Liberals. Meanwhile, the Alliance also had its share of liabilities on the issue front. The party had sought to distance itself from the Reform Party on matters like immigration, but the other parties were out to portray the Alliance as nothing more than Reform in a different guise. And they were bent on making political capital out of Stockwell Day's personal convictions by playing up issues like abortion and direct democracy.

These strategic calculations assume that issues matter to voters. There has been considerable controversy in the literature, though, over the question of whether—and how—issues affect the vote. The conventional wisdom in the 1960s was that issues did not really matter. The authors of *The American Voter* (Campbell et al., 1960: 183) concluded that "many people fail to appreciate that an issue exists, others are insufficiently involved to pay attention to recognized issues, and still others fail to make connections between issue opinions and party policy." This view was buttressed by the finding that many voters did not have stable (and hence "real") opinions on a variety of issues (Converse, 1964). However, it has been challenged by many critics.[1] It has been argued, in particular, that issue voting has become more important over time as partisan loyalties have declined (Franklin et al., 1992).

The most powerful theoretical exposition of why issues should matter was provided by Anthony Downs (1957) in his classic study, *An Economic Theory of Democracy*. In Downs's model, voters compare the utility they would derive from government activities if Party A or Party B or Party C were elected, and then they vote for the party that would benefit them the most. Issues are a central component of the vote decision in this model, because voters are assumed to estimate their expected utility by considering party positions on the most important issues of the election.

Many voting behaviour specialists have been sceptical of this rational choice model, on the ground that few voters are equipped to engage in the decision calculus that it presupposes. There is a good deal of evidence to suggest that many voters do not follow politics closely and are typically poorly informed about the issues and the parties' positions on them. In the 1997 Canadian election, for instance, only 11 per cent of Canadians were able to say that it was the NDP that was promising to cut unemployment in half, and as many as 53 per cent were apparently unaware that the Reform party was against the recognition of Quebec as a distinct society (Fournier, 2002: 95). How can voters vote on the basis of issues if they are so poorly informed?

The standard response is that they can resort to information shortcuts (Sniderman et al., 1991). The literature suggests at least three possible shortcuts. The first is that voters can consider "easy" issues rather than "hard" issues (Carmines and Stimson, 1984). Easy issues are symbolic rather than technical, deal with broad ends rather than specific means, and have been on the political agenda for a long time. Racial desegregation is an example of an "easy" issue in the US, while taxation is an example of a "hard" one. Second, voters can base their decision on whether they feel that the party shares their underlying value orientations. Third, voters may reason that it is too difficult to determine exactly where the various parties stand on a given issue, and so they focus instead on what the party in power has done during its mandate. If they are satisfied, they vote for the incumbent, and if not, they support one of the opposition parties. This is the retrospective voting model (Fiorina, 1981).

What is the situation in Canada? The basic thesis of the authors of *Absent Mandate* (Clarke et al., 1996: 143) is that elections "are not referendums on public policy, even though they are sometimes interpreted as such," and that "either the issues were not as important to the outcome of the election as generally thought, were phrased so generally as to defy a specific policy referent, or showed no clear trend of opinion." Clarke and his co-authors do *not* argue, though, that vote choice is unaffected by issues. In the case of the 1993 federal election, for example, they indicate that "what did matter a great deal was how the voters assessed the parties on the issues," and that "issues trumped leaders" (Clarke et al., 1996: 115). Their point is simply that issues are not as important as popular accounts seem to assume, that the issues are often defined in very general terms, and that opinion is usually divided so that the net effect on the outcome is minimal (with each party gaining votes among supporters of a position and losing votes among opponents).

The authors of *Letting the People Decide* (Johnston et al., 1992: 245) paid more attention to issues. They concluded that the "1988 campaign revolved around fundamental differences over the Canada-US Free Trade Agreement." Their data indicated that Canadians were deeply divided and that there was no mandate for the agreement. Our own assessment of the impact of issues in the 1997 election (Blais et al., forthcoming [b]) is that while they were decisive for a small, but important, segment (9 per cent) of the electorate, their net impact on the outcome of the election was practically nil. The question is: did issues matter more in the 2000 election?

Fiscal Issues

One of the central questions in the election was what should be done with the government surplus, or at least this was how the Prime Minister himself framed the campaign when he called the election. The Liberals argued in favour of their "balanced" approach. According to the Liberal's *Red Book* this involved devoting half of the surplus to increased spending and half to reducing taxes and the federal debt. Meanwhile, the NDP insisted on increased spending on social programs, while the Alliance and the Conservatives both wanted more substantial tax cuts. The Conservatives also committed themselves to paying off the federal debt in 25 years.

Almost half (47 per cent) of our respondents said that at least half of the surplus should be devoted to social programs; the percentage for tax cuts was 43 per cent (Figure 10.1). Views on fiscal matters did not differ substantially across regions[2] or socio-demographic groups (Table 10.1). Particularly noteworthy is the fact that almost the same percentage of Westerners (39 per cent) and Ontarians (36 per cent) were willing to devote at least half of the surplus to tax cuts. The implication is clear: the Alliance did not fail to break through in Ontario because Ontarians are less fiscally conservative than Westerners. This is the same conclusion that we reached with respect to the 1997 election (Gidengil et al., 1999).

We would expect voters who gave priority to tax cuts (20 per cent) to be more inclined to support the Alliance or the Conservatives in the 2000 election, while those who emphasized social programs (25 per cent) would be more inclined to support the

Figure 10.1   Distribution of Opinion on Issues

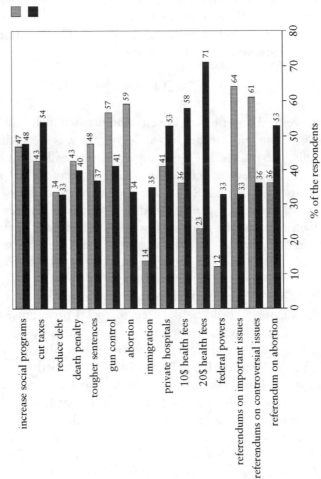

Table 10.1   Opinions on Fiscal Issues

	Cutting taxes	Social programs	Reducing debt
All	-.22	-.20	.01
Sex			
Men	-.21	-.23	.10
Women	-.23	-.16	-.08
Region			
Atlantic	-.26	-.22	-.07
Quebec	-.08	-.02	-.30
Ontario	-.29	-.25	.16
West	-.25	-.30	.12
Outside Quebec	-.27	-.26	.12
Residence			
Rural	-.23	-.21	.03
Urban	-.23	-.20	.01
Religion			
Catholic	-.16	-.12	-.13
Other religion	-.26	-.26	.14
No religion	-.32	-.24	.07
Origin			
North European	-.30	-.28	.16
Non-European	-.21	-.29	.09
Other origin	-.22	-.18	-.01
Language			
English	-.29	-.26	.11
French	-.10	-.03	-.25
Other language	-.18	-.25	.07
Marital Status			
Married	-.22	-.21	.04
Not married	-.24	-.17	-.04
Education			
Below high school	-.16	-.12	-.10
Middle	-.22	-.21	.03
University	-.30	-.23	.06

Note: Cell entries are mean scales scores. The scales range from –1 to 1.

NDP.[3] However, views about what should be done with the surplus did not have a statistically significant effect on vote choice. What really mattered were people's more general ideological beliefs about the legitimate role of the market: predictably, those who were more supportive of free enterprise thought that there should be significant tax cuts, while those who were more sceptical were more interested in improving social programs.[4] Views about fiscal issues as such did not have an independent impact on vote choice, once these broader values were taken into account.[5]

The same is true of views about the debt. The Conservatives had been the most explicit on this point, with a promise to reimburse the debt over a period of 25 years. It looks as if that promise did not pay any dividends. Only 16 per cent of those interviewed were even aware that the Conservatives had made such a promise, and views about the debt had no independent effect on vote choice.

Crime and Punishment

The Alliance did not fare any better with its tough stance on crime. The party seems to have been correct in its assessment that Canadians who wanted a tougher approach predominated. Almost half (48 per cent) favoured tougher sentences for young offenders who commit violent crimes, while only 37 per cent argued for spending more on rehabilitating them. However, the number favouring a get-tough approach had dropped 10 points since 1997. And there was a deep division when it came to the question of the death penalty: 43 per cent supported the death penalty for those convicted of murder and 40 per cent were opposed, leaving a substantial number who were ambivalent (Figure 10.1).

Combining these two issues into a single crime variable, we can see that support for a tough stance on crime was strongest in the West and in rural communities, while a softer approach was more popular among women, Quebecers, and, most strikingly, the better educated (Table 10.2).

Even in the West, though, views about crime had only a small effect on the Alliance vote. Overall, there was no relationship between toughness on crime and support for the Alliance, once more basic predispositions were taken into account. So, in contrast to Reform in 1997, the Alliance did not really benefit from its position on crime. Views on crime, of course, are related to social conservatism, but it was not because of their stance on crime that social conservatives were more likely to vote for the Alliance. Similarly, the Alliance was not stronger in the West because more people support the death penalty in the West (48 per cent) than in Ontario (42 per cent).

However, one crime-related issue did have an independent effect on vote choice (at least outside Quebec) and that was gun control. We asked people whether they agreed or disagreed with the rather

Table 10.2   Opinions on Crime and Punishment

	Crime	Gun control
All	.07	.16
Sex		
Men	.16	-.01
Women	-.02	.32
Region		
Atlantic	.01	-.01
Quebec	-.04	.28
Ontario	.09	.27
West	.17	-.05
Outside Quebec	.11	.11
Residence		
Rural	.15	-.09
Urban	.05	.22
Religion		
Catholic	.06	.24
Other religion	.10	.10
No religion	.04	.07
Origin		
North European	.15	-.09
Non-European	.15	.34
Other origin	.05	.16
Language		
English	.11	.08
French	-.03	.22
Other language	.09	.39
Marital Status		
Married	.10	.12
Not married	.01	.21
Education		
Below high school	.15	.14
Middle	.13	.13
University	-.13	.24

Note: Cell entries are mean scales scores. The scales range from –1 to 1.

radical statement that "only the police and the military should be allowed to have guns." Taken literally, this would imply a complete ban on guns, even for hunters. Surprisingly, 57 per cent said that they agreed (Figure 10.1), with as many as 40 per cent saying they *strongly* agreed. This is a good indication that the principle of gun control is widely accepted in Canada.

Interestingly, opinions on gun control were unrelated both to views about crime and to social conservatism. There were substantial differences of opinion between Ontario and Quebec, on the one hand, and the Atlantic provinces and the West, on the other. Canadians also divided along gender and urban/rural lines (Table 10.2). Support for a complete ban on guns ran as high as 72 per cent among urban Quebec women and as low as 23 per cent among rural Western men.[6] Support for gun control increased the odds of voting for the NDP (see Appendices A and C).

Abortion

The abortion issue received a lot of attention during the campaign, partly because of Stockwell Day's personal beliefs and partly because the other parties argued that an Alliance government would open the way for a referendum on the issue if as few as 300,000 Canadians put their name to a petition calling for a direct vote. When we asked our respondents whether they believed it should be very easy, quite easy, quite difficult, of very difficult to get an abortion, almost three-fifths (59 per cent) said it should be easy (Figure 10.1). While there are clearly many more pro-choice than pro-life voters in Canada, the percentage saying it should be very easy (16 per cent) was only slightly higher than the percentage saying it should be very difficult (13 per cent).

Interestingly, there was no difference between men and women when it came to views about abortion (Table 10.3). There was also little difference between Catholics and other religious denominations. Those with no religion, however, were overwhelmingly pro-choice. The pro-life position is strongest in Atlantic Canada (not the West) and weakest in Quebec. There is a striking difference between the views of Catholics in the two parts of the country: only 38 per cent of Catholics in Atlantic Canada said it should be easy to get an abortion, compared with fully 71 per cent of Catholics in Quebec. Finally, there was a huge gap between the university-educated and those who had not completed high school, the latter being divided on the issue and the former being strongly pro-choice. Views about abortion were also related to values. Social conservatives and those for whom religion is very important were more likely to be pro-life.[7] Finally, it is interesting to note that there was no correlation between opinions on abortion and opinions on the death penalty. Apparently, the "pro-life" position does not entail opposition to the death penalty.

Table 10.3 Opinions on Abortion and Immigration

	Abortion	*Immigration*
All	.14	-.21
Sex		
Men	.16	-.14
Women	.12	-.29
Region		
Atlantic	.06	-.25
Quebec	.30	-.22
Ontario	.13	-.21
West	.08	-.19
Outside Quebec	.09	-.21
Residence		
Rural	.07	-.28
Urban	.17	-.19
Religion		
Catholic	.12	-.27
Other religion	.06	-.16
No religion	.39	-.19
Origin		
North European	.05	-.18
Non-European	.01	.00
Other origin	.18	-.24
Language		
English	.13	-.25
French	.26	-.27
Other language	.03	.07
Marital Status		
Married	.11	-.19
Not married	.20	-.24
Education		
Below high school	.03	-.38
Middle	.14	-.27
University	.28	.07

Note: Cell entries are mean scales scores. The scales range from –1 to 1.

Abortion was clearly an issue that could potentially have hurt the Alliance. It turns out, though, that views on abortion did not have an independent effect on vote choice. True, pro-choice voters were less likely to vote Alliance: outside Quebec, only 26 per cent of those who said it should be easy to get an abortion opted for the Alliance, compared with 45 per cent of pro-life respondents. However, this difference disappeared when prior predispositions were taken into account. Again, what seemed to matter was voters' overall social conservatism rather than their specific opinions on abortion.

Immigration

The other issue that could potentially have hurt the Alliance was immigration. The Reform Party had been associated with the view that the number of immigrants admitted to Canada should be reduced. The Alliance hardly raised the issue in 2000, but that does not preclude the possibility that the anti-immigration perception lingered.

This turns out not to be the case. As with so many of the issues raised in the 2000 campaign, general ideological orientations appeared to count more than opinions on specific issues. Views about immigration were correlated (.23) with more general orientations towards racial minorities, and once these were taken into account, there is no evidence that Canadians' views about immigration had any independent effect on vote choice.

There was an important shift in public opinion on the immigration issue. In 1997, almost half (48 per cent) of those interviewed thought that Canada should admit fewer immigrants, but three years later, that percentage had dropped to 35 per cent, and the modal position (47 per cent) was to keep immigration at its present level. One consequence may be that immigration as such has become a non-issue. Table 10.3 shows that it was women and the less educated who were more likely to favour a reduction in immigration. The absence of regional variation on this issue is striking.

Health Care

If there was one issue that was relevant in the eyes of many voters, it was health. And at least two of the parties—the NDP and the Liberals—had made sure that it was near the top of the political agenda. The NDP's message throughout the campaign was that the Canadian public health system was threatened and that the NDP was the only party that was really committed to maintaining and improving the system. Instead of responding to the NDP's criticism, the Liberals made the wise strategic move of attacking the Alliance party, charging that it favoured a two-tier system.

The Liberal strategy was successful. Fully half (52 per cent) of those interviewed thought that the Alliance was in favour of such a system and 25 per cent could not tell. Only 23 per cent thought that the Alliance was against a two-tier system. Our data confirm that a majority of Canadians are opposed to the idea of privatization, though with as many as 41 per cent in favour of allowing some private hospitals in Canada—the *public* health care system is not a sacred cow. Support for a *free* system is much stronger. Only 36 per cent of Canadians expressed support for letting doctors charge patients a 10-dollar fee for each office visit, and support declined to 23 per cent for a 20-dollar fee.[8]

When we combined these two questions to create a "public health" variable, the average score was +.24 (on a −1 to +1 scale), confirming that public opinion was tilted in favour of the existing system.[9] Opinions on public health were correlated (-.29) with views about free enterprise: those who were more sceptical about the virtues of the market were more opposed to privatizing the health care system. Interestingly, support for the public health system was weakest in Quebec. Fifty-two percent of Quebecers indicated that they were in favour of having some private hospitals. It is possible that Quebecers are more open to privatization because they are slightly more supportive of free enterprise than other Canadians (see Table 7.1). However, the fact that Quebecers are even more dissatisfied with the state of health care is also likely to be part of the story. Seventy-six per cent of Quebecers believed that the quality of health care had deteriorated over the past five years, compared with 71 per cent in Canada as a whole. Whether their greater dissatisfaction stems from "objective" differences in the quality of health care or from media emphasis on waiting queues in emergency (Monière and Fortier, 2000) is an open question.

We would expect those who are dissatisfied with the existing public system to be open to change, but outside Quebec we observe exactly the opposite. Far from encouraging any willingness to experiment with some degree of privatization, the widespread perception that the quality of health care has deteriorated actually fuels support for the public system (findings not reported). The reasoning seems to be that things have worsened precisely because there has been some degree of privatization in the last few years. It may also be that public health is symbolically linked to Canadian identity in some voters' minds, and certainly the Liberal strategy had been to encourage this link. One indication of this may be that support for the public system was correlated with anti-American sentiment (findings not reported).

Outside Quebec, support for the public health system was strongest in Ontario[10] and weakest in the West. Still, the differences were not large: 41 per cent of Westerners were in favour of private

Table 10.4   Opinions on Public Health

	Public health
All	.24
Sex	
Men	.15
Women	.33
Region	
Atlantic	.30
Quebec	.09
Ontario	.35
West	.19
Outside Quebec	.28
Residence	
Rural	.17
Urban	.26
Religion	
Catholic	.22
Other religion	.25
No religion	.26
Origin	
North European	.25
Non-European	.27
Other origin	.23
Language	
English	.28
French	.08
Other language	.30
Marital Status	
Married	.20
Not married	.31
Education	
Below high school	.25
Middle	.25
University	.22

Note: Cell entries are mean scales scores. The scales range from –1 to 1.

hospitals, compared with 35 per cent of Ontarians. An important gender gap showed on this issue, with women being much more supportive of public health (see Gidengil et al., forthcoming). On the other hand, health is one of the few issues for which we find no difference among educational groups (Table 10.4).

Those who favoured a universal public health system were significantly more likely to vote Liberal and significantly less likely to sup-

port the Alliance (other things being equal). According to our estimates, the Alliance lost one percentage point outside Quebec because
of its perceived position on this issue. This is hardly a huge blow, but
health was one of the reasons that the party failed to make inroads
in Ontario.

Not only were the Liberals successful in convincing many voters
that they should not trust the Alliance to maintain the public health
care system, but they were also able to induce them to vote Liberal
rather than NDP. The fact that the NDP failed to attract the vote of
those concerned with the Canadian health system is one of the great
paradoxes of the 2000 election.

Because the Bloc is often perceived to be slightly to the left of the
political spectrum (Blais et al., 2002), we might have expected the
party to attract the votes of Quebecers who were opposed to privatization. This was not the case. In Quebec, as in the rest of Canada,
voters who supported the public health system were more likely to
opt for the Liberals. There was no difference between sovereignists
and federalists on this issue. As we saw in Chapter 1, the Bloc chose
to ignore the health issue in its program, and this strategic decision
was only partially reversed during the campaign. As a consequence,
opinions on health only affected the choice between the Liberals and
the Conservatives (see Appendix B). And, because opinions were
almost evenly divided, the issue did not have a net effect on the outcome of the election in Quebec.

Federal Powers

If health care hurt the Alliance, the issue of federal powers helped the
party. Throughout the campaign, the Liberals emphasized the importance of a strong federal government, while the Alliance and, in
Quebec, the Bloc indicated that they were willing to leave more room
for the provincial governments. A majority (55 per cent) of
Canadians seemed to be satisfied with the status quo, but many more
would like to strengthen the provincial (33 per cent) than the federal (12 per cent) government.[11]

Predictably, support for some degree of centralization was a little
higher in Ontario than in the West and Atlantic Canada (Table 10.5),
but even in Ontario there were slightly more people in favour of a
stronger provincial government (21 per cent) than a stronger federal
government (16 per cent). Equally predictably, there was a correlation (.23) with feelings of regional alienation: those who believed

Table 10.5   Opinions on Federal Powers and Direct Democracy

	Federal powers	Direct democracy
All	-.21	.02
Sex		
Men	-.21	.03
Women	-.21	.00
Region		
Atlantic	-.24	.03
Quebec	-.38	-.06
Ontario	-.05	.03
West	-.27	.07
Outside Quebec	-.16	.04
Residence		
Rural	-.24	.07
Urban	-.21	.01
Religion		
Catholic	-.27	.01
Other religion	-.16	.05
No religion	-.18	.03
Origin		
North European	-.21	.13
Non-European	-.02	.02
Other origin	-.23	.01
Language		
English	-.17	.04
French	-.39	-.03
Other language	-.05	.02
Marital Status		
Married	-.23	.01
Not married	-.17	.04
Education		
Below high school	-.18	.07
Middle	-.22	.06
University	-.19	-.13

Note: Cell entries are mean scales scores. The scales range from -1 to 1.

that their province is not fairly treated were more inclined to support some decentralization.

Outside Quebec, those who thought that the federal government should have more power were more inclined to vote Liberal, while those who would like to strengthen provincial governments were more likely to vote for the Alliance, even after controlling for a host of prior dispositions.[12] Since opinion was tilted towards decentralization, this was an issue that benefited the Alliance. According to our estimates, the Alliance may have gained one point thanks to its "decentralizing" stance. Note, though, that this does not explain the Alliance's lack of success in Ontario. As Appendix C shows, the Ontario/West disparity in Alliance support is almost entirely accounted for by underlying values and beliefs (mostly the latter) and party identification.

The party that was really helped by this issue was the Bloc. In Quebec, opinion was divided almost in half, with 46 per cent indicating that they would like a stronger provincial government and 47 per cent saying they would like things to remain more or less as they are. A mere 8 per cent expressed a preference for a stronger federal government. Not surprisingly, views on this matter were strongly related to opinion about sovereignty. Over two-thirds (69 per cent) of sovereignists wanted a devolution of powers from the federal to the provincial government, while three-fifths (59 per cent) of federalists were satisfied with the status quo. Still, there was a substantial minority (30 per cent) of federalists who believed that the provincial government should have more power. These "soft nationalists" represent about 20 per cent of the total electorate and they constitute a pivotal group. Many of them (44 per cent) voted for the Liberals, a reminder that views about sovereignty matter more than opinions about the division of power, but an important minority (30 per cent) voted for the Bloc.[13] Our results suggest that, everything else being equal, the probability of voting for the Bloc increased by six percentage points when someone shared this view. According to our estimates, the Liberals lost two points to the benefit of the Bloc on this issue.

Direct Democracy

Although the Reform party had been an advocate of direct democracy in general and of referendums in particular, the Alliance party did not advocate such measures during the campaign. This did not deter the party's critics. They were quick to point out that the Alliance's stand on direct democracy could well lead to referendums on divisive issues, given the leader's strong beliefs on matters like abortion. Did their attack pay off?

The idea of direct democracy has substantial appeal in Canada, at least in the abstract. Almost two-thirds (64 per cent) of Canadians thought that referendums should be held regularly or occasionally on *important* issues, and the percentage was almost as high (61 per cent) when the question referred to *controversial* issues.[14] This positive predisposition significantly eroded, however, in the case of abortion: fully half (53 per cent) indicated that it would be a bad thing to have a referendum on abortion (Figure 10.1). So Canadians' views on referendums can best be characterized as ambivalent. They like the idea of being consulted and not letting the politicians decide all of the issues, but they do not like the idea of getting into acrimonious debates on sensitive issues such as abortion.

When we constructed a scale from responses to these two questions, the mean score was close to the neutral point (0 on a −1 to +1 scale). View about direct democracy did not vary much across regions (Table 10.5). There was hardly more support for referendums in the West than in Ontario, and views about direct democracy were only very weakly related (.08) to political cynicism. This suggests that distrust of politicians is not driving Canadians' desire to have a direct say on important matters.[15] Socio-demographic differences on this question tended to be quite muted, except for the stronger resistance among the university-educated. More research is needed to determine whether that resistance reflects a better understanding of the pitfalls of direct democracy or some elitist bias (or both).

Opinions on referendums had a small independent impact on vote choice outside Quebec. Everything else being equal, those in favour of referendums were slightly more inclined to vote for the Alliance (especially in the West), while those who were opposed were more prone to vote for the NDP. However, the net effect on the outcome of the election was nil because opinions on the issue were evenly divided. Still, the critics' attacks may have served to neutralize an issue from which the Alliance could potentially have benefited, given that its stance on direct democracy was in tune with popular predispositions. In Quebec, the issue had no impact at all.

Given the attacks on the Alliance on the issues of health and referendums, we would expect the party to have lost ground in the second half of the campaign among those who were opposed to the privatization of the public health system and/or to direct democracy. However, this was not the case. The Alliance vote share among those who supported the public health care system[16] was the same (21 per cent) before and after the televised leaders' debates. Similarly, the party's share among opponents of direct democracy[17] was virtually the same in the first (25 per cent) and second (24 per cent) halves of the campaign. Indeed, we did not detect substantial shifts in the importance of any specific issue, suggesting that the campaign did little to prime issues. We reported a similar finding for values in Chapter 7, so the conclusion would have to be that the changes that took place during the campaign were not directly related to either issues or values.

Discussion

The two issues that mattered most to vote choice were health care and federal powers. However, their effects were relatively small. The propensity to vote Liberal outside Quebec, for instance, increased by only four points when someone was strongly supportive of the public health system.[18] That said, the combined impact of the two issues was more substantial: the propensity to vote Liberal increased by 7 points when someone was strongly opposed to the privatization of health care *and* thought that the federal government should have more power. On the other hand, opinions on what should be done with the government surplus and views about crime and abortion did not have an independent effect on voting behaviour.

The net overall effect of issues as such on the *outcome* of the election was limited. Our analyses suggest that the Alliance lost one point to the Liberals on health care, but won one point at the expense of the Liberals on the division of powers. There are two reasons why the net effect was so small. The first is that voters seemed to be making up their minds on the basis of general ideological orientations rather than on specific issue positions. To take one example, it was overall views about the merits and limits of free enterprise that mattered rather than opinions about taxes. The second reason is that opinions on most issues tended to be divided, and so a party often lost as many votes among those who opposed its position as it won among those who supported it. However, the implication is *not* that issues did not matter: gaining or losing one or two percentage points can mean a lot for a party, especially in a "first past the post" system.

Notes

1 For overviews of the debate, see Dalton and Wattenberg (1993: 206-08), Niemi and Weisberg (1984: 89-103), and Denver and Hands (1992: 170-73).

2 There is one exception: mean scores were close to 0 on both the taxes and social programs variables in Quebec. The most plausible explanation is that the response categories were not equivalent in English and French. These categories were: almost all of it (à peu près tout), most (la majeure partie), half (la moitié), some (une petite partie), almost none of it (à peu près rien). In English interviews, the most frequent response was "some," but in French it was "la moitié." In retrospect, it might have been preferable to use "a little" for the fourth category in English, since it is closer to "une petite partie." For a discussion of the problem of linguistic equivalence in surveys, see Blais and Gidengil (1993).

3 Twenty-one per cent were in favour of both tax cuts and improving social programs (that is, they said that at least half of the surplus should be devoted to each), whereas 27 per cent wanted neither.

4 The correlations were .20 and .21, respectively.

5 We also examined responses to another set of questions about whether spending on welfare, pensions, health, unemployment, and education should increase, decrease, or remain the same. Views on social spending were not correlated with vote choice, once antecedent variables were controlled for.

6 Sixty-two per cent of the latter strongly disagree with such a ban.

7 In each case, the correlation was .35.

8 One-half of the random sample was asked about a 10-dollar fee and the other half was asked about a 20-dollar fee. Privatizing some of the system and imposing user fees are theoretically two separate issues, since it is possible to privatize the whole health system while keeping it entirely free. However, the two issues were linked in the minds of voters (the correlation between the two sets of opinions was +.30).

9 At least in its broad principles. As a matter of fact, some health services are not free and some that are free require a long waiting period.

10 Opposition to user fees is much stronger in Ontario than in Atlantic Canada, but opposition to privatization is slightly stronger in the latter.

11 Half of a random sample were asked about the federal government and the other half were asked about the provincial governments. The two questions are pooled here, "more" for one level being interpreted as "less" for the other and vice-versa.

12 The multinomial logit regressions indicate, however, that this was not an issue that differentiated Liberal and Conservative voters. Furthermore, the issue appears not to have had any impact in Atlantic Canada.

13 In contrast, only 7 per cent of federalists who did not think that the provincial government should have more power voted for the Bloc.

14 Half of a random sample was asked about "important" issues and the other half was asked about "controversial" issues.

15 The correlation with opinion on abortion (.13) was only slightly higher. It is ironic that the minority group (the pro-life supporters) was favourable to a referendum that it would be bound to lose. The only rationale could be that they hope to be able to win a referendum that makes it a little more difficult to get an abortion.

16 These are those who scored +.5 or +1 on our public health scale.

17 That is, those who scored below -.25 on the direct democracy scale.

18 That is, compared to someone who was neutral on this issue. The difference is twice as large if the comparison is with someone who was strongly favourable to privatization.

CHAPTER 11

Liberal Performance

One intuitively plausible interpretation of the election is that the Liberals were re-elected because Canadians were broadly satisfied with what the Liberal government had done over the previous three years. This assumes that people vote *retrospectively*. In other words, they focus on what the incumbent government has—and has not—accomplished during its mandate, determine whether that performance is satisfactory or not, and vote for or against the government accordingly (Fiorina, 1981). This decision calculus makes fewer demands on voters than the classic rational choice model. That model assumes that voters vote *prospectively*, considering each party's positions in turn and opting for the party that seems most likely to defend their own views. We have just seen (in Chapter 10) that there was only weak evidence of prospective issue voting in the 2000 election. Was there more evidence of retrospective issue voting, and does this explain the Liberal victory?

Evaluating the Liberal Record

The second question is easily answered with "no." The only areas where the performance of the Liberal government was judged to be quite good were reducing the debt and handling international relations (see Table 11.1). Evaluations of the Liberals' performance in creating jobs were only modestly positive. The Liberals did get some credit for the drop in the unemployment rate from 9.6 per cent to 6.9 per cent during their mandate, and the judgments were clearly more positive than they had been in 1997, when the mean rating was negative (-.25). Still, barely half (54 per cent) thought that the Liberals had done a good job and as many as 37 per cent thought they had done a poor job on this front. Meanwhile, their performance was perceived to be quite poor with respect to health care, taxes, corruption, and (in Quebec) defending the interests of Quebec.[1] Health care was the domain that most frequently elicited negative evaluations (74 per cent). Only 21 per cent expressed satisfaction with what the government had been doing. Evaluations were only slightly less negative in the case of taxes, with 64 per cent offering negative evalua-

Table 11.1   Evaluations of Liberal Performance

	Canada	Atlantic	Quebec	Ontario	West
International relations	.22	.34	.19	.23	.20
Debt	.18	.16	.31	.22	.01
Jobs	.09	.03	.07	.17	.03
Environment	-.01	.06	.07	-.04	-.05
Crime	-.05	.17	-.22	.05	-.08
Provincial relations	-.08	.10	-.22	.02	-.13
Welfare	-.10	-.12	-.16	-.05	-.09
Corruption	-.16	-.07	-.29	-.07	-.19
Quebec	-.20	—	-.20	—	—
Cutting tax	-.23	-.28	-.22	-.11	-.37
Health	-.36	-.46	-.35	-.30	-.43

Note: Cell entries are mean scales scores. The scales range from -1 to 1.

tions and only 30 per cent offering positive ones. Moreover, 58 per cent thought that there had been "a lot" or some corruption under the Liberals, and only 31 per cent said "a little" or "none."[2] Finally, in Quebec, only 37 per cent indicated that the government had done a good job of defending the interests of the province.

There were significant regional variations in performance evaluations (see Table 11.1). Particularly striking are Westerners' negative ratings of Liberal performance on taxes, Ontarians' positive evaluations on job creation, and the contrast between the positive assessments in Atlantic Canada and the negative ones in Quebec concerning provincial relations and crime. The negative evaluations of Liberal performance with respect to crime in Quebec might well have been related to concerns about biker gangs. There was one noteworthy gender difference: women (-.41) tended to evaluate the Liberals more negatively than men (-.31) on health. Meanwhile, the better-educated provided more positive ratings for reducing the debt and creating jobs and more negative ones on protecting the environment (findings not reported).[3]

As we would expect, partisan predispositions affected evaluations of Liberals' performance. Predictably, Liberal partisans were more likely to provide positive evaluations. The median rating was -.21 among those who identified with the opposition parties, compared with a median rating of +.15 among Liberal partisans. The judgments of non-partisans were also quite negative, with a median rating of -.11. The domain that produced the greatest projection effect

Table 11.2 Evaluation of Liberal Performance and Party Identification

	Liberal identification	*Other party identification*[a]	*No identification*
International relations	.42	.13	.18
Debt	.42	.02	.14
Jobs	.31	-.04	.05
Environment	.17	-.15	-.07
Crime	.15	-.19	-.08
Provincial relations	.11	-.25	-.13
Welfare	.08	-.19	-.16
Corruption	.02	-.28	-.20
Quebec	.25	-.51	-.27
Cutting tax	-.07	-.33	-.26
Health	-.14	-.49	-.44

Note: Cell entries are mean scales scores. The scales range from -1 to 1.

[a] This column includes respondents who identified with the Alliance, Conservative, NDP, and Bloc.

was defending the interests of Quebec. The judgments of Liberal identifiers and federalists in this area were quite different from those of Bloc identifiers and sovereignists.

Performance Evaluations and Vote Choice

The crucial question, of course, is whether performance evaluations had an independent impact on vote choice. The short answer is that they did, at least outside Quebec. In Quebec, voting behaviour is so strongly structured by opinions about sovereignty that there is little room left for issues (or the economy) to have any additional impact.[4] Outside Quebec, though, the probability of voting Liberal increased by three to six points when someone thought that the Liberals had done a very good job in a given area, and decreased by the same amount if someone believed that they had not done a good job at all (see Appendix C).[5]

On taxes and corruption, the main beneficiary of dissatisfaction with Liberal performance was the Alliance. As we saw in Chapter 10, opinions on fiscal issues as such did not influence vote choice. What does seem to have mattered is general evaluations of how little the Liberals had cut taxes in the past. There was widespread dissatisfaction to that effect and that dissatisfaction nurtured support for the Alliance. Similarly, those who had come to the conclusion that there had been quite a lot of corruption under the Liberal government were led to vote Alliance, confirming once again that the Alliance vote had a strong protest component. The party was able to attract the support of those who were cynical about politicians in general, shared a sense of regional alienation, and thought that there was a lot of corruption under the Liberal government.

Many Canadians felt that the Liberal government had done a poor job of improving health care and this dissatisfaction was directly and strongly related to perceptions that the quality of health care had deteriorated over the past five years.[6] Tellingly, there was no correlation between views about what should be done (whether to privatize health care or not) and evaluations of Liberal performance. Dissatisfaction with Liberal performance was equally high among those who were willing to privatize and those who were opposed. Given the centrality of health care to its campaign, the NDP should have been the major beneficiary of this dissatisfaction with the Liberal record on health care. Instead, the main beneficiary was the Conservative party. Even among non-partisans, the NDP was able to attract the votes of only 15 per cent of those who were both dissatisfied with Liberal performance *and* opposed to privatization. This was less than half as many as the Liberals (38 per cent).

Discontent with their handling of health care certainly cost the Liberals votes: the party's vote share went up to 47 per cent when non-partisans were satisfied with the Liberal performance.[7] Still, it is puzzling that the cost was not higher. One reason is that the federal government did not shoulder all of the blame for the problems in the health-care system. Voters in general were quite divided when asked which level of government was most responsible for health care getting worse: one-third (35 per cent) pointed to the federal government, one-third (33 per cent) to the provincial government, and one-third (32 per cent) either could not tell or said both.[8] Moreover, only 32 per cent of Canadians thought that the main reason the quality of health care had deteriorated was lack of money (that is, federal funding).[9] The fact that many voters believed that the provincial governments were as much (or more) to blame helped limit the damage to the Liberals. This ability to share (or avoid) the blame was an important ingredient in the Liberal victory. The party's vote share fell to only 22 per cent when dissatisfied non-partisans thought that the federal government was most responsible for the problems in the health system, compared with 43 per cent among those who did not lay all of the blame at the feet of the federal government.

Health was not the only area where the Liberals were able to limit the damage caused by negative evaluations of their performance. In contrast to the Reform Party in the 1997 election (Nevitte et al., 2000), the Alliance was unable to benefit from dissatisfaction with Liberal performance on crime. Assessments of that performance did not exert an independent impact on vote choice, despite the fact that many voters seemed to consider fighting crime to be a very important issue in the election.[10] This may be because Canadians were quite divided about the best way to go about fighting crime (see Chapter 10).

On the environment, on the other hand, those who were dissatisfied with the Liberal government were inclined to support the NDP. Indeed, 26 per cent of those who said that the Liberal government had a very poor record on the environment voted NDP.[11] This is an issue on which the NDP did make some mileage, more so than on health, which was so central to the party's campaign.

Finally, the Liberals did not appear to benefit from the positive evaluations of their performance with respect to the federal debt and international relations. These evaluations simply did not matter very much when it came to vote choice.

On the three issues that did matter outside Quebec—health, taxes, and corruption—the Liberals were perceived not to have done a good job. Dissatisfaction with respect to taxes and corruption helped to nurture support for the Alliance. In the case of health, the Conservatives (and not the NDP) seem to have been the main beneficiary. According to our estimates, the Liberals lost about three points because of dissatisfaction on these three issues—to the benefit of the Alliance and, on the health-care issue, the Conservatives. However, neither opinions on the issues nor assessments of Liberal performance can account for the regionalization of the vote. Indeed, the regional coefficients did not weaken at all when issues and Liberal performance were entered into the equations (see Appendix A).

Finally, an examination of the relationships between evaluations of various aspects of Liberal performance and vote intentions in the first and second halves of the campaign shows that they remained quite similar. There is no evidence that the campaign primed some dimensions of the government record at the expense of others.

The Early Election Call

The other issue that hurt the Liberals in the 2000 election was the decision to call the election itself. There can be little doubt that Jean

Chrétien called an early election for no reason other than his belief that it was a good time for the party and himself. The Alliance had just elected its new leader and was not ready for a fall election. The Liberals were doing extremely well in the polls, enjoying a huge lead over all the other parties (see Chapter 4). And, finally, Mr. Chrétien could put an end to pressures within the Liberal Party for him to step down and to let the Finance Minister, Paul Martin, replace him.

Mr. Chrétien seems to have made the decision to go to the polls even though a majority in the Liberal caucus and among his close advisors were arguing against a fall election (*La Presse*, 27 September 2000, A19; *La Presse*, 5 October 2000, A13). The Prime Minister's advisors were concerned about the so-called Peterson effect. In July 1990, David Peterson, the Premier of Ontario, decided to call a snap election at a time when his Liberal Party was enjoying a huge lead in the polls. The campaign proved to be disastrous for the Liberals, and they lost the election. The lesson seemed to be that voters will react negatively to an election that appears to have been called for purely opportunistic reasons.

Only 10 per cent of our respondents indicated that they were very angry at the Prime Minister's decision to call an early election. Another 22 per cent said that they were somewhat angry.[12] Resentment about the early election call was typically highest among the better-informed. Even though it was limited to a small group, this resentment did have an independent effect on vote choice (see Appendices A to D). Everything else being equal, the likelihood of voting Liberal declined by 14 points outside Quebec when someone felt very angry about the election call. According to our estimations, it cost the Liberals two or three points, mainly to the benefit of the Alliance. In Quebec, too, resentment about the early election call had a small but significant effect on vote choice, costing the Liberals two or three per cent, to the benefit of the Conservatives. This may have been a relatively light punishment, but punishment it was. The Liberal victory would have been bigger if it had not been for resentment about the timing of the election among a small group of electors.

Discussion

The fact that the Liberal government was re-elected might seem to suggest that Canadians were broadly satisfied with what it had done over the previous three years. The findings reported in this chapter cast doubt on this interpretation. Retrospective evaluations did matter, but on the three issues that mattered most—health, taxes, and corruption—there was widespread dissatisfaction, and that dissatisfaction cost the Liberals votes. The Liberals also lost votes among those who resented the Prime Minister's decision to call an early election. If it had not been for this discontent, the Liberals would have won a sweeping victory.

The Liberals won *despite* the dissatisfaction with their performance. There were basically two reasons for this. The first and most obvious one is that those who were dissatisfied split their votes among the opposition parties. The second is that the Liberals started the campaign with a substantial edge among partisans. Thanks to that edge, they could manage to win an election even though many Canadians were not really satisfied with what they had been doing.

At the same time, it is probably true that the Liberals were re-elected because there was no *deep* discontent with their policies and performance. From that perspective, health was a crucial issue. Canadians were very concerned about the perceived deterioration in health care in the recent past and they expressed widespread dissatisfaction with Liberal performance in this area. That dissatisfaction did not result in the repudiation of the Liberals, though, in part because there was no consensus on what should be done and in part because Canadians felt that the blame had to be shared with the provincial governments.

Notes

1 The correlations among the various indicators were modest, with a median correlation of only .23, suggesting that respondents were able to differentiate the various domains, and did not simply offer systematically negative or systematically positive evaluations.

2 Unfortunately, the question in Quebec mistakenly referred to patronage rather than corruption. Comparisons between Quebec and the other regions should take that difference into account.

3 Those with a university education gave mean ratings of +.26, +.17 and -.11 for the Liberal record on the debt, jobs, and the environment; the corresponding ratings among those who did not complete high school were +.13, +.01 and +.04.

4 There is one small exception: those who were particularly dissatisfied with Liberal performance on cutting taxation were slightly more inclined to support the Alliance (see Appendix B.3).

5 The reference group is those with no opinion.

6 The correlation between these perceptions and evaluations of Liberal performance was .39.

7 The Liberals were particularly successful among those who were satisfied and opposed to privatization. They received only 33 per cent of the vote among non-partisans who were dissatisfied *and* favorable to privatization.

8 Note that these numbers refer to those (the great majority) who said that the quality of health care had deteriorated over the years.

9 Thirty-seven per cent attributed the problem to poor management, while 31 per cent thought it was both factors (or did not know).

10 Seventy-two per cent of our respondents said fighting crime was a very important issue. This was second to improving health care (84 per cent), and ahead of creating jobs (68 per cent) and cutting taxes (54 per cent).

11 Even more (34 per cent) voted for the Alliance but dissatisfaction as such led to a greater propensity to vote NDP.

12 The exact question was: "Are you very angry that the federal election was called early, somewhat angry, or not angry at all?" The level of anger did not decline during the campaign (see Blais et al., 2001d).

CHAPTER 12

The Leaders

An election is not just about choosing which party will form the government, it is also about who is going to be Prime Minister. There is evidence from a variety of settings that voters make up their minds in good part on the basis of how they feel about the leaders (see, especially, Bean and Mughan, 1989; Wattenberg, 1991; and McAllister, 1996). Indeed, according to conventional wisdom, "election outcomes are now, more than at any time in the past, determined by voters' assessments of party leaders" (Hayes and McAllister, 1997: 3). Typically, two reasons are cited for this pattern. The first is the growing importance of television and, more particularly, the extent to which television coverage has come to focus on the leaders and their personal qualities (Mendelsohn, 1993). The second reason is the decline of partisan attachments, which makes people more open to switching parties from one election to the next (Wattenberg, 1994; Dalton, 2000; Dalton et al., 2000).

There has been surprisingly little study, though, of whether leaders actually have become more important to vote choice. A recent series of studies of leader effects in Sweden and Norway (Aardal and Oscarsson, 2000), the Netherlands (Aarts, 2000), Germany (Schmitt and Ohr, 2000), and Canada (Gidengil et al., 2000) found no clear or consistent trends. The "presidentialization" of parliamentary elections may be one of those seemingly common-sense hypotheses that do not to square with the evidence.

This does not mean that leaders do not matter. They may just have mattered more in the past than we thought.[1] But how much do they matter? There have been relatively few attempts to provide a precise assessment of the impact of leaders on the vote. The first systematic attempt was Bean and Mughan's (1989) comparative study of leadership effects in the 1983 British and 1987 Australian elections. Focusing on the most popular leader in the respective elections, they estimate that Thatcher's popularity translated into a net gain of seven points for her party, while Hawke's popularity gave his party a net boost of four points. In the case of the Australian election, they point out, this was enough to reverse the outcome: in other words, if leadership had not played in Labour's favour, the party would have lost the election.

In a similar vein, Clarke and his colleagues (Clarke et al., 1996) have simulated how different the outcome of the Canadian 1993 election might have been if Kim Campbell had been as popular as her main rival, Jean Chrétien. According to their estimates, the Conservative vote share would have increased by five points. This is quite a substantial effect, and similar in magnitude to the ones observed in Britain and Australia (Bean and Mughan, 1989). It was not large enough, though, to reverse the outcome of the election. Our analyses of the 1997 election (Nevitte et al., 2000) indicate that Chrétien's popularity outside Quebec gave the Liberals a five-point boost. That effect paled, though, beside that of Charest's popularity in Quebec. The impact of leadership in Quebec was huge in 1997. Charest was the most popular leader and his popularity boosted the Conservative vote in Quebec by as much as 12 points.

These studies point to two conclusions. On the one hand, they confirm that leadership has quite a substantial effect on the vote: the party of the most popular leader can typically expect to get a boost of about five points. On the other hand, they suggest that these effects are usually not overwhelming, and seldom important enough to change the outcome of an election. In this chapter, we examine whether leader effects in the 2000 election fit this pattern, but first we need to know how popular the leaders were, and what made them popular (or not).

The most striking feature of leader evaluations in the 2000 election was how small the differences were in the leaders' overall popularity (see Table 12.1). The average ratings are based on a scale from 0 to 100, where 0 meant that the person really disliked the leader and 100 meant that the person really liked the leader. In the last week of the campaign, Chrétien and Duceppe (in Quebec only) were tied at 48, while Clark (47), McDonough (46), and Day (45) followed close behind.

There was a good deal of variability in the ratings, though, especially of Day and Duceppe. Day was more popular than Chrétien in the West, but lagged far behind the Prime Minister in Atlantic Canada and Ontario. Meanwhile, in Quebec, Duceppe was more popular than Chrétien, who trailed even Clark. However, Quebecers did not seem to be excited by any of the leaders, and all of the leaders received relatively low ratings in the province. Clark's ratings varied the least across regions.

We would expect leader evaluations to be influenced by people's partisan predispositions. Chrétien may have emerged as the most

Table 12.1   Leader Evaluations (Last Seven Days of Campaign)

	Chrétien	*Day*	*Clark*	*McDonough*	*Duceppe*
Canada	48 (45)	45 (46)	47 (49)	46 (46)	48 (50)
Atlantic	50 (49)	37 (37)	49 (48)	50 (53)	—
Quebec	42 (39)	41 (44)	44 (47)	42 (46)	48 (50)
Ontario	55 (51)	44 (46)	49 (50)	49 (47)	—
West	46 (43)	52 (51)	49 (48)	47 (45)	—
Outside Quebec	51 (48)	46 (47)	49 (49)	48 (47)	—

Note: Entries are mean evaluations on a 0 to 100 scale. Entries in parentheses refer to mean evaluations among those with no party identification.

popular leader in Ontario, for example, simply because there were more Liberal partisans, and those partisans tended to give "their" leader higher scores. Things do indeed look rather different if we just focus on non-partisans (see Table 12.1). With the exception of Atlantic Canada, Chrétien's ratings were appreciably lower among non-partisans across the country. In Ontario, the gap between Chrétien's average ratings and Day's narrows from 11 points to just five points. Meanwhile, in Quebec, Duceppe's lead over the Prime Minister in Canada increases from six points to 11 points.

The Popularity Stakes

The leaders' ratings were markedly different from 1997. Chrétien's average score outside Quebec in the last week of the campaign was six points below his score in 1997;[2] clearly the small Liberal gain in votes in the 2000 election cannot be attributed to Chrétien's personal popularity. This decline in Chrétien's ratings is consistent with a more general pattern: party leaders typically become less popular from one election to the next (see Clarke et al., 1991; Gidengil et al., 2000). McDonough bucked the trend:[3] her average score rose by five points, but this did not prevent the NDP from losing ground between 1997 and 2000. This is a salutary reminder that having a popular leader may not be enough to do well in an election.

Clark's ratings went up during the campaign and his strong performance allowed the Conservatives to retain official party status in the House of Commons, but his average rating was five points lower than Charest's in 1997. The opposite pattern applies to Day: his average score was seven points higher than Manning's had been three years before.

Figure 12.1 Evaluations of Leaders (5-Day Moving Averages)

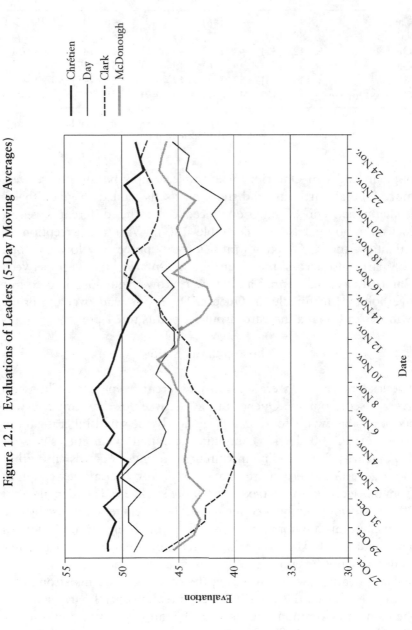

Chrétien's average ratings went down by only one point in Quebec. More importantly, he came in just a little way behind Clark. This was in sharp contrast to 1997, when he trailed Charest by 11 points. As for Duceppe, the widespread perception that he had a much better campaign this time is confirmed: his average score rose an impressive 10 points.[4]

There was some movement in leader evaluations over the course of the campaign, but not much (see Figure 12.1). The leaders who were more popular at the beginning of the campaign (Chrétien and Day) saw their ratings decline a little and those who were less popular (Clark and McDonough) saw their evaluations improve somewhat. Looking at Canada as a whole, Chrétien's average rating decreased from 51 to 49 between the first five days of interviewing (October 25 to October 29) and the last five days of the campaign, while Day's went from 49 to 46. Over the same period, Clark's average rating increased slightly from 46 to 48 and McDonough's hardly changed.[5]

The most important change concerned Joe Clark. His ratings initially declined, but then surged back in the aftermath of the English televised leaders' debate, which he was clearly perceived to have won (see chapter 4). Chrétien, meanwhile, was named most often as the leader who had performed worst in that debate, and his ratings went down by two or three points in the following days. The source of Day's decline is less clear. His daily mean score remained remarkably stable from 3 November to 15 November, so it was not the debates. His ratings appear to have dropped in the very first days of November. This was right after the 31 October headlines charging that his party was in favour of a two-tier health system. However, ratings of the party did not move during that period. It is possible that the drop in Day's ratings simply reflected a decay of the temporary boost that he had received in the very first days of the campaign (before the Canadian Election Study fieldwork started) or perhaps just before.[6] A second drop in Day's ratings occurred around November 15, following charges of racism against some of Day's supporters and CBC's report on "Fundamental Day." As we saw in Chapter 4, though, the effect seems to have been only temporary: Day's ratings rebounded in the last days of the campaign. The election campaign was a difficult one for Stockwell Day. Still, it was not as disastrous as it may have seemed. After all, Day's ratings declined by only three points and no specific event seems to have been responsible for the decline.[7]

By election day, the average ratings obtained by the five leaders were quite similar. There were marked differences, though, in the percentage of negative evaluations (below 50) that each leader received. Fully half (50 per cent) of those interviewed in the last week of the campaign gave Day a negative rating, compared with fewer than one third (31 per cent) for Chrétien.[8] Perhaps this was Chrétien's greatest achievement: less than one-third of the electorate actively disliked him, even though he had been Prime Minister for seven years.

Popularity and Personal Traits

We still need to understand what shaped these evaluations. One influential stream of research emphasizes leader traits. Kinder and his colleagues (Kinder et al., 1980) have argued that voters assess leaders on two basic dimensions: competence and trustworthiness. The former can be sub-divided into intellectual ability and leadership ability and the latter into integrity and empathy (Kinder, 1986; Johnston et al., 1992). This raises the question of which traits mattered most to voters' overall evaluations of the leaders in the 2000 election. It also raises the prior question of how people came to perceive a given leader as having a specific trait. One possibility is that these perceptions were mere projections. Liberal partisans, for example, might naturally tend to see the Liberal leader in a positive light on every dimension. Perceptions could also be influenced by voters' social background characteristics and by their fundamental beliefs and values. Finally, we need to consider the images that the leaders themselves projected.

In the post-election survey, voters were asked to say which leader they would describe as: arrogant, trustworthy, having new ideas, compassionate, dishonest, intelligent, extreme, and weak.[9] Table 12.2 gives the percentage of voters who associated a specific leader with a given trait. The most striking finding is that over 40 per cent of voters perceived Chrétien to be arrogant and 25 per cent considered him to be dishonest. Meanwhile, outside Quebec, Day was widely perceived (50 per cent) as having new ideas, but also as being extreme (45 per cent). The images of the other leaders were not as sharply defined. Outside Quebec, Clark was the most likely (24 per cent) to seen as trustworthy, while McDonough was the most likely (31 per cent) to be thought compassionate, but both Clark (28 per cent) and McDonough (26 per cent) were perceived to be weak lead-

Table 12.2 Perceptions of Leaders' Personal Traits

		Chrétien	*Day*	*Clark*	*McDonough*	*Duceppe*
Arrogant	Canada	44	22	3	1	3
	Quebec	48	11	3	1	11
	Outside Quebec	42	26	4	1	1
Trustworthy	Canada	17	12	22	11	4
	Quebec	18	9	17	5	16
	Outside Quebec	17	12	24	12	0
New Ideas	Canada	6	46	4	7	2
	Quebec	5	32	4	4	9
	Outside Quebec	7	50	4	8	0
Compassionate	Canada	13	9	12	27	4
	Quebec	9	6	11	16	15
	Outside Quebec	15	11	12	31	0
Dishonest	Canada	25	16	3	1	2
	Quebec	28	8	1	1	6
	Outside Quebec	24	19	3	1	1
Intelligent	Canada	24	11	16	4	4
	Quebec	16	7	12	3	14
	Outside Quebec	26	12	18	5	0
Extreme	Canada	11	43	3	7	5
	Quebec	11	35	2	1	12
	Outside Quebec	11	45	3	9	2
Weak	Canada	6	6	25	25	4
	Quebec	10	6	18	22	13
	Outside Quebec	4	7	28	26	1

Note: Cell entries represent the percentage of respondents saying they would describe the leader as having such a trait.

ers. As for Duceppe, few voters in Quebec associated him with any specific trait.

Traits clearly had an independent impact on voters' overall evaluations of the leaders, especially outside Quebec. Table 12.3 shows how much additional variance in leader evaluations was accounted for when voters' prior dispositions and their perceptions of leader traits were added sequentially. Personal traits were particularly important for feelings about Stockwell Day, suggesting that evaluations of the Alliance leader had a strong personal component. Feelings about Chrétien, on the other hand, were strongly influenced

Table 12.3   The Relative Impact of Socio-Economic Characteristics, Values and Beliefs, Party Identification, and Personal Traits on Leader Evaluations

	Additional Variance Explained			
	SES	*Values and Beliefs*	*Party ID*	*Traits*
Outside Quebec				
Chrétien	.08	.18	.13	.14
Day	.07	.13	.14	.20
Clark	.03	.06	.07	.14
McDonough	.05	.12	.06	.13
Quebec				
Chrétien	.07	.25	.06	.08
Duceppe	.03	.27	.07	.08
Day	.01	.04	.06	.22
Clark	.00	.09	.01	.20

by core beliefs, especially cynicism about politics: the more cynical voters were about politics and politicians, the less they liked the Prime Minister. In Quebec, opinion about sovereignty was the decisive factor in how voters felt about both Chrétien and Duceppe. Personal traits were only consequential for feelings about the two minor players in Quebec, Day and Clark.

Each of the eight traits appears to have had an independent effect on leader evaluations (results not shown). Different voters may well have attached different weights to the various dimensions, but the three traits that were consistently important in evaluating the leaders were "trustworthy," "dishonest," and "arrogant." There is no support for the view that negative traits would count more than positive ones. According to our estimations, the widespread perception that Chrétien is arrogant reduced his average ratings outside Quebec by three points on a 0 to 100 scale.[10] This was the sole negative trait that tarnished his image somewhat, and it may account for the decline in his personal popularity. This image of arrogance was perhaps only to be expected for someone who had been in power for seven years, though it may well have been reinforced by Chrétien's decision to call an early election. In Quebec, the negative trait that mattered the most for evaluations of Chrétien was "dishonest." The trait was not mentioned as often (only 28 per cent) but, even taking into account prior dispositions, those who shared this perception gave the Prime Minister much lower ratings, reducing his average score in Quebec by about three points.

As for Day, he seems to have lost three points outside Quebec because of his image of being extreme, but that was made up for by a five-point gain from being viewed as having new ideas.[11] Perceived trustworthiness gave Clark's ratings a three-point boost and being perceived as compassionate did the same for McDonough, but each received a two-point penalty because of their perceived weakness.[12] No specific trait appears to have struck voters about Duceppe.

There remains the question of Stockwell Day's personal religious convictions. One way to get at this is to determine whether voters' personal religious convictions played a greater role in 2000 than in previous elections. Respondents in the mail-back survey were asked whether they agreed or disagreed with the statement that "the Bible is the actual word of God and is to be taken literally word for word." Many more respondents disagreed (74 per cent) than agreed (19 per cent) with the statement, an indication that relatively few Canadians adhere to religious fundamentalism. Still, one Canadian in five does believe that the Bible should be taken word for word. That percentage varies only slightly across regions. Interestingly, religious fundamentalism is more widespread in Atlantic Canada. As expected, those who believed that the Bible is the actual word of God tended to like Stockwell Day more than those who did not: outside Quebec, Day's average rating was 55 among Christian fundamentalists, but only 39 among other respondents. Since the latter group was much larger, this implies a negative net effect.

Of course, this difference could simply reflect the greater propensity of religious fundamentalists to support a socially conservative party. In other words, perhaps it was not so much Day's personal religious convictions as the party he was leading. However, views about the Bible were only weakly related to evaluations of Manning in 1993 (the question about the Bible was not asked in 1997). In 1993, Manning's average rating outside Quebec was 52 among those who believed that the Bible should be taken word for word and 49 among those who disagreed. Day was clearly more disliked (39) among the latter than Manning had been in 1993. The obvious inference is that Day was hurt by the fact that a clear majority of Canadians reject Christian fundamentalist beliefs.[13]

Table 12.4   The Impact of Reactions to Religious Fundamentalism on Evaluations of Stockwell Day, Outside Quebec (OLS Regressions)

	Day's evaluations
Party identification	
Liberal	-8.68 (1.95)
Alliance	29.46 (2.44) [a]
Conservative	2.62 (2.76)
New Democrat	-16.28 (3.10) [a]
Socio-demographics	
Atlantic	-3.34 (2.67)
West	1.99 (1.73)
Catholic	-2.09 (1.91)
Non-religious	-2.52 (2.26)
North European	-3.08 (2.22)
Non-European	-8.56 (3.42) [b]
Male	1.90 (1.58)
Other Language	1.62 (2.59)
Married	4.38 (1.81) [b]
Below high school	-1.20 (2.19)
Rural	-.40 (1.86)
Bible as word of God	
Strongly agree	3.88 (2.81)
Strongly disagree	-10.14 (1.77) [a]
Constant	42.23 (2.54) [a]
Adjusted R^2	.33
N	874

a: significant $\alpha \leq .01$; b: significant $\alpha \leq .05$

Note: Cell entries are unstandardized regression coefficients and standard errors are in parentheses.

This inference is strengthened when we look at those who strongly disagreed with the notion that the Bible should be taken literally. Table 12.4 shows that, irrespective of social background characteristics and partisan predispositions, those who strongly disagreed with the statement that the Bible is the word of God gave Stockwell Day much lower ratings, on average. These respondents represented about 40 per cent of the electorate, and their ratings were about 10 points lower.[14] This suggests that Day's ratings were about four points lower than they would have been if his religious convictions had played no role in voters' assessments. Interestingly, those who strongly agreed with a literalist interpretation of the Bible did not give Day significantly higher ratings, once social background characteristics and party identification were taken into account. So the conclusion has to be that Day's religious fundamentalism made him a less attractive leader overall.

Day's religious views were particularly important for the widespread perception that he was "extreme." Forty-five per cent of respondents outside Quebec attributed this trait to Day. The percentage reached 67 per cent among those who disagreed strongly with the view that the Bible is the literal word of God.

These findings raise the question: Did Day's religious beliefs come to play an important role because the media decided to focus on them? If so, we would expect to see the relationship strengthen as the campaign progressed. Systematic assessments of the impact of the media would require more complex analyses than we can provide here, but some pieces of evidence suggest that it may be misleading to blame the media. The relationship between religious beliefs and vote intention was basically the same in the first and second halves of the campaign. After the debates, 30 per cent of those who said that the Bible should not be taken word for word intended to vote for the Alliance (outside Quebec), almost the same percentage (31 per cent) as before the debates.[15] This is consistent with the finding, reported in Chapter 4, that the CBC's "Fundamental Day" report had no lasting impact on the vote. Concerns about Day's religious beliefs were there from the very beginning.

The Impact of Leader Evaluations

Evaluations of the leaders had a substantial effect on vote choice (see Appendices C and D). Typically, the probability of voting for a party increased by 25 to 30 points when a voter gave its leader a rating of 100, even controlling for causally prior variables.[16] The effect was even stronger in the case of Day. Feelings about the Alliance leader had twice as much impact as feelings about the other leaders. This confirms the conventional wisdom that the election was in good part about Stockwell Day.

There was no indication of a negativity bias. This is the notion that negative ratings have a greater impact on vote choice than positive ones (Lau, 1982; Holbrook et al., 2001). However, there was no evidence that voters were more likely to vote against leaders they disliked than to vote in favour of those they liked.[17] Voters were as likely to be attracted to a party by a leader they liked as they were to be repelled by one they disliked.

Our approach allows us to estimate the fraction of the electorate for whom leaders were a decisive factor. On the basis of the multinomial logit regressions presented in Appendix A, we can determine the party that each respondent is predicted to support, given his or her social background characteristics, values and beliefs, party identification, economic perceptions, issue opinions, evaluations of liberal performance, and evaluations of leaders.[18] We can then compare this prediction with the party that each respondent would be predicted to support if leader ratings had not mattered at all, but all other considerations had remained the same.[19] If a respondent is predicted to support the same party under both scenarios, we can infer that leaders did not play a decisive part in his or her vote choice. Conversely, if the two predictions diverge, we can infer that leader ratings were decisive: but for leader evaluations, the respondent would have voted differently. According to our estimates, leaders played a crucial role in the vote choice of one voter in five (21 per cent) outside Quebec. This is a very substantial effect. Voters made up their minds in good part on the basis of how they felt about the party leaders. However, the overall net impact of leader evaluations on the outcome of the election was quite small.[20] This was because leader evaluations did not differ very much overall (in contrast to 1997 when two of the leaders—Chrétien and Charest—were quite popular and two of the others—Manning and McDonough—were unpopular).

Previous studies have indicated that voters may attach greater importance to party leaders as the campaign progresses because media coverage is so leader-centred (Mendelsohn, 1994; Gidengil et al., forthcoming). As we saw in Chapter 2, television news did pay a lot of attention to the leaders during the 2000 campaign. This raises the question of whether leader evaluations carried more weight towards the end of the campaign.

We see little trace of such an effect in 2000. For instance, before the debates, 68 per cent of those (outside Quebec) who gave Stockwell Day a positive score (above 50) said they intended to vote for the Alliance, compared with only 5 per cent of those who have him a negative score (below 50). After the debates, the figures were 67 per cent and 3 per cent, respectively. There is no indication, then, that leaders were more important in the second half of the campaign.

There is one small exception, and that concerns Joe Clark. Before the debates, only 15 per cent of those who had positive feelings (above 50) towards Clark were intending to vote Conservative.[21] After the debates, that percentage rose to 27 per cent, suggesting that Clark was successful in transforming favourable evaluations of his performance into actual support for the party. These gains were made at the expense of the Liberals: "only" 34 per cent of those who viewed Clark positively after the debates voted Liberal, compared with fully 46 per cent before the debates.[22] This was the basic source of Conservative gains during the campaign.

Discussion

Voters' evaluations of leaders may not have greatly affected the actual outcome of the election, but they played a critical role in many people's vote decision. And for one voter in five, they were the decisive consideration. Feelings about Stockwell Day were particularly important. His religious beliefs were a source of concern for some Canadians and this helped to make him a less appealing leader. Still, the impact of his religious fundamentalism should not be overstated. In the last week of the campaign, Day was as popular as Chrétien among non-partisans, and more popular than Manning had been in 1997. Indeed, in the 2000 election, no leader was markedly more popular—or unpopular—than the others, and this is why the net overall impact on the outcome of the election turned out to be quite small.

Notes

1 Indeed, Jon Pammett (1997) suggests that leaders matter less to vote choice in Canada than they did in the past. See also Turcotte (2001).

2 The 1997 numbers are corrected because respondents in the campaign survey were not asked to evaluate a leader if they had said they knew nothing about him or her (see Blais, Nadeau, Gidengil, and Nevitte, 2000). The correction involved attributing lower scores to those who were not asked to rate the leader. The uncorrected mean scores (outside Quebec) in 1997 were: 56 for Chrétien and Charest, 46 for McDonough, and 44 for Manning. The corrected scores were: 54 for Chrétien, 52 for Charest, 41 for McDonough, and 38 for Manning.

3 Interestingly, the previous exception was Ed Broadbent.

4 The uncorrected mean ratings in Quebec were: 57 for Charest, 45 for Chrétien, and 42 for Duceppe. The corrected (see note 2) scores were: 54 for Charest, 43 for Chrétien, and 38 for Duceppe.

5 We do not present data on the evolution of Duceppe's ratings during the campaign because the number of interviews in Quebec does not allow such comparisons. Our data suggest that his ratings were slightly higher at the end of the campaign than at the beginning.

6 Consistent with this interpretation is the fact that public polls showed vote intentions for the Alliance at around 30 per cent in the last days of October, compared with around 25 per cent in mid-October, just before the campaign began.

7 For a more thorough analysis, see Blais et al. (Forthcoming [a]).

8 The comparable figures for Clark and Duceppe were 43 per cent, and 47 per cent for McDonough.

9 This was the order in which the traits were presented.

10 That is, if no voter had named him as arrogant, his mean evaluation outside Quebec would have increased by 42 per cent times 7.90. The effect is slightly lower in Quebec.

11 The effects are much smaller in Quebec.

12 In Quebec, Clark appears to have benefited from perceptions of trustworthiness, but not to have suffered from an image of weakness.

13 When we asked respondents whether the leaders' religious beliefs had influenced their vote, 19 per cent outside Quebec said "yes" and so did 6 per cent in Quebec. People were slightly more likely to say that they had been influenced if religion was either very important or not important at all in their lives. However, those who said they were influenced gave Day the same overall rating as those who said they were not influenced, and there was no difference in actual vote choice between the two groups. Outside Quebec, 36 per cent of those who said they were influenced by the leaders' religious beliefs voted for the Alliance; the percentage was 34 per cent among those who claim not to have been influenced. Multivariate analyses confirmed the lack of effect. These data seem to indicate that some voters may have voted Alliance because of Day's beliefs while others may have decided not to vote Alliance because they disagreed with his convictions, and the two effects more or less cancelled one other out. But we have more confidence in the "objective" test reported in the text than in results that are based on respondents' introspective assessments. We would not rule out the validity of some introspective questions (see Blais et al., 1998), but we are concerned that some people may not want to admit that they are affected by religious

considerations. Our verdict is, therefore, that Day's personal religious views did negatively affect his ratings.

14 The reference group is composed of those who somewhat agreed or somewhat disagreed.

15 Similarly, average ratings of Day remained the same among those who believed that the Bible is the word of God (55) and among those who disagreed (39) in both halves of the campaign.

16 The referent here is someone who felt neutral (that is, they gave the leader a rating of 50). We also performed separate analyses for Atlantic Canada, Ontario, and the West. There was no indication that leaders were systematically more—or less—important in one region than another.

17 We performed two tests. For the first, we created a *negative* dummy variable for each leader that equaled 1 when the respondent gave the leader a score below 50. If there was a negativity bias, any score below 50 would reduce the propensity to vote for the leader's party. For the second, we created a series of interactive variables (leader evaluation times negative). If there was a negativity bias, ratings below 50 would have more impact than positive ratings. However, neither set of variables had statistically significant effects when each was added to the multinomial logit estimations.

18 More precisely, the regressions allow us to estimate each respondent's probability of voting for each of the parties. The respondent is predicted to vote for the party with the highest probability.

19 This entails setting the leader evaluation coefficients to 0 and keeping all the other coefficients intact.

20 Our estimations suggested that the Alliance would have obtained five percentage points more if leader evaluations had had no effect, which implies that the Alliance lost 5 points (to the benefit of the Liberals and the Conservatives) because of Day's relative unpopularity. This estimate is biased, however, because it is based on post-election ratings, and Day's ratings (outside Quebec) were significantly lower (43) after the election than they were in the last week of the campaign (46), while Chrétien's were substantially higher (54) than they were in the last week of the campaign (51). Accordingly, we performed a second estimation substituting leader ratings in the last week of the campaign. Although this re-estimation was necessarily based on a small sample size, it is more realistic. The results suggest that the Liberals lost two points to the benefit of the Conservatives and the NDP because of leader evaluations. There was no net effect for the Alliance. The bottom line is that leader evaluations had a very small net impact on the vote.

21 In comparison, 23 per cent of those who gave McDonough a positive rating were intending to vote NDP. All of these numbers refer to the situation outside Quebec.

22 All of these before/after differences are statistically significant.

CHAPTER 13

Strategic Voting

Most accounts of voting behaviour work from the assumption that citizens vote for the party that they most prefer. And indeed the evidence suggests that the vast majority of voters really do vote for the party they most prefer. By the same token, there is evidence that, under some circumstances, a significant number of people will deliberately vote for a party that is not their first choice, because of strategic considerations. Any explanation of voting behaviour has to consider the possibility that in any election at least some proportion of the electorate might vote strategically. This chapter examines the evidence of strategic voting in the 2000 election.

The opportunities/incentives for strategic or tactical voting depend on the electoral rules (Cox, 1997). In a "first past the post" system like Canada's, some voters may vote for a party other than the one they really prefer because they do not want to "waste" their vote on a party that has little chance of winning in their constituency. Rather than voting for their preferred party, they vote for the party that is perceived to have the best chance of defeating the party that they dislike the most. This sort of strategic voting has been documented in previous Canadian elections, though on a smaller scale than often seems to be assumed (Blais and Nadeau, 1996; Blais et al., 2001e). The question in the 2000 election is *how much* strategic voting took place and, more importantly, whether it hurt the two weaker parties: the NDP and the Conservatives.

How did voters think the parties would do?

If a strategic voter is defined as a voter who does not vote for his/her preferred party because that party is perceived to have little chance of winning in his/her constituency, then the place to start is with perceptions of the local race. Just how did voters perceive the race in their constituency? We asked our survey respondents to estimate each party's chances of winning in their constituency, using a scale from 0 to 100. Zero meant no chance at all, while 100 meant certain victory.

Aggregate perceptions were broadly accurate (see Table 13.1).[1] The Liberals were perceived to be ahead in every region except the

Table 13.1   Perceptions of Parties' Chances of Winning

	Liberal	Alliance	Conservative	NDP	Bloc
Canada	39.2	23.6	14.7	12.6	–
Atlantic	40.2	12.1	30.1	17.6	–
Quebec	39.5	7.1	8.3	4.9	39.9
Ontario	49.3	20.2	16.6	13.9	–
West	26.6	44.2	13.4	15.7	–
Outside Quebec	39.1	29.0	16.8	15.1	–

Note: Cell entries represent the average standardized score on a 0 to 100 scale.

West where the Alliance was (correctly) viewed as the strongest party. Conservatives' prospects were viewed to be particularly bleak in Quebec, but were considered to be much better in Atlantic Canada. The NDP, meanwhile, was not seen as having much chance in any region of the country. For their part, Quebecers expected a close fight between the Liberals and the Bloc.

Interestingly, voters tended to overestimate the chances of the smaller parties and to underestimate those of the Liberals. The Liberals won 57 per cent of the seats, but their mean chances were perceived to be only 39 per cent. By contrast, the Conservatives and the NDP won only 4 per cent of the seats, but voters gave them almost a 15 per cent chance of winning, on average.[2]

This drives home an important point. Voters should expect a party that is traditionally weak in their constituency to have little chance of winning, but a party's perceived chances of winning are not just a function of objective factual information. On the contrary, there is a substantial amount of wishful thinking among those who identify with a party and this can lead them to overestimate its chances of winning (Uhlaner and Grofman, 1986). Perceptions are affected by both "objective" and "subjective" factors. This comes out clearly when voters' perceptions of each party's chances of winning are regressed on the party's actual vote share in 1997 in the respondent's constituency, on the one hand, and on whether or not the respondent identified with the party, on the other. Controls were included for the various social background characteristics that affected vote choice.

Both objective and subjective factors shaped voters' perceptions of the race (see panel A of Table 13.2). The more votes a party had obtained in the respondent's constituency in 1997, the better its chances of winning were perceived to be. Typically, a party's per-

Table 13.2 Determinants of Perceptions of Chances of Winning in the Local Constituency (OLS Regressions)

	Liberal	Alliance	Conservative	NDP	Bloc
A. All					
1997 Constituency vote	.79 (.05) [a]	.72 (.04) [a]	.28 (.04) [a]	.69 (.03) [a]	1.17 (.10) [a]
Party identification	7.70 (1.00) [a]	15.04 (1.18) [a]	6.83 (1.04) [a]	6.39 (1.15) [a]	9.49 (2.44) [a]
Constant	6.51 (2.55) [b]	1.81 (1.27)	14.26 (1.00) [a]	7.28 (.86) [a]	-5.13 (5.49)
N	2184	2184	2184	2184	516
Adjusted R^2	.32	.54	.23	.31	.29
B. Better informed					
1997 Constituency vote	.91 (.06) [a]	.88 (.06) [a]	.35 (.05) [a]	.83 (.04) [a]	1.54 (.14) [a]
Party identification	7.13 (1.43) [a]	12.54 (1.62) [a]	2.78 (1.33) [b]	-.08 (1.42)	6.13 (3.61) [c]
Constant	7.48 (3.71) [b]	-1.21 (1.86)	9.44 (1.43) [a]	3.21 (1.15) [a]	-8.62 (6.87)
N	1047	1047	1047	1047	225
Adjusted R^2	.45	.64	.25	.41	.40
C. Less informed					
1997 Constituency vote	.67 (.06) [a]	.53 (.05) [a]	.23 (.05) [a]	.54 (.05) [a]	.88 (.14) [a]
Party identification	8.18 (1.34) [a]	14.43 (1.67) [a]	12.47 (1.58) [a]	13.19 (1.73) [a]	12.30 (3.33) [a]
Constant	6.33 (3.42) [c]	6.98 (1.67) [a]	16.88 (1.38) [a]	10.34 (1.21) [a]	-3.07 (9.51)
N	1132	1132	1132	1132	288
Adjusted R^2	.21	.43	.22	.28	.21

a: significant $\alpha \leq .01$; b: significant $\alpha \leq .05$; c: significant $\alpha \leq .10$

Note: Cell entries are unstandardized regression coefficients and standard errors are in parentheses. The regressions also include socio-economic variables that are omitted from the table due to space constraints but are available from the authors.

ceived chances rose (fell) about 7 points for every 10 points higher (lower) its vote share had been in 1997. For instance, among those who did not identify with the Alliance, its perceived chances of winning were 9 per cent, on average, in a constituency where the Reform party had obtained 10 per cent in 1997.[3] In constituencies where the Reform party had received 20 per cent of the vote in 1997, this figure rose to 16 per cent, and where Reform had received 30 per cent of the vote, the Alliance's perceived chances increased to 23 per cent. There was one exception to this pattern, and this concerned the Conservatives. Perceptions of the Conservatives' chances of winning in a given constituency were more loosely connected to the actual outcome of the 1997 election.[4] Perhaps the collapse of the Conservatives in 1993 meant that many voters just did not know how strong or weak the party was in their constituency. Still, voters did know that the party was doing better in Atlantic Canada and much worse in Quebec (Table 13.1).

Voters' perceptions were influenced also by their partisan orientations. Everything else being equal, those who identified with a party gave their party a higher chance of winning in their constituency. The typical bias in favour of their own party's winning was of the order of 8 points. Alliance partisans exhibited the highest level of wishful thinking: in a typical constituency where Reform had obtained 20 per cent of the vote in 1997, Alliance identifiers gave the party a 31 per cent chance of winning, on average, compared to 16 per cent among other voters. It could be that partisans of the party that has gained the most since the previous election are the most susceptible to wishful thinking. Whatever the case, it seems that Alliance identifiers were expecting to win about 30 per cent of the constituencies in Ontario, and many of them must have been deeply disappointed with the actual outcome of the election. And it is entirely possible that this disappointment could have been one important reason why many of them subsequently raised questions about Stockwell Day's leadership.

As we would expect, the better-informed were less susceptible to wishful thinking, especially in the case of the NDP and the Conservatives (see Panels B and C of Table 13.2).[5] The better-informed were more likely to have been aware of the results of the 1997 election in their constituency, and so they were less swayed by their partisan attachments. For every party, the actual vote obtained by the party in 1997 in the respondent's constituency had a greater impact on the perceptions of the better-informed. Conversely, party identification exerted a greater influence on the less-informed. Take perceptions of the Conservatives' chances, for example. The coefficient for the 1997 vote is larger among the better-informed (.35) than among the less-informed (.23). The reverse holds for party identification: the party identification coefficient is much smaller among the former (2.78) than among the latter (12.47).

Did strategic voting hurt the weaker parties?

The real question, though, is whether the perception that a party had little chance of winning in a constituency induced some voters to vote for a party other than the one they preferred the most, and whether this hurt the less competitive parties. To address this question, we need a measure of voters' preferences among the parties. These preferences are assumed to be reflected in their overall evaluations of the parties, the leaders, and the local candidates, as well as in their party identification (Blais et al., 2001e).[6] Overall evaluations of the parties and leaders were measured on a 0 to 100 scale where 100 meant that respondents really liked the party or leader and 0 meant that they really disliked them. Party identification was a dummy variable that took the value of 1 if respondents thought of themselves as Liberal, Alliance, Conservative, NDP, or Bloc supporters. Feelings towards local candidates was also a dummy variable that equaled 1 if respondents indicated that they particularly liked a local candidate.

Perceptions of the race were tapped through the "no chance" variables. These indicate the extent to which a party was perceived to be *trailing* in a constituency. "No chance" equaled 0 if a party was perceived to be ahead or tied for first place. If the party was perceived to be behind, it equaled the distance between the chances of the top contender and those of the party. The higher the value, the more hopeless the party's perceived chances, and the greater the predicted likelihood of a shift away from the party.

If strategic considerations really matter, vote choice should depend not only on preferences but also on whether the voter thinks that a given party has any chance of winning in his/her constituency. We tested this hypothesis by relating vote choice outside Quebec to the four dimensions of preference (evaluations of parties, leaders, local candidates, and party identification) and to perceptions of the race (as represented by the "no chance" variable),

Table 13.3   The Impact of Perceptions of Chances of Winning on Vote Choice Outside Quebec (Multinomial Probit, Liberal Coefficients Normalized to Zero)

	Choice specific	Alliance/ Liberal	Conservative/ Liberal	NDP/ Liberal
Party identification	.96 (.14) [a]			
Feelings about local candidates	1.51 (.17) [a]			
Leader evaluations	3.22 (.33) [a]			
Party evaluations	3.76 (.39) [a]			
NO CHANCE	-.67 (.23) [a]			
Atlantic		-.40 (.53)	.33 (.43)	.35 (.34)
West		-.34 (.27)	-.56 (.33)[c]	.14 (.28)
Constant		.91 (.18)[a]	-.35 (.24)	.01 (.20)
σ (Liberals, Conservatives)	-.94 (.42)			
σ (Alliance, NDP)	.40 (.16)			
σ (Conservatives, NDP)	-.07 (.37)			
N	1352			
Log likelihood	-384.93			
% Correctly predicted	85			

a: significant $\alpha \leq .01$; b: significant $\alpha \leq .05$; c: significant $\alpha \leq .10$

Note: Cell entries are unstandardized regression coefficients and standard errors are in parentheses.

as well as to region. Predictably, vote choice was highly dependent on whether or not voters identified with one of the parties and on how they felt about the parties, their leaders, and their local candidates (see Table 13.3).

The question is whether perceptions of the race had an additional independent effect, once all these dimensions of preferences are taken into account. Table 13.3 shows that indeed respondents were less likely to support a party if they thought that the party had little chance of winning in his/her constituency. It can be seen, however, that perceptions of the race had a much smaller impact than preferences (the coefficient of "leader evaluations," for instance, is five times larger than that of "no chance").

Based on these results, we estimated the proportion of voters who cast a strategic vote. These are voters who would have voted differently had they not thought that their preferred party had little chance of winning in their constituency. We determined which party each respondent was predicted to support based first both on their preferences and on their perceptions of the race, and then on their preferences alone (that is, when the "no chance" coefficient was set to 0 and all other coefficients were left the same). When the two predictions diverged, this implied that perceptions of the race were decisive, in the sense that respondents would have voted differently if they had not considered the various parties' chances.

According to these estimations, 3 per cent of voters outside Quebec cast a strategic vote for a party that was not the one that they most preferred. Typically, these strategic voters were people who preferred the Conservatives or the NDP, but decided to vote for the Liberals or the Alliance. So, there was a certain amount of strategic voting, and this hurt the smaller parties to the benefit of the stronger ones. All in all, almost one voter in 10 whose first choice was the Conservatives or the NDP decided to vote for another party because of strategic considerations. If no strategic considerations had been in play, the NDP would have obtained 12 per cent of the vote outside Quebec, instead of 11 per cent, and the Conservatives would have obtained 16 per cent, instead of 15 per cent. The same analysis was replicated for vote choice in Quebec. In this case, the results are even more clear-cut: the "no chance" variable turned out to be insignificant (findings not shown). In Quebec, there was no evidence at all of strategic voting.

Discussion

There was some strategic voting in the 2000 election, at least outside Quebec. A number of voters who preferred the NDP or the Conservatives decided to vote for their second-choice party because they believed that their first choice was not likely to win the race. However, these strategic voters were few in number and, consequently, their impact on the outcome of the election was quite small. If there had been no strategic voting, the NDP and the Conservatives each would have seen their vote share increase by just one percentage point. This is not good news for either party. The great majority of Canadians voted for the party they liked the most (or disliked the least). The problem confronting the Conservatives and the NDP was simple: they were the first choice of few people.

Notes

1 We use standardized scores: each party's score is divided by the total scores given to the four (five in Quebec) parties, and multiplied by 100.

2 Perceptions of the race moved somewhat during the campaign. The greatest change concerned the Alliance. Its average chances were perceived to be 27 per cent at the beginning of the campaign and 21 per cent at the end.

3 The perceived chances were 4 points higher in the West, an indication that voters were aware that this was the region where the party was making the greatest gains. These numbers apply to our reference category (an urban woman, not married, under 55 ...), but perceptions did not vary much across social groups, once party identification was taken into account.

4 While the coefficient for the 1997 vote (.28) was highly significant for the Conservatives' chances, it was much weaker than it was for the other parties.

5 The best-informed were able to name the Premier of their province, the federal Minister of Finance, the Prime Minister at the time of the Free Trade Agreement with the United States, and the capital of the United States.

6 Another approach would have been to use our seven blocs of variables as proxies for preferences and to add perceptions of the race as the eighth bloc. We prefer to rely on more direct measures of preferences.

Conclusion

Our goal in this book has been to explain why Canadians voted the way they did in the 2000 election, and why some parties were more successful than others. To that end, we adopted quite deliberately a broad analytical framework, one that would help us to sort out how much impact a variety of factors had on the vote choice of individual voters and on the final outcome of the election. Broad analytic frameworks may be cumbersome, but their strength is that they hold open the possibility that vote choice can be affected by so many things. What, then, has been learned about Canadian voting behaviour by adopting this approach? And, at the end of the day, do the results of this analysis reinforce or challenge conventional wisdom?

There are two major sources of conventional wisdom about what kinds of considerations are most important to citizens making their vote decisions: those informed by the cumulative studies of voting behaviour in advanced industrial states, and those that come from the systematic study of Canadian voting behaviour, a tradition that goes back to 1965 (see Gidengil, 1992). The main findings from this investigation converge with some, but they challenge other, conventional wisdoms.

The analytical framework identified eight blocs of factors that could potentially affect vote choice: socio-demographic characteristics, broad values and beliefs, partisan loyalties, economic perceptions, issue opinions, evaluations of government performance, feelings towards the leaders, and strategic considerations.

Our findings indicate that, of these eight blocs, four were quite important to Canadians' vote choices in the 2000 election: socio-demographic characteristics, values and beliefs, party attachment, and leader evaluations. Each one of these blocs of variables accounted for at least an additional 10 percentage points in the variance in vote choice. Economic perceptions, issue opinions, evaluations of government performance, and strategic considerations proved to be much less important.

First, consider the case of socio-demographic characteristics. The conventional wisdom is that socio-demographic factors are relatively unimportant determinants of vote choice. Franklin and colleagues (1992) tracked the relationship between social structure and partisan preferences over 14 countries from the 1960s to the 1980s and found a consistent decline in the impact of socio-demographic characteristics on vote choice. Dalton's (1996: 329) review essay on political cleavages refers to Franklin's conclusion as the new conventional wisdom of comparative electoral research. LeDuc (1984: 467) similarly argues that socio-demographic variables explain only 11 per cent of the variance in vote choice and that, consequently, attention should focus on more short-term factors.

Our empirical findings are similar to LeDuc's but our interpretation is different and so on this matter, we stand against conventional wisdom. Like LeDuc, we find that socio-demographic characteristics account for "only" 12 per cent of vote choice outside Quebec. Explaining 10 or 12 per cent of the variance is no small achievement, as our bloc-recursive approach has shown. A fundamental aspect of the 2000 election would be missed if we failed to acknowledge the importance of the huge regional divide to the vote, or if we ignored the appeal of the Liberals to Catholics and Canadians of non-European origin, of the Alliance to rural men, and of the NDP among those with no religion. Some of these patterns, especially those related to region and religion, are long- standing ones; they are an integral ingredient of Canadian political life. Others, such as the gender gap, are more recent.

The impact of social cleavages on vote choice may well have declined in most advanced industrial states between the 1960s and the 1980s. Whether the trend has continued along this same trajectory is not clear. What is clear is that there is no such pattern in Canada. Region and religion remain as crucial now as they once were. The strong support enjoyed by the Liberals among Catholics and Canadians of non-European origin is also a remarkably consistent fault line. It is the sustained impact of these social cleavages on structuring the vote that help to make sense of the 2000 and preceding elections. Certainly, social cleavages are not entirely frozen. Union membership, for example, seems to have become a less important determinant of vote choice. By the same token, gender has now become more important. The Canadian case, then, contradicts the conventional wisdom that social cleavages are inexorably eroding.

The second important bloc of considerations concerns values and beliefs. Here, the conventional wisdom is that Canadian elections are based on brokerage politics, in which styles and leaders predominate. Accounts of Canadian voting behaviour, such as those in the *Absent Mandate* tradition, do not examine the role of values in vote choice. The implicit assumption is that battles about ideas matter little to the outcomes of Canadian elections and that individual vote decisions are disconnected from values. The findings for the 2000 election, however, emphatically challenge that conventional wisdom. Core values and beliefs had a substantial impact on vote choice, and the implication of these findings is that ideas and world views played a major role in the 2000 election.

Values, of course, are only one part of the story; other factors also contributed to citizens' vote choice. Still, for many voters, the vote does express deep beliefs concerning the proper role of the market, the state, the family, and of religion in society. Our results indicate that the main ideological divide, in Canada as elsewhere, concerns orientations towards markets. Those who believe in the virtue of the market tend to support right-wing parties, and those who are more sceptical about market values, tend to vote for center or left-wing parties. Canadian elections do not take place in an ideological vacuum, they engage voters' competing world views. Like elections in the United States and Europe (Scarbrough, 1984), Canadian elections are ideological battlegrounds. In this respect, there is no evidence of Canadian exceptionalism.

Third, there is the matter of partisan loyalties. Conventional wisdom maintains that partisan attachments are weak in Canada and that the country is peopled by voters who are "flexible partisans;" these are voters who are always willing to consider all the options and who will shift from one party to another depending on the circumstances. Clarke and colleagues (Clarke et al., 1996: 55), estimate that flexible partisans constitute somewhere between three-fifths and two-thirds of the entire Canadian electorate. Some voters undoubtedly qualify as "flexible partisans". But our view is that there is an important core of "not so flexible" partisans in Canada as elsewhere. The proportion of the Canadian electorate that qualifies as partisan may be slightly smaller than in other countries, but it forms a crucial component of the electorate that deserves close attention.

The point turns on a combination of methodological and conceptual questions. As explained in Chapter 8, much depends on the question that is used to measure party identification and on how responses to that question are treated. We set a stricter standard and consider as partisans only those respondents who said they think of themselves as Liberals and who feel very or fairly strongly Liberal. Following that approach reduces the estimated number of partisans to around 50 per cent of the electorate. Significantly, these partisans are not completely inflexible: about 15 per cent of them did not vote for "their" party in the 2000 election. But they do lean heavily in one direction.

The volatility of the vote in Canadian elections is viewed often as a consequence of weak party attachments. Evidence of such volatility can be found in such instances as the 1993 election, which saw the Conservative vote share plummet from 43 per cent (in 1988) to 16 per cent. But that raises the question: Is the Canadian electorate more volatile than its counterparts in other advanced industrial states? The comparative evidence (Dalton et al., 1984: 10) indicates that Canada rates slightly above average with respect to vote volatility; party attachments are slightly weaker in Canada. Other evidence points to the same conclusion. A smaller percentage of the Canadian electorate say they think of themselves as "close to" a party than is the case for their British or American counterparts (Blais et al., 2001a).

These findings correspond to the conventional view that there are fewer "true" partisans in Canada than in Britain or the United States. But our point is a rather different one: a substantial number of Canadians do have a feeling of attachment to a particular party and these Canadian partisans are no more fickle than their American or British counterparts. These partisan attachments, we argue, need to be considered in any account of the more stable aspects of Canadian electoral politics. The volatility of the vote may be above average in Canada but an important element of stability is provided by the Liberal party, the dominant party in Canadian politics. In the post-war period, it has won a plurality of the vote in 14 elections out of 18, leading Johnston (2001: 11) to observe that, "the Liberal party may not be indispensable, but it is, in effect, irreplaceable."

The key to Liberal dominance is partisanship, or more particularly the distribution of partisan orientations throughout the electorate: the simple and impressive reality is that of those Canadians who identify with a party a full half think of themselves as Liberals. This has very real consequences. One is that the Liberals go into an election with a significant head start. The Liberals begin an election campaign knowing that they can count on the votes of a crucial core of loyal supporters, and that core is significantly larger than the reservoir of loyal support available to any of the other parties. As Johnston (2001: 11) puts it, "the deck is stacked in favour of the Liberal party."

Concluding that a significant number of people are voting Liberal because they think of themselves as Liberals raises the question of *why* the Liberals are able to retain the loyalty of so many Canadians. In the case of these staunch partisans, what needs to be explained is not so much their vote, but why they identify with their chosen party. One strength of our explanatory framework is that it enables us to shed some light on this question. Consider, once again, the evidence presented in Appendix C.1. Working back across the columns in Appendix C.1 from party identification (column 1-3), it becomes clear who is the most likely to be a Liberal partisan outside Quebec. The answer is: Catholics, people of non-European ancestry, and people whose first language is other than English or French. The fact that the impact of these socio-demographic factors shrink when party identification is taken into account indicates a causal connection between these social-background characteristics and party identification.

The ethno-linguistic basis of Liberal partisanship might be explained by pointing to such Liberal initiatives as official multi-culturalism and immigration policy. Far more difficult to explain is the connection between religious denomination, Catholic, and Liberal partisanship. One possibility is that religious denomination is a proxy for fundamental beliefs and values. But there is no empir-ical support for that hypothesis. The evidence in Appendix C.1 clearly demonstrates that values and beliefs do not mediate the relationship between religious affiliation and party identification. This does not mean that values and beliefs provide no help in explaining party identification. They clearly do. There is a strong link between social conservatism and support for free enterprise, on the one hand, and identifying with the Alliance, on the other. Conversely, socially liberal social views and scepticism about the virtues of free enterprise also help to explain why people identify with the Liberals. The point, though, is that this does not provide any additional explanatory leverage to help us understand the roots of the religious divide.

Precisely why the Liberals are so much more successful than other parties in nurturing a sense of partisan attachment certainly requires a more complete explanation, but what we can conclude is that the advantage of Liberals is so substantial that their chances of winning a federal election are huge unless some powerful overriding short-term factor, or set of factors, goes clearly against them. There was no such factor at work in 2000.

The fourth block of variables that make a substantial contribution to Canadians' vote choice in 2000 concerns political leaders. In this instance, our findings reinforce conventional wisdom. Canadians pay more attention to party leaders than do voters from most other countries and for good reason. The personal power of the Canadian Prime Minister is very substantial indeed (Savoie, 1999; Simpson, 2001). Unlike many other countries where governments either rest on the unsteady foundations of coalitions or face the uncertainty of a minority situation, the party of the Canadian Prime Minister usually enjoys full control over Parliament, and that control bestows huge personal power upon the leader of the party in government. Canadians seem to understand this very well.

According to our estimations, about one voter out of five would have voted differently were it not for how they felt about the leaders. Leader evaluations are a crucial element of the vote decision in Canada, probably more so than in many other countries. The fact that leader evaluations are extremely important to individual vote choice calculations does not mean that leaders will always be a decisive factor in the final outcome of the election. Indeed, this is precisely the case in the 2000 election. No single leader emerged as clearly more, or clearly less, popular than any of the others, and so the net effect of the leadership factor on the parties' vote shares was minimal.

Socio-demographic factors, values and beliefs, partisanship, and party leaders all had a substantial impact on individual vote choice in 2000, although some of those effects do not correspond to conventional wisdom. What about the effects of the other factors that were under consideration?

Perhaps the single most counter-intuitive finding to emerge from this entire study concerns economic perceptions. As Chapter 9 noted, it has become common to think that the fate of incumbent governments hinges on the state of the economy. Our results challenge that conventional wisdom; it turns out that economic perceptions mattered very little to the outcome of the 2000 election. Furthermore, this finding is not so different from a similar analysis of the 1997 election. In 1997, economic perceptions contributed a meagre two percentage points in the Liberal vote variance (Nevitte et al., 2000).

One reason why economic perceptions were not that decisive in the vote decision is that many Canadians do not assign credit, or blame, to the government for good or bad economic times. For those who think the government is not responsible for the ups and downs of the economy, there is no reason to reward or punish the government for its "economic performance." Furthermore, economic perceptions are coloured by partisan attachments. Liberal partisans, in particular, were more likely to see the economy in rosy terms.

On balance, the evidence does not point to the conclusion that the economy was the main cause of the Liberal victory in 2000. Economic forecasting models would have predicted an easy Gore victory in the 2000 American presidential election. They were well off the mark and provide a powerful reminder of the pitfalls of making simple connections between economic conditions and electoral outcomes. By the same token, there are also reasons to be cautious about rushing too quickly to the conclusion that the economy does not matter. It seems to us indisputable that governments generally do better in good times than in bad times. Our point is rather that this is only a general pattern. There are many exceptions to the pattern, and the economy, like all factors, plays only at the margin.

One possibility is that individual economic perceptions matter more when there is an economic downturn. The asymmetric hypothesis that, at the individual level, voters punish the government for bad economic times, but do not reward it for good times, was both tested and rejected. It is possible that the interactions between the state of the aggregate economy and individual economic perceptions are more complex. Analyses pooling data from different elections and different economic contexts are needed to explore this important question.

Our findings do converge with conventional wisdom evinced in the Canadian voting literature (see, especially, *Absent Mandate*) by attributing little effect to issues as such. As Clarke and his colleagues (1996: 143) have argued, elections are seldom referendums on public policies. There is contemporary evidence, of course, that elections *can* be fought on easy issues such as free trade with the US (Johnston et al., 1992). But even if issues typically matter little, general ideological orientations are important. It should also be pointed out that the Liberal position on what Canadians thought was the "most important" issue of the campaign—public health care—was entirely in line with majority public opinion. Even though a substantial minority of Canadians expressed support for a dose of privatization, public opinion was clearly tilted in favour of maintaining the existing system.

The retrospective model of voting supposes that individual vote choices reflect citizens' evaluations of the performance of the incumbent government. Our analysis yields evidence indicating that these evaluations mattered relatively little. And our findings are similar to those obtained in the 1997 election. It might be that the retrospective model applies best in those rare countries (basically the United States) with a two-party system in which there is a clear government party and opposition party. Most Canadians, it would seem, were voting neither for nor against the Liberal government; they were supporting the party that they liked best.

Finally, our analyses indicate that there was little strategic voting in the 2000 election. According to our estimates, only 3 per cent of the voters voted for a party that was not their most preferred because they did not want to waste their vote for a party that had no chance of winning in their constituency. This estimate corresponds almost precisely to that found in the 1997 election (Blais et al., 2001e). Some voters do cast a strategic vote but there are few of them even in a "first past the post" system that is assumed to induce such strategic considerations.

Why is there so little strategic voting? Blais (forthcoming) suggests two reasons. First, many voters have a strong preference for one party over all others and thus are reluctant to rally to another. Second, many supporters of weak parties overestimate their party's chances of winning and in so doing they are less likely to reckon that their vote will be wasted.

During the course of this study we have raised a variety of questions about the 2000 federal election. Having sketched out the broad lines of our overall findings, we can conclude by supplying direct answers to those questions.

Q1: **Why was turnout so low? Was it because this election happened to be a "boring" one or is there a deeper structural change going on?**

Answer: The basic source of declining turnout is structural, not conjunctural. Turnout did not decrease among the cohorts born before 1970, who apparently did not find the 2000 election more boring than previous ones. And voters did not feel systematically more negative about the parties than in previous elections.

Q2: Is turnout decline the result of generational replacement? Is it taking place mainly among the youngest generation?

Answer: Yes, and yes. Turnout declined only among the youngest generation. If there had been no generational replacement between 1988 and 2000, turnout would have been 71 per cent instead of 61 per cent.

Q3: What attitudes and beliefs are most strongly correlated with the decision not to vote?

Answer: First and foremost the overall level of political interest and information. The younger generation is much less interested and informed about politics, and that is the main reason for its lower turnout. Cynicism is *not* the main source of declining turnout. Cynicism has declined slightly over the last 10 years and the younger generation is slightly *less* cynical than the other generations.

Q4: What impact did the campaign have on the overall evolution of vote intentions? Which campaign events mattered?

Answer: The campaign event that mattered most was the English debate, which Joe Clark won. It gave the Conservatives a three-point boost that allowed the party to keep its official status in the House of Commons. These gains were made at the expense of the Liberals. No other campaign event seems to have had a lasting impact on the vote. And we found no evidence that the campaign changed the considerations underlying vote choice.

Q5: What happened to the Alliance? How much support did it lose during the campaign and why?

Answer: Support for the Alliance remained relatively stable throughout the campaign. The party gained some ground at the very beginning of the campaign. Those gains are likely the public opinion dividend resulting from the attention paid by the media to the Alliance leadership race. But those gains dissipated in early November. The Alliance suffered slightly from allegations of racism and media reporting on Day's religious beliefs, around November 15, but these effects also disappeared by Election Day.

Q6: Among which groups did the parties do best? Which socio-demographic characteristics were more strongly related to vote choice?

Answer: The most important lines of electoral cleavage were: region, religion, ethnicity, gender, community type (urban/rural), and language (in Quebec). The two groups constituting the core of Liberal support are the Catholics and Canadians of non-European origin. Support for the Alliance was concentrated among rural Protestant men of Northern European origin.

Q7: Did vote choice reflect deep values and beliefs? Which ones mattered and which ones did not?

Answer: Yes, vote choice reflected values and beliefs, although it was also affected by other considerations. Outside Quebec, the most important value dimension was voters' views about the free enterprise system. Those most supportive of the free enterprise system were inclined to vote Alliance or Conservative, while those more sceptical about the virtues of free enterprise were prone to vote Liberal or NDP. These market orientations, however, do not explain the regional divide. Within Quebec, as in 1997, the basic cleavage was between the sovereignists and the federalists. Unlike the 1997 election, views about Quebec in the rest of the country did not have any impact in 2000.

Q8: What fraction of the electorate can be construed as partisans, who are strongly inclined to vote for the same party at every election? Do the Liberals have many more partisans than the other parties? Does this "explain" the Liberal victory?

Answer: About half of the electorate can be construed as partisan. About half of these partisans are Liberals. The fact that the Liberals have a strong lead among partisans provides them with a huge advantage. This goes a considerable distance towards explaining the Liberal victory.

Q9: Did Canadians perceive the economy, both the national economy and their own financial situation, in rosy terms? Does this "explain" the Liberal victory?

Answer: Economic perceptions were moderately positive at the time of the election. But these economic perceptions had little independent effect on vote choice, once general predispositions are taken into account. At the aggregate level, it makes sense to suppose that the Liberals were helped somewhat by the decline in the unemployment rate, though the fact that Liberal support actually declined in Alberta makes us reluctant to give too much credit to the economy. All in all, the economy does not appear to have been a crucial factor in the Liberal victory.

Q10: What were Canadians' positions on the major issues of the day? How did issue opinions relate to vote choice?

Answer: Canadians were quite divided on most of the issues that were debated in the election. The principal exception was abortion: the pro-choice position had far more supporters than the pro-life one. On balance, issue opinions had a very modest effect on vote choice. Underlying values mattered more.

Q11: How satisfied were voters with what the Liberal government had done over the previous three years? Does this explain the Liberal victory?

Answer: On the three issues that mattered most—health, taxes, and corruption—there was widespread public dissatisfaction. The Liberals won despite that dissatisfaction for a combination of three reasons: First, the dissatisfied split their votes among many parties. Second, the Liberals had a substantial edge among non-partisans. Third, discontent was not too deep. The Liberal victory is more aptly interpreted as a reflection of the absence of deep dissatisfaction rather than as the presence of satisfaction.

Q12: How were the party leaders perceived? Did these perceptions merely reflect voters' partisan and ideological orientations or were they also affected by the leaders' personal traits?

Answer: By Election Day, all leaders were about equally popular; their average rating was close to the neutral point. Many voters perceived Chrétien to be "arrogant" and Day to have "new ideas" but also to be "extreme." Leaders' personal traits were at least as important as partisan orientations in shaping overall evaluations of the leaders.

Q13: How much did party leaders matter for vote choice? For how many voters were the leaders a decisive consideration? How much net impact did the leaders have on the final outcome of the election?

Answer: Leaders were quite important in the vote decision; they were a decisive consideration for about one voter out of five, but they were less important in Quebec than elsewhere. Because all the leaders were about equally popular, the net impact of these leadership evaluations on the outcome of the election turned out to be minimal.

Q14: Was Stockwell Day particularly unpopular? Was he the main reason for the Alliance's lack of success in Ontario? Did the voters reject him because of his personal religious beliefs?

Answer: Day was not particularly unpopular. Among non-partisans, Day was as popular as Chrétien, and he was more popular than Manning in 1997. The Alliance's lack of success cannot be attributed primarily to the leader. Day's religious beliefs were a source of concern for some Canadians, however, and this contributed to making him a less appealing leader.

Q15: Did the "weak" parties, the Conservatives and the NDP, fail to get significant support because they were the first choice of few voters or because many voters did not want to waste their vote on parties that had no chance of winning?

Answer: Mostly the former. There was some strategic voting and this was mostly to the benefit of the Liberals and the Alliance. An overwhelming majority of Canadians, however, voted for the party they liked most. The Conservatives and the NDP were the first choice of few people.

Q16: Why did the Alliance fail to make substantial progress in Ontario?

Answer: Perhaps the question should be rephrased: Why was the Alliance so strong in the West and so weak in Ontario, and the reverse for the Liberals? The focus should be on comparing the two regions and the two parties. We can start by dismissing two factors. The Liberals were not stronger in Ontario because the economy was stronger in that province. And the Alliance was not stronger in the West because there is more support for right-wing positions in that region (there is only a little more support). The Alliance did better in the West because it could build on a sense of regional alienation and because the Liberals have a smaller core of partisans.

The 2000 election has confirmed the dominance of the Liberal Party. The Liberals easily won the election even though there was widespread dissatisfaction on health care, even though many Canadians had come to perceive Jean Chrétien as arrogant, even though the party lost some ground after the English debate. It is difficult to see how the Liberals could fail to win a plurality of the vote in the next few elections.

The Liberals, of course, won "only" 41 per cent of the vote, and it is only because of the "first past the post" system that they were able to win a majority of seats. But their lead over their main opponent was a comfortable 15 percentage point on Election Day, and typically over 30 points between 1997 and 2000. Getting 40 per cent of the vote in a five-party system is enough to be dominant. And the CES survey indicates that if one of the opposition parties were to disappear many of its supporters would rally to the Liberals rather than to another opposition party.

The old party system was shattered in 1993, with the surge of two new parties, the Bloc Québécois and the Reform party. The results of the 2000 election confirm that the Bloc Québécois is the logical shelter of those Quebecers who support Quebec sovereignty. The party receded slightly, relative to the Liberals, in 2000, in part because support for sovereignty slightly declined. But the Bloc remains the only serious contender with the Liberals in Quebec. It represents a solid bloc of voters, who had no voice at the federal level before 1993, and its fate hinges on the flux in the sovereignist movement. Whether the Bloc will endure or not depends primarily on what will happen in Quebec provincial politics, a reminder that federal and provincial party politics affect each other.

Then, there is the Reform party, and its successor, the Alliance. Its situation can be characterized as unsteady. On the positive side, the party has continued to make some progress, increasing its vote share by six points. On the negative side, the Alliance failed to make a substantial inroad in Ontario and the party is the second choice of very few Canadians.

The big question, of course, is whether there is room for two right-wing parties in Canada, and, if there is none, which of the two parties, the Alliance and the Conservatives, is better positioned to survive.

Consider the number of parties. The standard view is that the plurality rule should produce a two-party system (Duverger, 1951). Cox (1997) specifies, however, that this equilibrium should be achieved at the constituency level: there should be two parties running in each constituency, but they need not be the same two parties in each and every constituency across the country. In Canada, we typically have three or four candidates with at least 5 per cent of the vote in the constituencies. The Duverger law does not seem to hold. Is Canada an exceptional case? It does not look so. In Britain, there are usually three candidates with at least 5 per cent of the vote in a constituency. The idea that there is room for only two parties in a plurality system should be rejected. The point remains, however, that the plurality system is biased against small parties and that it is more difficult for small parties to survive in such a system.

In the absence of merger or electoral coalition, which of these two parties is least likely to survive? Different indicators point in different directions. The Alliance/Reform has had more votes and seats than the Conservatives for three successive elections and it could more easily retain a small core of seats because its support is more regionally concentrated. The two parties are tied in terms of growth potential: outside Quebec, the two parties are the first or second choice of about 40 per cent of the electorate—a limited growth potential, it should be stressed. The Conservatives have the advantage of resilience: they have been there for a long time, they appear willing to be patient. The Alliance, because of its young age, is more prone to ideological in-fighting. The whole saga of the leadership issue reminds us that the party is still fragile.

So it is not clear which of the two parties is less likely to disappear, leaving aside a merger or an electoral coalition. A lot depends, in fact, on what the parties themselves will do and, in particular, on who will lead them. This is particularly important for the Alliance, the youngest of the two parties. Many Canadians perceive the party to be too extreme and the challenge for the party is whether that perception can be changed.

Then there is the possibility of a merger. At first sight, this is an appealing option. Together, the Alliance and the Conservatives had almost as many votes as the Liberals. The Liberals seem to win because the right is divided. The CES data show that things are far from that simple. Alliance and Conservative voters share a general positive orientation towards the market, but they diverge on many issues, especially social ones, where Conservative voters are much closer to the Liberals (Blais et al., 2002). This is why the most frequent second choice of Conservative voters is the Liberal Party, not the Alliance. It cannot be taken for granted that present Conservative supporters would rally to the new party, after an eventual merger of the Alliance and the Conservatives. A lot would depend on how far to the right the new party would stand, but it is fair to assume that some Conservative supporters would prefer to vote Liberal or abstain.

Another option is an electoral coalition, under which the Alliance and the Conservatives would agree on fielding only one candidate per constituency. Under such a scenario, the Conservatives would not have candidates in the West and the Alliance would not run in Atlantic Canada. It is not clear however whether this would really help the Alliance to win more seats in the West or the Conservatives in Atlantic Canada. And the moot point would be Ontario. Dividing up the province between constituencies with an Alliance candidate and those with a Conservative one would be an extraordinarily delicate exercise. And even if it could be done, there is no guarantee that Conservative supporters would be willing to rally to the Alliance. And, finally, would the electoral coalition prevent the two party leaders from attacking each other during the campaign? As can be seen, there is no easy solution on the horizon.

What about the NDP? For a third successive election, the party has reveived less votes than each of the two right-wing parties. Clearly, the party is treated by the media as a minor actor. Does this mean that there is no future for a centre-left party in Canada? We do not think so. We have seen, in particular, that there is about a quarter of the Canadian population that is highly sceptical about the virtues of free enterprise. The challenge for the party is to convince Canadians that it can renew its approaches to fit the new environment of the 21st century. A formidable task, but not an insurmoutable one.

Meanwhile, under the existing electoral system, the Liberals seem poised to maintain their dominance of Canadian electoral politics. And turnout is likely to get even lower.

Appendices

Appendix A: Multinomial Estimations of Vote Choice Outside Quebec

A.1 Multinomial Estimation of Alliance versus Liberal Vote Choice Outside Quebec

	1	1-2	1-3	1-4	1-5	1-6	1-7
1. Socio-demographics							
Atlantic	-.74 [b]	-.99 [a]	-.94 [b]	-.95 [b]	-1.09 [a]	-.98 [b]	-1.08
West	1.27 [a]	.84 [a]	.38	.37	.25	.26	.36
Catholic	-.78 [a]	-.83 [a]	-.69 [a]	-.67 [a]	-.58 [b]	-.46	-.39
Non-religious	-.63 [a]	-.39	-.47	-.44	-.36	-.18	-.74
North European	.54 [a]	.41	.52	.57	.56	.61	.53
Non-European	-1.67 [a]	-1.62 [a]	-1.16 [b]	-1.13 [b]	-1.04 [b]	-.99 [b]	-.72
Male	.54 [a]	.37 [b]	.10	.12	.08	.01	-.20
Other language	-.60 [a]	-.81 [a]	-.63	-.63	-.58	-.54	-.74
Married	.36 [b]	.17	.21	.22	.17	.02	.25
Below high school	-.04	-.30	-.04	-.09	-.09	-.01	-.47
Rural	.61 [a]	.51 [b]	.29	.28	.29	.22	.79 [b]
2. Values and beliefs							
Social conservatism		.67 [a]	.37 [b]	.32	.21	.17	.10
Free enterprise		.91 [a]	.59	.65 [b]	.61	.71 [b]	-.44
Racial minorities		-.53 [a]	-.58 [b]	-.53 [b]	-.49 [b]	-.49 [b]	-.24
Feminism		-.64 [a]	-.46 [a]	-.48 [a]	-.47 [a]	-.48 [b]	-.43
Religiosity		.06	.12	.12	.19	.19	-.04
Regional alienation		.69 [a]	.46	.42	.41	.10	.18
Cynicism		.89 [a]	.53	.53	.43	.10	.37
3. Party identification							
Liberal			-2.18 [a]	-2.18 [a]	-2.09 [a]	-2.13 [a]	-1.55 [a]
Alliance			26.52 [a]	26.52 [a]	26.31 [a]	26.18 [a]	26.39 [a]
Conservative			1.25 [a]	1.26 [a]	1.20 [a]	1.12 [a]	1.70 [a]
New Democrat			-1.52 [b]	-1.56 [b]	-1.51 [b]	-1.56 [b]	-1.46
4. Economic perceptions							
Personal past				-.31 [b]	-.25	-.14	-.23
5. Issues							
Federal powers					-.48 [a]	-.37 [b]	-.16
Public health					-.42 [a]	-.48 [a]	-.38
Gun control					-.08	-.06	.04
Direct democracy					.24	.30	.20
6. Liberal performance							
Environment						.12	.44
Health						-.38	-.43
Taxes						-.73 [a]	-.38
Corruption						-.46 [b]	.00
Early call						1.31 [a]	.76
7. Leader evaluation							
Chrétien							-3.77 [a]
Day							6.43 [a]
Clark							-.60
McDonough							-.11
Constant	-.93 [a]	-.61 [b]	-.17	-.15	-.11	-.57	-.27
Pseudo R[2]	.12	.22	.46	.46	.48	.50	.65
Log likelihood	-1412.54	-1189.37	-819.43	-813.90	-790.54	-745.12	-516.86
N	1280	1221	1217	1215	1202	1193	1181

a: significant $\alpha \leq .01$; b: significant $\alpha \leq .05$

A.2   Multinomial Estimation of PC versus Liberal Vote Choice Outside Quebec

	1	1-2	1-3	1-4	1-5	1-6	1-7
1. Socio-demographics							
Atlantic	1.06 [a]	.91 [a]	.88 [a]	.90 [a]	.87 [a]	1.00 [a]	1.22 [a]
West	.33	.05	.15	.16	.17	.31	-.07
Catholic	-.89 [a]	-.92 [a]	-.70 [a]	-.72 [a]	-.60 [b]	-.53	-.44
Non-religious	-.42	-.62	-.66	-.66	-.63	-.47	-.58
North European	-.37	-.43 [b]	-.07	-.05	-.02	-.11	-.06
Non-European	-1.32 [a]	-1.22 [b]	-1.10 [b]	-1.11 [b]	-1.08	-1.19 [b]	-.32
Male	-.15	-.24	-.26	-.29	-.32	-.35	-.63 [b]
Other language	-.56	-.74 [b]	-.53	-.56	-.52	-.54	-.79
Married	.07	.14	.14	.14	.14	-.03	-.19
Below high school	-.78 [b]	-.84 [b]	-.62	-.61	-.55	-.47	-.80
Rural	.27	.25	.10	.09	.06	-.03	.25
2. Values and beliefs							
Social conservatism		-.09	-.01	-.01	-.05	-.05	.17
Free enterprise		.86 [a]	.59	.57	.54	.79 [b]	.60
Racial minorities		-.28	-.17	-.18	-.11	-.12	-.02
Feminism		.05	.06	.06	.06	.06	.17
Religiosity		-.22	-.11	-.10	-.09	-.04	-.06
Regional alienation		-.20	-.10	-.10	-.11	-.47	-.53
Cynicism		.82 [a]	.45 [b]	.49	.49	.06	-.00
3. Party identification							
Liberal			-1.84 [a]	-1.85 [a]	-1.85 [a]	-1.73 [a]	-1.35 [a]
Alliance			22.05 [a]	22.07 [a]	21.98 [a]	21.81 [a]	22.87 [a]
Conservative			2.85 [a]	2.85 [a]	2.84 [a]	2.76 [a]	2.27 [a]
New Democrat			-.69	-.67	-.57	-.66	-.49
4. Economic perceptions							
Personal past				.13	.11	.22	.36
5. Issues							
Federal powers					.08	.14	-.08
Public health					-.28	-.32	-.31
Gun control					-.06	-.03	-.13
Direct democracy					-.02	.05	.25
6. Liberal performance							
Environment						-.46 [b]	-.07
Health						-.75 [b]	-.86 [b]
Taxes						-.50 [b]	-.47
Corruption						-.31	-.17
Early call						.73	.29
7. Leader evaluation							
Chrétien							-2.51 [a]
Day							.33
Clark							3.95 [a]
McDonough							.09
Constant	-.85 [a]	-.55 [b]	-.50	-.51	-.45	-.96 [b]	-.91
Pseudo R^2	.12	.22	.46	.46	.48	.50	.65
Log likelihood	-1412.54	-1189.37	-819.43	-813.90	-790.54	-745.12	-516.86
N	1280	1221	1217	1215	1202	1193	1181

a: significant $\alpha \leq .01$; b: significant $\alpha \leq .05$

A.3 Multinomial Estimation of NDP versus Liberal Vote Choice Outside Quebec

	1	1-2	1-3	1-4	1-5	1-6	1-7
1. Socio-demographics							
Atlantic	.76 [a]	.65	.88 [b]	.93 [b]	.95 [b]	1.20 [a]	.87
West	.85 [a]	.86 [a]	.90 [a]	.91 [a]	1.00 [a]	1.06 [a]	.96 [b]
Catholic	-.19	-.17	.34	.37	.46	.52	.60
Non-religious	.94 [a]	.17	.08	.09	.12	.27	.23
North European	.08	.25	.30	.39	.44	.39	.25
Non-European	-1.06 [a]	-.75	-.50	-.31	-.36	-.15	.28
Male	-.44 [a]	-.41	-.36	-.33	-.27	-.48	-.30
Other language	-.63 [b]	-.48	-.21	-.24	-.38	-.32	-.89
Married	-.47 [b]	-.26	-.24	-.28	-.28	-.50	-.42
Below high school	.33	.46	.00	-.02	.10	.14	.09
Rural	.05	.00	-.27	-.31	-.26	-.24	.04
2. Values and beliefs							
Social conservatism		-.45 [b]	-.31	-.39	-.40	-.34	-.30
Free enterprise		-2.06 [a]	-1.65 [a]	-1.55 [a]	-1.54 [a]	-1.44 [a]	-1.37 [a]
Racial minorities		.17	.11	.13	.13	.13	-.07
Feminism		.05	.12	.14	.08	.05	.03
Religiosity		-.43 [b]	-.36	-.37	-.34	-.38	-.32
Regional alienation		.35	.26	.18	.09	-.03	-.16
Cynicism		1.26 [a]	.92 [a]	.80 [b]	.94 [b]	.47	.26
3. Party identification							
Liberal			-1.56 [a]	-1.53 [a]	-1.52 [a]	-1.55 [a]	-1.31 [a]
Alliance			-12.43	-6.43	-6.52	-6.41	-9.40
Conservative			.48	.47	.47	.40	.53
New Democrat			2.91 [a]	2.86 [a]	2.87 [a]	2.78 [a]	2.14 [a]
4. Economic perceptions							
Personal past				-.47 [b]	-.57 [a]	-.53 [b]	-.50 [b]
5. Issues							
Federal powers					-.14	-.16	-.10
Public health					-.16	-.05	-.00
Gun control					.37 [b]	.38 [b]	.38 [b]
Direct democracy					-.40	-.30	-.22
6. Liberal performance							
Environment						-.79 [a]	-.55
Health						.24	.18
Taxes						-.19	-.12
Corruption						-.05	-.15
Early call						1.16 [b]	.75
7. Leader evaluation							
Chrétien							-1.86 [a]
Day							.16
Clark							-.19
McDonough							2.79 [a]
Constant	-1.18 [a]	-1.65 [a]	-1.82 [a]	-1.80 [a]	-1.96 [a]	-2.08 [a]	-1.82 [a]
Pseudo R2	.12	.22	.46	.46	.48	.50	.65
Log likelihood	-1412.54	-1189.37	-819.43	-813.90	-790.54	-745.12	-516.86
N	1280	1221	1217	1215	1202	1193	1181

a: significant $\alpha \leq .01$; b: significant $\alpha \leq .05$

A.4   Multinomial Estimation of Alliance versus PC Vote Choice Outside Quebec

	1	1-2	1-3	1-4	1-5	1-6	1-7
1. Socio-demographics							
Atlantic	-1.80[a]	-1.90[a]	-1.82[a]	-1.85[a]	-1.96[a]	-1.99[a]	-2.30[a]
West	.93[a]	.80[a]	.23	.21	.08	-.05	.43
Catholic	.11	.09	.02	.05	.02	.06	.04
Non-religious	-.20	.23	.18	.21	.27	.29	-.15
North European	.91[a]	.84[b]	.60	.62	.58	.72	.59
Non-European	-.35	-.40	-.06	-.02	.05	.20	-.39
Male	.69[a]	.61[a]	.36	.41	.41	.36	.44
Other language	-.04	-.07	-.10	-.07	-.05	.00	.06
Married	.29	.04	.07	.07	.03	.04	.44
Below high school	.75[b]	.54	.58	.52	.46	.46	.32
Rural	.34	.26	.19	.19	.23	.25	.53
2. Values and beliefs							
Social conservatism		.59[a]	.39	.33	.25	.22	-.07
Free enterprise		.05	-.01	.08	.06	-.09	-1.05
Racial minorities		-.25	-.41	-.35	-.37	-.37	-.22
Feminism		-.69[a]	-.51[b]	-.53[b]	-.53[b]	-.54[b]	-.60[b]
Religiosity		.28	.23	.22	.28	.24	.02
Regional alienation		.49[b]	.58[b]	.52	.51	.57	.71
Cynicism		.07	.08	-.04	-.05	.04	.37
3. Party identification							
Liberal			-.34	-.32	-.25	-.40	-.19
Alliance			4.47[a]	4.46[a]	4.34[a]	4.37[a]	3.52[b]
Conservative			-1.60[a]	-1.59[a]	-1.64[a]	-1.64[a]	-.56
New Democrat			-.83	-.89	-.94	-.89	-.97
4. Economic perceptions							
Personal past				-.44[b]	-.36	-.36	-.59[b]
5. Issues							
Federal powers					-.56[a]	-.51[b]	-.08
Public health					-.13	-.15	-.07
Gun control					-.02	-.03	.17
Direct democracy					.26	.25	-.05
6. Liberal performance							
Environment						.59[b]	.51
Health						.37	.43
Taxes						-.23	.09
Corruption						-.15	.18
Early call						.58	.47
7. Leader evaluation							
Chrétien							-1.26[b]
Day							6.10[a]
Clark							-4.55[a]
McDonough							-.20
Constant	.08	.06[a]	-.33	-.35	.34	.39	.64
Pseudo R^2	.12	.22	.46	.46	.48	.50	.65
Log likelihood	-1412.54	-1189.37	-819.43	-813.90	-790.54	-745.12	-516.86
N	1280	1221	1217	1215	1202	1193	1181

a: significant $\alpha \leq .01$; b: significant $\alpha \leq .05$

A.5   Multinomial Estimation of Alliance versus NDP Vote Choice Outside Quebec

	1	1-2	1-3	1-4	1-5	1-6	1-7
1. Socio-demographics							
Atlantic	-1.50 [a]	-1.64 [a]	-1.83 [a]	-1.88 [a]	-2.04 [a]	-2.18 [a]	-1.94 [a]
West	.42	-.02	-.52	-.54	-.75 [b]	-.80 [b]	-.60
Catholic	-.60 [b]	-.66 [b]	-1.02 [a]	-1.04 [a]	-1.04 [a]	-.98 [a]	-1.00 [b]
Non-religious	-1.56 [a]	-.55	-.55	-.54	-.48	-.45	-.97
North European	.46	.17	.23	.18	.12	.22	.28
Non-European	-.61	-.88	-.66	-.82	-.67	-.84	-.99
Male	.98 [a]	.78 [a]	.46	.45	.35	.48	.10
Other language	.03	-.33	-.41	-.39	-.19	-.21	.15
Married	.83 [a]	.43	.45	.50	.45	.52	.66
Below high school	-.37	-.76 [a]	-.04	-.06	-.19	-.15	-.56
Rural	.55 [b]	.51	.56	.60	.55	.45	.74
2. Values and beliefs							
Social conservatism		1.12 [a]	.68 [b]	.71 [a]	.61 [b]	.51	.40
Free enterprise		2.97 [a]	2.23 [a]	2.21 [a]	2.14 [a]	2.14 [a]	.93
Racial minorities		-.70 [b]	-.69 [b]	-.65 [b]	-.61	-.62	-.17
Feminism		-.69 [a]	-.57 [b]	-.61 [b]	-.55	-.53	-.46
Religiosity		.49 [a]	.48	.48	.53 [b]	.57 [b]	.28
Regional alienation		.34	.20	.24	.32	.13	.34
Cynicism		.38	.39	.34	-.50	-.37	.11
3. Party Identification							
Liberal			-.63	-.64	-.57	-.58	-.24
Alliance			36.95	35.96	25.84 [a]	25.59 [a]	24.79 [a]
Conservative			.77	.79	.73	.72	1.17
New Democrat			-4.43 [a]	-4.42 [a]	-4.38 [a]	-4.33 [a]	-3.60 [a]
4. Economic perceptions							
Personal past				.16	.32	.39	.27
5. Issues							
Federal powers					-.35	-.20	-.06
Public health					-.26	-.43	-.38
Gun control					-.45 [b]	-.45 [b]	-.34
Direct democracy					.64 [a]	.60 [b]	.43
6. Liberal performance							
Environment						.91 [a]	.99 [a]
Health						-.61	-.60
Taxes						-.54	-.26
Corruption						-.40	.15
Early call						.15	.01
7. Leader evaluation							
Chrétien							-1.91 [a]
Day							6.27 [a]
Clark							-.42
McDonough							-2.90 [a]
Constant	-.25	-1.04 [a]	-1.65 [a]	-1.605 [a]	1.85 [a]	1.51 [a]	1.55 [b]
Pseudo R^2	.12	.22	.46	.46	.48	.50	.65
Log likelihood	-1412.54	-1189.37	-819.43	-813.90	-790.54	-745.12	-516.86
N	1280	1221	1217	1215	1202	1193	1181

a: significant $\alpha \leq .01$; b: significant $\alpha \leq .05$

A.6   Multinomial Estimation of NDP versus PC Vote Choice Outside Quebec

	1	1-2	1-3	1-4	1-5	1-6	1-7
1. Socio-demographics							
Atlantic	-.30	-.25	.00	.03	.08	.19	-.35
West	.52	.82 [b]	.75	.75	.83 [b]	.75	1.03 [b]
Catholic	.71 [b]	.75 [b]	1.04 [a]	1.10 [a]	1.06 [a]	1.04 [a]	1.04 [b]
Non-religious	1.36 [a]	.78 [b]	.74	.75	.75	.75	.81
North European	.45	.68	.37	.44	.46	.50	.31
Non-European	.26	.48	.60	.80	.72	1.05	.60
Male	-.29	-.17	-.10	-.04	.05	-.12	.33
Other language	-.07	.26	.32	.33	.14	.21	-.09
Married	-.54 [b]	-.39	-.38	-.43	-.43	-.47	-.23
Below high school	1.12 [a]	1.29 [a]	.62	.59	.65	.61	.89
Rural	-.21	-.25	-.37	-.40	-.31	-.20	-.21
2. Values and beliefs							
Moral traditionalism		-.53 [b]	-.30	-.38	-.36	-.29	-.47
Free enterprise		-2.91 [a]	-2.24 [a]	-2.12 [a]	-2.08 [a]	-2.23 [a]	-1.98 [a]
Racial minorities		.46	.28	.31	.24	.25	-.05
Feminism		.00	.06	.08	.02	-.01	-.14
Religiosity		-.21	-.25	-.27	-.25	-.33	-.26
Regional alienation		.15	.37	.28	.20	.44	.37
Cynicism		.44	.46	.30	.45	.42	.26
3. Party identification							
Liberal			.28	.32	.32	.18	.05
Alliance			-30.48	-32.50	-33.50	-31.22	-34.27
Conservative			-2.37 [a]	-2.38 [a]	-2.37 [a]	-2.36 [a]	-1.73
New Democrat			3.60 [a]	3.54 [a]	3.44 [a]	3.44 [a]	2.63 [a]
4. Economic perceptions							
Personal past				-.60 [b]	-.69 [a]	-.75 [a]	-.86 [a]
5. Issues							
Federal powers					-.22	-.31	-.02
Public health					.13	.27	.31
Gun control					.43 [b]	.41 [b]	.51 [b]
Direct democracy					-.38	-.35	-.48
6. Liberal performance							
Environment						-.32	-.48
Health						.99 [b]	1.03 [b]
Taxes						.31	.35
Corruption						.25	.03
Early call						.43	.46
7. Leader evaluation							
Chrétien							.65
Day							-.17
Clark							-4.14 [a]
McDonough							2.69 [a]
Constant	-.34	-1.10 [a]	-1.32 [a]	-1.29 [a]	-1.50 [a]	-1.12 [b]	-.91
Pseudo R2	.12	.22	.46	.46	.48	.50	.65
Log likelihood	-1412.54	-1189.37	-819.43	-813.90	-790.54	-745.12	-516.86
N	1280	1221	1217	1215	1202	1193	1181

a: significant $\alpha \leq .01$; b: significant $\alpha \leq .05$

Appendix B: Multinomial Estimations of Vote Choice in Quebec

B.1   Multinomial Estimation of Bloc versus Liberal Vote Choice, Quebec

	1	1-2	1-3	1-5	1-6	1-7
1. Socio-demographics						
French language	2.00 [a]	1.62 [a]	1.55 [b]	1.16	1.32 [b]	1.83 [b]
Age 55+	-.69 [a]	.22	.62	.54	.42	.99
2. Values and beliefs						
Quebec sovereignty		2.96 [a]	2.26 [a]	2.17 [a]	2.19 [a]	2.10 [a]
Social conservatism		-.58	-.57	-.41	-.40	-.40
Regional alienation		1.24 [a]	.86 [b]	.63	.48	.31
Cynicism		1.28 [b]	.84	.82	.64	.83
3. Party identification						
Liberal			-2.37 [a]	-2.31 [a]	-2.37 [a]	-1.96 [a]
Bloc Québécois			24.09 [a]	24.15 [a]	24.20 [a]	23.74 [a]
Alliance			20.39 [a]	21.09 [a]	20.77 [a]	21.10 [a]
Conservative			-43.01 [a]	-42.78 [a]	-42.45 [a]	-43.72 [a]
5. Issues						
Public health				-.24	-.25	.00
Federal powers				-.97 [a]	-.89 [a]	-.46
6. Liberal performance						
Taxes					-.39	-.45
Early call					1.01 [b]	.98
7. Leader evaluation						
Chrétien						-2.07 [a]
Day						-.05
Clark						-.11
Duceppe						3.61 [a]
Constant	-1.40 [a]	-1.16 [b]	-1.38 [b]	-1.35 [b]	-1.67 [b]	-2.12 [a]
Pseudo R^2	.06	.40	.55	.56	.57	.69
Log likelihood	-617.90	-386.53	-287.58	-279.69	-270.77	-194.33
N	617	604	602	600	600	596

a: significant $\alpha \le .01$; b: significant $\alpha \le .05$

B.2   Multinomial Estimation of PC versus Liberal Vote Choice, Quebec

	1	1-2	1-3	1-5	1-6	1-7
1. Socio-demographics						
French language	3.09[b]	2.71	3.74[a]	3.44	3.49	2.51
Age 55+	-.27	-.02	-.14	-.13	-.41	.25
2. Values and beliefs						
Quebec sovereignty		1.23[a]	1.14[a]	1.15[a]	1.18[a]	.82
Social conservatism		-.56	-.40	-.23	-.24	-.53
Regional alienation		.73	.63	.62	.49	.24
Cynicism		1.20[b]	1.21	1.16	1.07	1.70
3. Party identification						
Liberal			-1.39[b]	-1.55[b]	-1.65[b]	-.77
Bloc Québécois			-15.35	-10.30	-9.23	-17.24
Alliance			-21.67[a]	-17.55	-16.76	-20.62[a]
Conservative			4.70[a]	5.04[a]	5.30[a]	5.54[b]
5. Issues						
Public health				-.74[b]	-.70[b]	-.38
Federal powers				-.36	-.21	.43
6. Liberal performance						
Taxes					.10	.09
Early call					2.06[a]	1.40
7. Leader evaluation						
Chrétien						-2.85[a]
Day						-1.58[b]
Clark						3.29[a]
Duceppe						1.19
Constant	-4.82[a]	-4.17[a]	-5.01[a]	-4.85[b]	-5.26[a]	-4.63[a]
Pseudo R^2	.06	.40	.55	.56	.57	.69
Log likelihood	-617.90	-386.53	-287.58	-279.69	-270.77	-194.33
N	617	604	602	600	600	596

a: significant $\alpha \leq .01$; b: significant $\alpha \leq .05$

B.3   Multinomial Estimation of Alliance versus Liberal Vote Choice, Quebec

	1	1-2	1-3	1-5	1-6	1-7
1. Socio-demographics						
French language	1.03 b	.66	.55	.35	.57	2.41 b
Age 55+	-1.46 a	-1.64 a	-1.59 a	-1.65 a	-1.83 a	-2.19 b
2. Values and beliefs						
Quebec sovereignty		.50	.01	-.07	-.08	.54
Social conservatism		.42	.52	.69	.71	.41
Regional alienation		1.34 a	1.26 a	1.11 b	.87	1.07
Cynicism		.94 b	.61 a	.58	.25	.44
3. Party identification						
Liberal			-1.68 a	-1.73 a	-1.74 a	-.55
Bloc Québécois			22.70 a	22.74 a	22.82 a	23.37 a
Alliance			25.37 a	26.15 a	25.85 a	25.29 a
Conservative			-42.56 a	-42.90 a	-41.51 a	-37.23 a
5. Issues						
Public health				-.32	-.39	.18
Federal powers				-.67	-.57	-.73
6. Liberal performance						
Taxes					-.81 b	-1.09 b
Early call					1.22 b	1.09
7. Leader evaluation						
Chrétien						-2.65 a
Day						6.49 a
Clark						.32
Duceppe						-1.62
Constant	-2.13 a	-1.91 a	-1.97 a	-1.96 a	-2.47 a	-5.03 a
Pseudo R^2	.06	.40	.55	.56	.57	.69
Log likelihood	-617.90	-386.53	-287.58	-279.69	-270.77	-194.33
N	617	604	602	600	600	596

a: significant $\alpha \le .01$; b: significant $\alpha \le .05$

B.4   Multinomial Estimation of Bloc versus PC Vote Choice, Quebec

	1	1-2	1-3	1-5	1-6	1-7
1. Socio-demographics						
French language	-1.09	-1.09	-2.19	-2.28	-2.16	-.68
Age 55+	-.42	.24	.75	.67	.83	.74
2. Values and beliefs						
Quebec sovereignty		1.73 [a]	1.13 [a]	1.03 [a]	1.02 [b]	1.28 [a]
Social conservatism		-.02	-.17	-.18	-.16	.13
Regional alienation		.51	.23	.01	-.02	.07
Cynicism		.08	-.37	-.34	-.43	-.88
3. Party identification						
Liberal			-.98	-.77	-.72	-1.19
Bloc Québécois			25.44 [a]	25.46 [a]	25.43 [a]	24.98 [a]
Alliance			21.06 [a]	21.64 [a]	21.53 [a]	20.72 [a]
Conservative			-47.72 [a]	-47.82 [a]	-47.75 [a]	-49.26 [a]
5. Issues						
Public health				.50	.45	.38
Federal powers				-.62	-.68	-.89
6. Liberal performance						
Taxes					-.49	-.53
Early call					-1.04	-.42
7. Leader evaluation						
Chrétien						.78
Day						1.53 [b]
Clark						-3.40 [a]
Duceppe						2.42 [a]
Constant	-3.43 [b]	-3.01 [b]	-3.63	3.50	3.59	2.51
Pseudo R^2	.06	.40	.55	.56	.57	.69
Log likelihood	-617.90	-386.53	-287.58	-279.69	-270.77	-194.33
N	617	604	602	600	600	596

a: significant $\alpha \leq .01$; b: significant $\alpha \leq .05$

B.5   Multinomial Estimation of Bloc versus Alliance Vote Choice, Quebec

	1	1-2	1-3	1-5	1-6	1-7
1. Socio-demographics						
French language	.97	.96	1.00	.81	.76	-.58
Age 55+	.77	1.86 [a]	2.20 [a]	2.19 [a]	2.25 [a]	3.18 [a]
2. Values and beliefs						
Quebec sovereignty		2.46 [a]	2.26 [a]	2.24 [a]	2.28 [a]	1.55 [a]
Social conservatism		-.99 [a]	-1.08 [a]	-1.10 [b]	-1.11 [a]	-.81
Regional alienation		-.10	-.40	-.48	-.40	-.76
Cynicism		.34	.23	.24	.38	.39
3. Party identification						
Liberal			-.69	-.58	-.63	-1.41
Bloc Québécois			1.39 [b]	1.42 [b]	1.38 [b]	.37
Alliance			-4.98 [a]	-5.07 [a]	-5.08 [a]	-4.19 [b]
Conservative			-21.45 [a]	-20.88 [a]	-20.94 [a]	-25.49 [a]
5. Issues						
Public health				.07	.14	-.18
Federal powers				-.30	-.32	.27
6. Liberal performance						
Taxes					.41	.64
Early call					-.21	-.11
7. Leader evaluation						
Chrétien						.58
Day						-6.55 [a]
Clark						-.43
Duceppe						5.23 [a]
Constant	.74	.75	.58	.61	.80	2.91 [b]
Pseudo R^2	.06	.40	.55	.56	.57	.69
Log likelihood	-617.90	-386.53	-287.58	-279.69	-270.77	-194.33
N	617	604	602	600	600	596

a: significant $\alpha \leq .01$; b: significant $\alpha \leq .05$

B.6   Multinomial Estimation of Alliance versus PC Vote Choice, Quebec

	1	1-2	1-3	1-5	1-6	1-7
1. Socio-demographics						
French language	-2.06	-2.05	-3.19	-3.09	-2.92	-.09
Age 55+	-1.18 [b]	-1.62 [b]	-1.45	-1.51	-1.42	-2.44 [b]
2. Values and beliefs						
Quebec sovereignty		-.73	-1.12 [b]	-1.22 [b]	-1.26 [b]	-.28
Social conservatism		.97 [b]	.92	.92	.95	.94
Regional alienation		.62	.63	.49	.38	.83
Cynicism		-.26	-.60	-.58	-.81	-1.27
3. Party identification						
Liberal			-.29	-.19	-.09	.22
Bloc Québécois			24.05 [a]	24.04 [a]	24.05 [a]	24.61 [a]
Alliance			26.04 [a]	26.71 [a]	26.61 [a]	24.91 [a]
Conservative			-47.26 [a]	-47.94 [a]	-46.81 [a]	-42.77 [a]
5. Issues						
Public health				.43	.31	.56
Federal powers				-.31	-.36	-1.16
6. Liberal performance						
Taxes					-.91	-1.18
Early call					-.83	-.31
7. Leader evaluation						
Chrétien						.21
Day						8.07 [a]
Clark						-2.97 [a]
Duceppe						-2.81 [a]
Constant	2.69	2.26	3.04	2.89	2.79	-.40
Pseudo R^2	.06	.40	.55	.56	.57	.69
Log likelihood	-617.90	-386.53	-287.58	-279.69	-270.77	-194.33
N	617	604	602	600	600	596

a: significant $\alpha \leq .01$; b: significant $\alpha \leq .05$

Appendix C: The Estimated Impact of Variables on the Propensity to Vote for the Parties Outside Quebec

C.1 The Estimated Impact of Variables on the Propensity to Vote for the Parties Outside Quebec: Liberal

	1	1-2	1-3	1-4	1-5	1-6	1-7
1. Socio-demographics							
Atlantic	-6.0	-2.8	-3.9	-4.3	-3.8	-5.8	-5.6
West	-20.8	-13.0	-6.4	-6.3	-6.0	-6.4	-4.4
Catholic	14.3	13.6	5.6	5.4	4.1	2.6	0.4
Non-religious	1.7	5.7	5.0	4.8	4.1	1.7	3.1
North European	-5.2	-3.6	-4.3	-5.0	-5.1	-4.7	-2.4
Non-European	30.8	25.7	13.1	12.1	11.7	10.1	2.1
Male	-2.9	-0.2	1.7	1.6	1.7	2.9	3.7
Other language	13.1	14.1	6.7	7.0	7.0	6.2	7.8
Married	-1.7	-1.0	-1.0	-0.9	-0.5	1.8	1.4
Below high school	1.7	3.7	2.3	2.8	2.2	1.2	3.5
Rural	-8.4	-6.1	-1.3	-1.1	-1.2	-0.4	-3.5
2. Values and beliefs							
Social conservatism		-6.2	-1.6	-1.0	0.1	0.2	0.0
Free enterprise		-11.4	-3.4	-3.9	-3.3	-5.1	2.3
Racial minorities		5.5	3.7	3.4	2.8	2.7	1.0
Feminism		5.2	2.0	2.0	2.1	2.1	0.6
Religiosity		2.6	1.0	1.0	0.4	0.3	1.4
Regional alienation		-9.4	-3.6	-3.0	-2.5	1.2	1.6
Cynicism		-17.6	-8.6	-7.8	-8.2	-2.5	-2.1
3. Party identification							
Liberal			30.8	30.7	29.8	27.4	15.2
Alliance			-45.6	-45.6	-45.2	-45.1	-44.0
Conservative			-25.5	-25.5	-25.3	-22.5	-16.6
New Democrat			-16.4	-15.6	-15.2	-12.8	-8.2
4. Economic perceptions							
Personal past				3.0	2.9	1.6	1.1
5. Issues							
Federal powers					2.8	1.8	1.1
Public health					4.2	4.1	2.2
Gun control					-0.7	-0.9	-1.1
Direct democracy					-0.2	-1.1	-0.8
6. Liberal performance							
Environment						3.3	0.5
Health						3.2	2.8
Taxes						6.4	3.1
Corruption						3.9	1.1
Early call						-14.2	-6.0
7. Leader evaluation							
Chrétien							27.4
Day							-36.8
Clark							-23.2
McDonough							-16.0

C.2   The Estimated Impact of Variables on the Propensity to Vote for the Parties Outside Quebec: Alliance

	1	1-2	1-3	1-4	1-5	1-6	1-7
1. Socio-demographics							
Atlantic	-18.8	-19.0	-12.5	-12.6	-13.3	-12.9	-8.9
West	20.1	11.3	2.4	2.2	0.7	0.2	1.4
Catholic	-10.6	-9.3	-5.6	-5.4	-4.8	-3.7	-2.0
Non-religious	-13.4	-4.3	-3.1	-2.9	-2.1	-0.7	-3.3
North European	11.3	7.4	5.9	6.1	5.7	6.4	3.0
Non-European	-20.1	-17.7	-7.8	-7.7	-6.8	-6.0	-3.6
Male	12.0	7.6	2.5	2.8	2.3	1.8	0.3
Other language	-6.9	-8.7	-4.6	-4.6	-3.9	-3.3	-2.1
Married	8.0	2.8	2.2	2.3	1.7	0.9	2.1
Below high school	0.2	-3.3	1.5	0.9	0.5	1.1	-1.4
Rural	10.3	7.1	3.3	3.3	3.3	2.7	4.1
2. Values and beliefs							
Social conservatism		12.5	5.0	4.4	3.0	2.4	0.5
Free enterprise		13.3	6.1	7.1	6.4	5.9	-3.0
Racial minorities		-7.5	-5.6	-5.1	-4.8	-4.6	-1.2
Feminism		-9.9	-5.1	-5.3	-5.0	-4.9	-2.7
Religiosity		2.8	2.2	2.1	2.8	2.6	0.1
Regional alienation		9.4	5.2	4.7	4.7	2.5	2.1
Cynicism		6.4	2.8	2.1	1.5	0.2	1.9
3. Party identification							
Liberal			-16.7	-16.6	-15.5	-14.8	-5.7
Alliance			71.8	71.8	70.7	70.5	47.1
Conservative			-1.5	-1.2	-1.9	-2.3	4.5
New Democrat			-16.3	-16.4	-15.9	-15.1	-8.9
4. Economic perceptions							
Personal past				-3.2	-2.3	-1.6	-1.7
5. Issues							
Federal powers					-4.7	-3.7	-0.7
Public health					-3.3	-3.7	-1.6
Gun control					-1.2	-1.1	0.1
Direct democracy					3.3	3.4	0.9
6. Liberal performance							
Environment						3.6	3.1
Health						-2.2	-1.4
Taxes						-4.9	-1.2
Corruption						-3.4	0.4
Early call						10.1	3.2
7. Leader evaluation							
Chrétien							-13.6
Day							59.3
Clark							-14.0
McDonough							-5.2

C.3　The Estimated Impact of Variables on the Propensity to Vote for the Parties Outside Quebec: PC

	1	1-2	1-3	1-4	1-5	1-6	1-7
1. Socio-demographics							
Atlantic	15.6	14.9	10.2	10.3	10.4	10.7	10.0
West	-3.1	-4.1	-1.1	-1.0	-0.6	0.4	-2.1
Catholic	-5.9	-5.9	-3.9	-4.1	-3.5	-3.2	-2.4
Non-religious	-4.1	-4.7	-3.8	-3.9	-3.9	-3.3	-2.4
North European	-5.3	-5.5	-2.7	-2.7	-2.5	-3.2	-1.6
Non-European	-6.4	-5.9	-4.5	-4.8	-4.8	-5.5	-1.0
Male	-2.8	-3.3	-2.1	-2.4	-2.7	-2.4	-3.2
Other language	-2.7	-3.9	-2.1	-2.3	-2.1	-2.2	-2.6
Married	0.3	1.1	0.7	0.8	0.9	0.3	-1.2
Below high school	-7.1	-6.8	-4.5	-4.3	-4.0	-3.6	-3.7
Rural	0.3	0.6	0.1	0.1	-0.2	-0.7	0.0
2. Values and beliefs							
Social conservatism		-1.5	-1.2	-0.9	-0.8	-0.7	1.2
Free enterprise		7.4	4.6	4.0	3.9	5.9	6.3
Racial minorities		-1.4	0.2	0.0	0.4	0.4	0.4
Feminism		2.8	1.8	1.9	1.9	1.9	1.8
Religiosity		-1.9	-1.0	-0.9	-1.0	-0.6	0.0
Regional alienation		-1.1	-2.7	-2.4	-2.3	-3.9	-3.2
Cynicism		2.5	0.8	1.7	1.5	-0.4	-0.9
3. Party identification							
Liberal			-8.1	-8.3	-8.5	-7.0	-4.7
Alliance			-13.3	-13.2	-12.7	-12.8	9.1
Conservative			31.3	31.0	31.3	28.9	13.9
New Democrat			-7.9	-7.6	-6.9	-6.9	-4.0
4. Economic perceptions							
Personal past				2.6	2.4	2.9	3.2
5. Issues							
Federal powers					2.4	2.6	-0.1
Public health					-0.9	-1.1	-1.2
Gun control					-0.7	-0.5	-1.2
Direct democracy					-0.6	-0.3	1.4
6. Liberal performance							
Environment						-3.2	-0.8
Health						-3.8	-3.6
Taxes						-1.7	-1.9
Corruption						-1.0	-0.9
Early call						-0.1	-0.4
7. Leader evaluation							
Chrétien							-7.8
Day							-13.3
Clark							44.2
McDonough							-3.6

C.4   The Estimated Impact of Variables on the Propensity to Vote for the Parties Outside Quebec: NDP

	1	1-2	1-3	1-4	1-5	1-6	1-7
1. Socio-demographics							
Atlantic	9.2	6.8	6.2	6.6	6.7	8.0	4.5
West	3.7	5.8	5.1	5.1	5.8	5.8	5.1
Catholic	2.1	1.6	3.9	4.2	4.3	4.3	4.1
Non-religious	15.8	3.4	1.9	1.9	1.9	2.4	2.5
North European	-0.8	1.7	1.1	1.6	1.9	1.5	0.9
Non-European	-4.3	-2.2	-0.8	0.5	-0.1	1.4	2.5
Male	-6.3	-4.1	-2.1	-1.9	-1.4	-2.4	-0.8
Other language	-3.4	-1.5	0.0	-0.1	-1.1	-0.7	-3.2
Married	-6.7	-3.0	-1.9	-2.2	-2.1	-2.9	-2.3
Below high school	5.1	6.4	0.7	0.6	1.3	1.3	1.6
Rural	-2.2	-1.6	-2.1	-2.3	-1.9	-1.6	-0.7
2. Values and beliefs							
Social conservatism		-4.8	-2.2	-2.5	-2.3	-1.9	-1.6
Free enterprise		-9.3	-7.3	-7.2	-7.1	-6.8	-5.6
Racial minorities		3.4	1.7	1.8	1.6	1.5	-0.2
Feminism		1.9	1.3	1.5	1.1	0.8	0.3
Religiosity		-3.5	-2.2	-2.2	-2.2	-2.3	-1.5
Regional alienation		1.1	1.1	0.6	0.1	0.2	-0.5
Cynicism		8.8	5.0	4.1	5.2	2.7	1.1
3. Party identification							
Liberal			-6.0	-5.8	-5.8	-5.6	-4.8
Alliance			-12.9	-13.0	-12.8	-12.7	-12.3
Conservative			-4.3	-4.3	-4.2	-4.0	-1.8
New Democrat			40.6	39.5	37.9	34.9	21.0
4. Economic perceptions							
Personal past				-2.5	-3.0	-2.9	-2.6
5. Issues							
Federal powers					-0.4	-0.7	-0.3
Public health					-0.1	0.7	0.6
Gun control					2.5	2.5	2.2
Direct democracy					-2.5	-2.0	-1.5
6. Liberal performance							
Environment						-3.6	-2.8
Health						2.9	2.2
Taxes						0.1	0.0
Corruption						0.5	-0.6
Early call						4.3	3.2
7. Leader evaluation							
Chrétien							-5.9
Day							-9.2
Clark							-7.0
McDonough							24.8

Appendix D: The Estimated Impact of Variables on the Propensity to Vote for the Parties in Quebec

D.1 The Estimated Impact of Variables on the Propensity to Vote for the Parties, Quebec: Bloc

	1	1-2	1-3	1-5	1-6	1-7
1. Socio-demographics						
French language	35.6	12.0	9.1	6.3	7.0	6.5
Age 55+	-11.1	5.0	8.2	7.5	7.2	8.8
2. Values and beliefs						
Quebec sovereignty		34.3	26.5	25.1	24.8	17.9
Social conservatism		-6.5	-6.2	-5.5	-5.5	-3.0
Regional alienation		8.9	3.7	1.9	1.3	0.1
Cynicism		9.1	3.7	3.6	2.8	1.8
3. Party identification						
Liberal			-15.3	-14.0	-14.1	-12.0
Bloc Québécois			41.3	41.8	41.9	37.7
Alliance			-30.8	-30.9	-30.4	-4.3
Conservative			-46.7	-46.2	-46.3	-46.1
5. Issues						
Public health				-0.3	-0.3	0.4
Federal powers				-6.4	-6.1	-3.8
6. Liberal performance						
Taxes					-2.4	-2.3
Early call					1.3	2.6
7. Leader evaluation						
Chrétien						-9.0
Day						-33.5
Clark						-12.7
Duceppe						30.3

D.2   The Estimated Impact of Variables on the Propensity to Vote for the Parties, Quebec: Liberal

	1	1-2	1-3	1-5	1-6	1-7
1. Socio-demographics						
French language	-41.8	-17.1	-14.0	-10.6	-11.8	-14.7
Age 55+	16.5	3.8	0.8	1.4	2.6	-1.9
2. Values and beliefs						
Quebec sovereignty		-23.1	-19.1	-18.4	-18.2	-13.3
Social conservatism		2.2	1.1	-0.8	-0.8	1.7
Regional alienation		-16.1	-10.4	-8.3	-6.0	-3.4
Cynicism		-14.8	-8.8	-8.2	-5.8	-7.3
3. Party identification						
Liberal			21.5	20.9	20.6	10.0
Bloc Québécois			-42.9	-43.4	-43.6	-42.6
Alliance			-40.1	-40.6	-40.7	-40.6
Conservative			-24.0	-25.1	-25.4	-23.7
5. Issues						
Public health				3.3	3.4	0.2
Federal powers				7.5	6.2	1.6
6. Liberal performance						
Taxes					3.4	2.9
Early call					-12.7	-8.0
7. Leader evaluation						
Chrétien						17.3
Day						-29.5
Clark						-13.6
Duceppe						-19.7

D.3   The Estimated Impact of Variables on the Propensity to Vote for the
Parties, Quebec: PC

	1	*1-2*	*1-3*	*1-5*	*1-6*	*1-7*
1. Socio-demographics						
French language	5.0	4.8	5.7	5.5	5.3	4.2
Age 55+	0.9	0.1	-1.1	-1.0	-1.6	-0.6
2. Values and beliefs						
Quebec sovereignty		-4.5	-2.1	-1.5	-1.5	-2.2
Social conservatism		-1.5	-1.0	-0.7	-0.8	-1.2
Regional alienation		-0.1	0.3	0.9	0.7	0.0
Cynicism		2.6	3.9	3.6	3.6	5.9
3. Party identification						
Liberal			-1.6	-2.2	-2.2	0.6
Bloc Québécois			-7.1	-7.2	-7.2	-7.6
Alliance			-5.4	-5.5	-5.4	-6.1
Conservative			53.9	54.4	54.6	51.8
5. Issues						
Public health				-2.0	-1.8	-1.3
Federal powers				0.5	1.2	3.9
6. Liberal performance						
Taxes					1.8	1.7
Early call					7.6	3.6
7. Leader evaluation						
Chrétien						-4.0
Day						-3.7
Clark						27.5
Duceppe						-3.2

D.4   The Estimated Impact of Variables on the Propensity to Vote for the Parties, Quebec: Alliance

	1	1-2	1-3	1-5	1-6	1-7
1. Socio-demographics						
French language	1.3	0.4	-0.8	-1.3	-0.5	4.0
Age 55+	-6.3	-8.9	-7.9	-7.9	-8.2	-6.4
2. Values and beliefs						
Quebec sovereignty		-6.7	-5.3	-5.2	-5.1	-2.5
Social conservatism		5.8	6.1	7.1	7.0	2.6
Regional alienation		7.2	6.3	5.6	4.1	3.3
Cynicism		3.0	1.2	1.0	-0.6	-0.3
3. Party identification						
Liberal			-4.6	-4.7	-4.3	1.5
Bloc Québécois			8.7	8.8	8.9	12.6
Alliance			76.3	76.9	76.6	50.9
Conservative			16.9	16.9	17.0	18.0
5. Issues						
Public health				-1.0	-1.3	0.7
Federal powers				-1.7	-1.3	-1.6
6. Liberal performance						
Taxes					-2.8	-2.3
Early call					3.8	1.8
7. Leader evaluation						
Chrétien						-4.3
Day						66.8
Clark						-1.3
Duceppe						-7.4

Appendix E: Description of Variables[1]

Values and beliefs

Variables were coded on a scale from -1 to 1, unless specified otherwise.

SOCIAL CONSERVATISM is an index made up of two questions:

> Do you strongly agree, somewhat agree, somewhat disagree, or strongly disagree with the following statements?
> a) Society would be better off if more women stayed home with their children. (cpsf3)
> b) Gays and lesbians should be allowed to get married. (cpsf18)

The index is the sum of the two scores divided by 2.

Cronbach's Alpha – Quebec: .30   Outside Quebec: .45

FREE ENTERPRISE in an index made up of five questions:

> Do you strongly agree, somewhat agree, somewhat disagree, or strongly disagree with the following statements?
> a) The government should leave it entirely to the private sector to create jobs. (cpsf6)
> b) People who don't get ahead should blame themselves, not the system. (pesg15)
> c) When businesses make a lot of money, everyone benefits, including the poor. (pesg16)

> How much power do you think business should have: much more, somewhat more, about the same as now, somewhat less, or much less? (pesd3)

> How much power do you think unions should have: much more, somewhat more, about the same as now, somewhat less, or much less? (pesd2)

The index is the sum of the five scores divided by 5.

Cronbach's Alpha – Quebec: .34   Outside Quebec: .47

---

[1] The parentheses refer to the question number in the survey; "cps" refers to the campaign survey and "pes" to the post-election survey.

RACIAL MINORITIES:

How much do you think should be done for racial minorities: much more, somewhat more, about the same as now, somewhat less, or much less? (cpsc11)

FEMINISM:

Are you very sympathetic towards feminism, quite sympathetic, not very sympathetic, or not sympathetic at all? (pesg20)

RELIGIOSITY:

In your life, would you say religion is very important, somewhat important, not very important, or not important at all? (cpsm10b)

REGIONAL ALIENATION:

In general, does the federal government treat your province better, worse, or about the same as other provinces? (cpsj12)

CYNICISM is an index made up of four questions:

Do you strongly agree, somewhat agree, somewhat disagree, or strongly disagree with the following statement?
a) I don't think the government cares much what people like me think. (cpsb10d)
b) All federal parties are basically the same; there isn't really a choice. (cpsb11)

Use any number from zero to one hundred. Zero means you really dislike them and one hundred means you really like them.
a) How do you feel about politicians in general? (cpspolit)
b) How do you feel about political parties? (pesc2d)

The index is the sum of the four scores divided by 4.

Cronbach's Alpha – Quebec: .58   Outside Quebec: .62

QUEBEC SOVEREIGNTY (Quebec only)

Are you very favourable, somewhat favourable, somewhat opposed, or very opposed to Quebec sovereignty, that is Quebec is no longer a part of Canada? (pesc6)

Party identification

In federal politics, do you usually think of yourself as a Liberal, Bloc Québécois, Alliance, Conservative, NDP, or none of these? (pesk1)

How strongly (name of the party) do you feel: very strongly, fairly strongly, or not very strongly? (pesk2)

Five variables were created, one for each party. Each variable takes the value of 1 if the respondent has a strong or a fairly strong identification with the party, and 0 otherwise.

Economic perceptions

Variable was coded on a scale from −1 to +1.

PERSONAL PAST

Financially, are you better off, worse off, or about the same as a year ago? (cpsc1)

Issues

Variables were coded on a scale from −1 to +1.

FEDERAL POWERS

When it comes to the division of power between the federal and provincial governments, do you think the provincial governments should have more power than now, less power, or about the same as now? (pese1a)

PUBLIC HEALTH is an index made up of two questions:

Would you favour or oppose having some private hospitals in Canada? (pesd7)

And would you favour or oppose letting doctors charge patients a 10-dollar [or 20-dollar] fee for each office visit? (pesd8)

The index is the sum of the two scores divided by 2.

Cronbach's Alpha – Quebec: .47   Outside Quebec: .46

GUN CONTROL

Do you strongly agree, somewhat agree, somewhat disagree, or strongly disagree with the following statement? Only the police and the military should be allowed to have guns. (cpsf19)

DIRECT DEMOCRACY is an index made up of two questions:

Do you think that referendums on important [or controversial] issues should be held regularly, occasionally, rarely, or never? (pesg4)

Do you think it would be a good thing or a bad thing to have a referendum on abortion? (pesg14)

The index is the sum of the two scores divided by 2.

Cronbach's Alpha – Quebec: .39   Outside Quebec: .46

Liberal performance

Variables were coded on a scale from -1 to 1, unless specified otherwise.

ENVIRONMENT

How good a job has the Liberal government done of protecting the environment? Has the Liberal government done a very good job, quite good job, not good, or not good at all? (cpsf10a)

HEALTH

How good a job has the Liberal government done of improving health care? Has the Liberal government done a very good job, quite good job, not good, or not good at all? (cpsf10c)

TAXES

How good a job has the Liberal government done of cutting taxes? Has the Liberal government done a very good job, quite good job, not good, or not good at all? (cpsf10f)

CORRUPTION

Do you think there has been a lot of corruption under the present Liberal government, some, a little, or none? (cpsf11)

EARLY CALL

Are you very angry that the Federal election was called early, somewhat angry, or not angry at all? (cpsl20)

This variable was coded on a scale from 0 to 1.

Leader evaluation

Variables were coded on a scale from -1 to 1.

CHRÉTIEN

Use any number from zero to one hundred. Zero means you really dislike him and one hundred means you really like him. How do you feel about Jean Chrétien? (pesf2)

DAY

Use any number from zero to one hundred. Zero means you really dislike him and one hundred means you really like him. How do you feel about Stockwell Day? (pesf4)

CLARK

Use any number from zero to one hundred. Zero means you really dislike him and one hundred means you really like him. How do you feel about Joe Clark? (pesf1)

McDONOUGH

Use any number from zero to one hundred. Zero means you really dislike her and one hundred means you really like her. How do you feel about Alexa McDonough? (pesf3)

DUCEPPE (Quebec only)

Use any number from zero to one hundred. Zero means you really dislike him and one hundred means you really like him. How do you feel about Gilles Duceppe? (pesf5)

References

Aardal, Bernt O., and Henrik Oscarsson. 2000. "The Myth of Increasing Personalization of Politics: Party Leader Effects on Party Choice in Sweden and Norway, 1979-1998," Paper presented at the Annual Meeting of the American Political Science Association, Washington, September 2000.

Aarts, Kees. 2000. "Are Party Leaders Becoming More Important in Dutch Elections?" Paper presented at the Annual Meeting of the American Political Science Association, Washington, September 2000.

Ansolabehere, Stephen, Roy Behr, and Shanto Iyengar. 1993. *The Media Game*. New York: Macmillan.

Archer, Keith. 1985. "The Failure of the New Democratic Party: Unions, Unionists, and Politics in Canada," *Canadian Journal of Political Science* 18: 353-66.

Bartels, Larry M., and John Zaller. 2001. "Presidential Vote Models: A Recount," *Political Science & Politics* 34: 9-20.

Bean, Clive, and Anthony Mughan. 1989. "Leadership Effects in Parliamentary Elections in Australia and Britain," *American Political Science Review* 83: 1165-79.

Blais, André. 2000. *To Vote or Not to Vote? The Merits and Limits of Rational Choice Theory*. Pittsburgh: Pittsburgh University Press.

Blais, André. Forthcoming. "Why is There So Little Strategic Voting in Canadian Plurality Rule Elections?" *Political Studies*.

Blais, André, Donald Blake, and Stéphane Dion. 1993. "Do Parties Make a Difference? Parties and the Size of Government in Liberal Democracies," *American Journal of Political Science* 37: 40-62.

Blais, André, and Elisabeth Gidengil. 1992. *Making Representative Democracy Work: The Views of Canadians*. Ottawa, Royal Commission on Electoral Reform and Party Financing.

—. 1993. "Things Are Not Always What They Seem: French-English Differences and the Problem of Measurement Equivalence," *Canadian Journal of Political Science* 26: 541-56.

Blais, André, Elisabeth Gidengil, Richard Nadeau, and Neil Nevitte. 2001a. "Measuring Party Identification: Canada, Britain and United States," *Political Behavior* 23: 5-22.

—. 2001b. "The Evolving Nature of Non-Voting: Evidence from Canada," Paper prepared for the Annual Meeting of the American Political Science Association, San Francisco, September 2001.

—. 2001c. "Making Sense of The Vote in The 2000 Canadian Election," Paper presented at the annual meeting of the Canadian Political Science Association, Université Laval, May 2001.

—. 2001d. "Do (Some) Voters Punish a Prime Minister for Calling an Early Election?" Paper presented at the annual meeting of the Public Choice Society, San Antonio, Texas, March 21.

—. Forthcoming (a). "Campaign Dynamics in the 2000 Canadian Election: How the Leader Debates Salvaged the Conservative," *PS: Political Science and Politics*.

—. 2002. "Do Party Supporters Differ?" in Everitt and O'Neill, eds. (2002).

Blais, André, Pierre Martin, and Richard Nadeau. 1998. "Can People Explain Their Own Vote? Introspective Questions as Indicators of Salience in the 1995 Quebec Referendum on Sovereignty," *Quality and Quantity* 32: 355-66.

Blais, André, and Richard Nadeau. 1992. "To Be or Not to Be Sovereignist: Quebeckers' Perennial Dilemma," *Canadian Public Policy* 18: 89-103.

—. 1996. "Measuring Strategic Voting: A Two-Step Procedure," *Electoral Studies* 15: 39- 52.

Blais, André, Richard Nadeau, Elisabeth Gidengil, and Neil Nevitte. 2000. "Do People Have Feelings Towards Leaders about Whom They Say They Know Nothing?" *Public Opinion Quarterly* 64: 452-64.

—. 2001e. "Measuring Strategic Voting in Multiparty Plurality Elections," *Electoral Studies* 20: 343-52.

—. Forthcoming (b). "The Impact of Issues and the Economy in the 1997 Canadian Election," *Canadian Journal of Political Science*.

Blais, André, and Robert Young. 1999. "Why Do People Vote? An Experiment in Rationality," *Public Choice* 99: 39-55.

Blake, Donald E. 1982. "The Consistency of Inconsistency: Party Identification in Federal and Provincial Politics," *Canadian Journal of Political Science* 15: 691-710.

Bloom, Howard S., and H. Douglas Price. 1975. "Voter Response to Short-Run Economic Conditions," *American Political Science Review* 69: 1240-54.

Brady, Henry E., Sydney Verba, and Kay Lehman Schlozman. 1995. "Beyond SES: A Resource Model of Political Participation," *American Political Science Review* 89: 271-95.

Budge, Ian, and Dennis Farlie. 1983. *Explaining and Predicting Elections.* London: Allen and Unwin.

Butler, David, and Donald Stokes. 1971. *Political Change in Britain.* London: Macmillan.

Campbell, Angus, Philip E. Converse, Warren E. Miller, and Donald Stokes. 1960. *The American Voter.* New York: Wiley.

Campbell James E., and James C. Garand, eds. 2000. *Before the Vote:*

Forecasting American National Elections. Thousand Oaks, Calif.: Sage.

Carmines, Edward G., and James A. Stimson. 1984. "The Dynamics of Issue Evolution," in Russell Dalton, Paul Allen Beck, and Scott Flanagan, eds., *Electoral Change in Industrial Democracies.* Princeton: Princeton University Press.

Clarke, Harold, Jane Jenson, Lawrence LeDuc, and Jon Pammett. 1979. *Political Choice in Canada.* Toronto: McGraw-Hill Ryerson.

—. 1984. *Absent Mandate: The Politics of Discontent in Canada.* Toronto: Gage.

—. 1991. *Absent Mandate: Interpreting Change in Canadian Elections.* Toronto: Gage.

—. 1996. *Absent Mandate: Canadian Electoral Politics in an Era of Restructuring.* Toronto: Gage.

Clarke, Harold D., and Allan Kornberg. 1992. "Support for the Canadian Federal Progressive Conservative Party since 1988: The Impact of Economic Evaluations and Economic Issues," *Canadian Journal of Political Science* 25: 29-53.

Converse, Philip. 1964. "The Nature of Belief Systems in Mass Publics," in David E. Apter, ed., *Ideology and Discontent.* New York: Free Press.

—. 1969. "Of Time and Partisan Stability," *Comparative Political Studies* 2: 139-71.

Cox, Gary W. 1997. *Making Votes Count: Strategic Coordination in the World's Electoral Systems.* Cambridge: Cambridge University Press.

Crête, Jean. 1984. "La presse quotidienne et la campagne électorale de 1981." *Recherches Sociographiques* 25: 103-14.

Cutler, Fred. 2002. "The Simplest Shortcut of All: Vote-Candidate Socio-Demographic Similarity and Electoral Choice," *Journal of Politics* 64.

Dalton, Russell J. 1988. *Citizen Politics in Western Democracies.* Chatham: Chatham House.

—. 1996. "Political Cleavages, Issues, and Electoral Change," in LeDuc et al. (1996).

—. 2000. "The Decline of Party Identifications," in Russell J. Dalton and Martin P. Wattenberg, eds. (2000).

Dalton, Russell J., Paul Beck, and Scott Flanagan, eds. 1984. *Electoral Change in Advanced Industrial Democracies: Realignment or Dealignment?.* Princeton: Princeton University Press.

—. 1984. "Electoral Change in Advanced Industrial Democracies," in Dalton et al., eds. (1984).

Dalton, Russell J., Ian McAllister, and Martin P. Wattenberg. 2000. "The Consequences of Partisan Dealignment," in Dalton and Wattenberg (2000).

Dalton, Russell J., and Martin P. Wattenberg. 1993. "The Not So Simple Act of Voting," in Finifter, ed. (1993).

—. eds. 2000. *Parties without Partisans*. Oxford: Oxford University Press.

Dennis, Jack, and Diana Owen. 2001. "Popular Satisfaction with the Party System and Representative Democracy in the United States," *International Political Science Review* 22: 399-415.

Denver, David, and Gordon Hands. 1992. *Issues and Controversies in British Electoral Behaviour*. New York: Harvester Wheatsheaf.

Downs, Anthony. 1957. *An Economic Theory of Democracy*. New York: Harper and Row.

Durand, Claire, André Blais, and Sébastien Vachon. 2001. "A Late Campaign Swing or a Failure of the Polls? The Case of the 1998 Quebec Election," *Public Opinion Quarterly* 65: 108-23.

Duverger, Maurice. 1951. *Les partis politiques*. Paris: Armand Colin.

Elkins, David. 1978. "Party Identification: A Conceptual Analysis," *Canadian Journal of Political Science* 11: 419-35.

Erickson, Lynda, and Brenda O'Neill. Forthcoming. "The Gender Gap and the Changing Woman Voter in Canada," *International Political Science Review*.

Everitt, Joanna, and Brenda O'Neill, eds. 2002. *Citizen Politics: Research and Theory in Canadian Political Behaviour*. Toronto: Oxford University Press.

Farrell, David M. 1996. "Campaign Strategies and Tactics," in LeDuc et al. (1996).

Finifter, Ada W., ed. 1993. *Political Science: The State of the Discipline II*. Washington, D.C.: American Political Science Association.

Fiorina, Morris P. 1981. *Retrospective Voting in American National Elections*. New Haven: Yale University Press.

Fletcher, Frederick J., ed. 1991. *Media, Elections and Democracy* Volume 10 of the Research Studies of the Royal Commission on Electoral Reform and Party Financing. Toronto: Dundurn Press.

Fletcher, Frederick J, and Robert Everett. 1991. "Mass Media and Elections in Canada," in Fletcher, ed. (1991).

Fournier, Patrick. 2002. "The Uninformed Canadian Voter," in Everitt and O'Neill, eds. (2002).

Franklin, Mark N. 1996. "Electoral Participation," in LeDuc et al. (1996).

Franklin, Mark, Thomas T. Mackie, and Henry Valen. 1992. *Electoral Change: Responses to Evolving Social and Attitudinal Structures in Western Democracies*. Cambridge: Cambridge University Press.

Gidengil, Elisabeth. 1992. "Canada Votes: A Quarter Century of Canadian National Election Studies," *Canadian Journal of Political Science* 25: 219-48.

—. 2002. "The Class Voting Conundrum," in Douglas Baer, ed., *Political Sociology: Canadian Perspectives*. Toronto: Oxford University Press.

Gidengil, Elisabeth, André Blais, Richard Nadeau, and Neil Nevitte. 1999. "Making Sense of Regional Voting in the 1997 Federal Election: Liberal and Reform Support Outside Quebec," *Canadian Journal of Political Science* 32: 247-72.

—. 2000. "Are Leaders Becoming More Important To Vote Choice in Canada?" Paper presented at the Annual Meeting of the American Political Science Association, Washington, September 2000.

—. 2001. "The Correlates and Consequences of Anti-Partyism in the 1997 Canadian Election," *Party Politics* 7: 491-513.

—. Forthcoming. "Women to the Left? Gender Differences in Political Beliefs and Policy Preferences," in Manon Tremblay and Linda Trimble, eds., *Women and Electoral Representation in Canada*. Oxford University Press.

Granberg, Donald, and Soren Holmberg. 1992. "The Hawthorne Effect in Election Studies," *British Journal of Political Science* 22: 240-48.

Hayes, Bernadette C., and Ian McAllister. 1997. "Gender, Party Leaders, and Election Outcomes in Australia, Britain, and the United States," *Comparative Political Studies* 30: 3-26.

Holbrook, Thomas. 2001. "Forecasting with Mixed Economic Signals: A Cautionary Tale," *Political Science & Politics* 34: 39-44.

Holbrook, Allyson J., Jon A. Krosnick, Penny S. Visser, Wendy L. Gardner, and John T. Capiocco. 2001. "Attitudes Toward Presidential Candidates and Political Parties: Initial Optimism, Initial First Impressions, and a Focus on Flaws," *American Journal of Political Science* 45: 930-50.

Irvine, William P. 1974. "Explaining the Religious Basis of the Canadian Partisan Identity: Success on the Third Try," *Canadian Journal of Political Science* 7: 560-63

Jenson, Jane. 1975. "Party Loyalty in Canada: The Question of Party Identification," *Canadian Journal of Political Science* 8: 419-35.

Johnston, Richard. 1985. "The Reproduction of the Religious Cleavage in Canadian Elections," *Canadian Journal of Political Science* 18: 99-113.

—. 1992. "Party Identification Measures in the Anglo-American Measures: A National Survey Experiment," *American Journal of Political Science* 36: 542-59.

—. 2001. "A Conservative Case for Electoral Reform," *Policy Options* 22 (July/August): 7-14.

Johnston, Richard, André Blais, Henry E. Brady, and Jean Crête. 1992. *Letting the People Decide: Dynamics of a Canadian Election*. Montréal: McGill-Queen's University Press.

Kanji, Mebs, and Keith Archer. 2002. "The Theories of Voting and Their Applicability" in Everitt and O'Neill, eds. (2002).

Kinder, Donald R. 1986. "Presidential Character Revisited," in Richard R. Lau and David O. Sears, eds., *Political Cognition*. Hillsdale: Lawrence Erlbaum.

Kinder, Donald R., Mark D. Peters, Robert P. Abelson and Susan T. Fiske. 1980. "Presidential Prototypes," *Political Behavior* 2: 315-37.

Kleppner, Paul. 1982. *Who Voted? The Dynamics of Electoral Turnout, 1970-1980*. New York: Praeger.

Lambert, Ronald D., James E. Curtis, Steven D. Brown and Barry J. Kay. 1986. "In Search of Left/Right Beliefs in the Canadian Electorate," *Canadian Journal of Political Science* 19: 541-63.

Lanoue, David. 1996. "The State of Debate Research in the United States," Paper presented at Les Entretiens Jacques-Cartier, Montréal, October 1996.

Lau, Richard. 1982. "Negativity in Political Perception," *Political Behavior* 4: 353-77.

—. 1985. "Two Explanations for Negativity Effects in Political Behavior," *American Journal of Political Science* 29: 119-38.

LeDuc, Lawrence. 1984. "Canada: The Politics of Stable Dealignment," in Dalton et al. eds. (1984).

LeDuc, Lawrence, Richard G. Niemi, and Pippa Norris, eds. 1996. *Comparing Democracies: Elections and Voting in Global Perspective*. Thousand Oaks, Calif.: Sage.

LeDuc, Lawrence, Harold Clarke, Jane Jenson, and Jon Pammett. 1984. "Partisan Instability in Canada: Evidence from a New Panel Study," *American Political Science Review* 78: 470- 84.

Lewis-Beck, Michael S. 1988. *Economics and Elections: The Major Western Democracies*. Ann Arbor: University of Michigan Press.

Lewis-Beck, Michael S., and Martin Paldam. 2000. "Economic Voting: An Introduction," *Electoral Studies* 19: 113-21.

Lewis-Beck, Michael S., and Mary Stegmaier. 2000. "Economic Determinants of Electoral Outcomes," *Annual Review of Political Science* 3: 183-219.

Lewis-Beck, Michael, and Charles Tien. 2001. "Modeling the Future: Lessons from the Gore Forecast," *Political Science & Politics* 34: 21-23.

Martinez, Michael D. 1984. "Intergenerational Transfer of Canadian Partisanships," *Canadian Journal of Political Science* 17: 133-143.

Massicotte, Louis, and André Blais. 1999. "Dernières élections: le PLQ aurait eu besoin de 300,000 votes de plus,"*La Presse* 7 Jan., B3.

McAllister, Ian. 1996. "Leaders," in LeDuc et al., eds. (1996).

Meisel, John. 1975. *Working Papers on Canadian Politics*. Montreal: McGill-Queen's University Press.

Mendelsohn, Matthew. 1993. "Television's Frames in the 1988 Canadian Election," *Canadian Journal of Communication* 18: 149-71.

—. 1994. "The Media's Persuasive Effects: The Priming of Leadership in the

1988 General Election," *Canadian Journal of Political Science* 27: 81-97.

Mendelsohn, Matthew, and Richard Nadeau. 1997. "The Religious Cleavage and the Media in Canada," *Canadian Journal of Political Science* 30: 129-46.

Miller, Warren E., and J. Merrill Shanks. 1996. *The New American Voter*. Cambridge: Harvard University Press.

Miller, Arthur, and Martin Wattenberg. 1984. "Politics and the Pulpit: Religiosity and the 1980 Elections," *Public Opinion Quarterly* 48: 301-17.

Monière, Denis, and Julie Fortier. 2000. *Radioscopie de l'information télévisée au Canada*. Montréal: Presses de l'Université de Montréal.

Nadeau, Richard. 1987. Modélisation et analyse empirique des fluctuations de court terme du comportement électoral: le cas canadien. Montréal: Université de Montréal. PH.D. dissertation.

Nadeau, Richard, and André Blais. 1993. "Explaining Election Outcomes in Canada," *Canadian Journal of Political Science* 26: 775-90.

Nadeau, Richard, André Blais, Elisabeth Gidengil, and Neil Nevitte. 2000. "It's Unemployment Stupid! Why Perceptions about the Job Situation Hurt the Liberals in the 1997 Election," *Canadian Public Policy* 26: 77-94.

Nadeau, Richard, and Matthew Mendelsohn. 1994. "Short-Term Popularity Boost Following Leadership Change in Great Britain," *Electoral Studies* 13: 222-28.

Nevitte, Neil. 1996. *The Decline of Deference: Canadian Value Change in Cross-National Perspective*. Peterborough, Ont.: Broadview Press.

Nevitte, Neil, André Blais, Elisabeth Gidengil, and Richard Nadeau. 2000. *Unsteady State: The 1997 Canadian Federal Election*. Toronto: Oxford University Press.

Niemi, Richard G., and Herbert F. Weisberg. 1984. *Controversies in Voting Behaviour*. 2nd ed. Washington, D.C.: Congressional Quarterly Press.

Norpoth, Helmut. 1996. "The Economy," in LeDuc et al. eds. (1996).

—. 2001. "Primary Colors: A Mixed Blessing for Gore," *Political Science & Politics* 34: 45-48.

Norris, Pippa, John Curtice, David Sanders, Margaret Scammell, and Holli A. Semetko. 1999. *On Message: Communicating the Campaign*. London: Sage.

Oppenhuis, E. 1995. *Voting Behaviour in Europe*. Amsterdam: Het Spinhuis.

Pammett, Jon H. 1997. "The Voters Decide," in Allan Frizzell and Jon H. Pammett, eds., *The Canadian General Election of 1997*. Toronto: Dundurn.

—. 2001. "The People's Verdict," in Jon H. Pammett and Christopher Dornan, eds., *The Canadian General Election of 2000*. Toronto: Dundurn.

Petrocik, John R. 1996. "Issue Ownership in Presidential Elections, with a 1980 Case Study," *American Journal of Political Science* 40: 825-50.

Poguntke, Thomas. 1996. "Anti-Party Sentiment – Conceptual Thoughts and Empirical Evidence: Explorations into a Minefield," *European Journal of Political Research* 29: 319- 44.

Robinson, Michael J., and Margaret A. Sheehan. 1983. *Over the Wire and on TV*. New York: Russell Sage Foundation.

Rose, Richard. 1974. *Electoral Behaviour: A Comparative Handbook*. New York: The Free Press.

Rosenstone, Steven J., and John Mark Hansen. 1993. *Mobilization, Participation, and Democracy in America*. New York: Macmillan.

Savoie, Donald J. 1999. *Governing from the Centre: The Concentration of Political Power in Canada*. Toronto: University of Toronto Press.

Scarbrough, Elinor. 1984. *Ideology and Voting Behaviour: An Exploratory Study*. Oxford: Clarendon Press.

Schickler, Eric, and Donald P. Green. 1997. "The Stability of Party Identification in Western Democracies: Results from Eight Panel Surveys," *Comparative Political Studies* 30: 450-83.

Schmitt, Hermann, and Dieter Ohr. 2000. "Are Party Leaders Becoming More Important in German Elections?" Paper presented at the annual meeting of the American Political Science Association, Washington, September 2000.

Semetko, Holli A. 1996. "The Media," in Leduc et al., eds. (1996).

Simpson, Jeffrey. 2001. *The Friendly Dictatorship*. Toronto: McClelland & Stewart.

Sniderman, Paul M. 1993. "The New Look in Public Opinion Research," in Finifter, ed. (1993).

Sniderman, Paul M., David A. Brody, and Philip E. Tetlock. 1991. *Reasoning and Choice: Explorations in Political Psychology*. New York: Cambridge University Press.

Sniderman, Paul, H. D. Forbes, and Ian Meltzer. 1974. "Party Loyalty and Electoral Volatility: A Study of the Canadian Party System," *Canadian Journal of Political Science* 7: 268-88.

Strom, Kaare. 1990. "A Behavioral Theory of Competitive Political Parties," *American Journal of Political Science* 34: 565-98.

Teixeira, Ruy A. 1992. *The Disappearing American Voter*. Washington: Brookings Institute.

Topf, Richard. 1995. "Electoral Participation," in Hans-Diter Klingemann and Dieter Fuchs, eds., *Citizens and the State*. Oxford: Oxford University Press.

Turcotte, André. 2001. "Fallen Heroes: Leaders and Voters in the 2000 Canadian Federal Election," in Jon H. Pammett and Christopher Dornan, eds., *The Canadian General Election of 2000*. Toronto: Dundurn.

Uhlaner, Carole, and Bernard Grofman. 1986. "The Race May Be Close but My Horse is Going to Win: Wish Fulfillment in the 1980 Presidential Election," *Political Behaviour* 8: 101-29.

Van Deth, Jan W., and Elinor Scarbrough, eds. 1995. *The Impact of Values*. Oxford: Oxford University Press.

Verba, Sidney, and Norman H. Nie. 1972. *Participation in America: Political Democracy and Social Equality*. New York: Harper and Row.

Verba, Sidney, Kay Lehman Schlozman, and Henry Brady. 1995. *Voice and Equality: Civic Voluntarism in America Politics*. Cambridge: Harvard University Press.

Wattenberg, Martin. 1991. *The Rise of Candidate-Centered Politics: Presidential Elections of the 1980s*. Cambridge: Harvard University Press.

Wattenberg, Martin. 1994. *The Decline of American Political Parties: 1952-1992*. Cambridge: Harvard University Press.

West, Darrell M. 1997. *Air Wars*. Washington, D.C.: CQ Press.

Wittman, Donald A. 1990. "Spatial Strategies When Candidates Have Policy Preferences," in James M. Enelow and Melvin J. Hinich, eds., *Advances in the Spatial Theory of Voting*. Cambridge: Cambridge University Press.

Wolfinger, Raymond, and Steven J. Rosenstone. 1980. *Who Votes?* New Haven: Yale University Press.